GW00771083

Nomads, Empires, States

Nomads, Empires, States

Modes of Foreign Relations and Political Economy

Volume I

KEES VAN DER PIJL

Pluto Press

LONDON

First published 2007 by Pluto Press
345 Archway Road, London N6 5AA

www.plutobooks.com

Copyright © Kees van der Pijl 2007

The right of Kees van der Pijl to be identified as the author of this work
has been asserted by him in accordance with the Copyright, Designs,
and Patents Act 1988.

British Library Cataloguing in Publication Data
A catalogue record for this book is available from the British Library

ISBN-13   978 0 7453 2601 6
ISBN-10   0 7453 2601 3
ISBN 978 0 7453 2601 6
Library of Congress Cataloging in Publication Data applied for

This book is printed on paper suitable for recycling and made from fully
managed and sustained forest sources. Logging, pulping and manufacturing
processes are expected to conform to the environmental regulations of
the country of origin.

10 9 8 7 6 5 4 3 2 1

Designed and produced for Pluto Press by
Chase Publishing Services Ltd, Fortescue, Sidmouth, EX10 9QG, England
Typeset from disk by Newgen Imaging Systems, Chennai, India
Printed and bound in the European Union by
Marston Book Services Ltd, Didcot

Contents

Preface

My aim in the present study is to broaden the domain covered by the discipline of International Relations (IR) to *relations between communities occupying separate spaces and dealing with each other as outsiders*. This is an ambitious project vastly enlarging the field and raising a host of intellectual challenges. But there are simply too many contemporary world–political phenomena beyond the self-imposed horizon of the discipline to escape the conclusion that the very notion of the 'international' must be re-examined if we want to come to grips, theoretically and practically, with the world politics of today. This after all is the central terrain on which the survival of the human species and the preservation of the biosphere, under threat from an impending catastrophe, will be decided. All others are 'dependent variables'.

The current conjuncture of an unravelling world order in fact facilitates such a rethink. As in the 'twenty years crisis' between the two world wars, 'global governance' by the West (this time to impose neoliberal market discipline and competitively elected government) has turned out to be an illusion. In the 1930s and 1940s, the *realism* of Anglo-American theorists and practitioners of international relations, such as E.H. Carr, George Kennan, and others, articulated the insight that power politics cannot force the world into compliance with something materially out of reach. Unfortunately it also gave IR a state-centric and, by placing the 'nation-state' at the centre of analysis, Eurocentric and ahistoric imprint. Theories of imperialism (dominated by Marxism) and geopolitics (perverted by Nazi thinkers) were discarded; the study of historic civilisations and their relation to world order, exemplified by the work of Toynbee and others, was dismissed as woolly headed idealism, antithetical to science. True, aspects of all these traditions were later allowed back in to some extent. Global or international political economy (IPE) in this respect deserves a place of honour, especially once we accept, to quote Robert Cox (2002: 79), that 'the real achievement of IPE was not to bring in economics, but to open up a critical investigation into change in historical structures.'

In this study I seek to push this investigation a step further in the area of relations among communities occupying separate spaces and considering each other as outsiders. The 'international' is a historically specific, but not the final form of such relations. People today are exposed to 'foreigners' to a degree and on a scale never before seen in history. With more than half of the world's population now living in cities, each containing large non-native or otherwise different communities, due to unprecedented migratory pressures, global politics is present on every street corner – but not as a balance of power among states, although that too is part of the complex of historical forces which brought about the frontiers and boundaries cutting across the present world.

Indeed the contemporary crisis of globalisation and the proliferation of conflict it entails, points into the past as much as it reveals a possible future. It lays bare an underworld of foreign relations of earlier provenance which cannot be dealt with by a global governance for which the West writes the rules, nor by diplomacy backed up by military means. A crisis, Kaviraj writes (1992: 81),

opens up the future dramatically by forcing us to abandon the lines of extrapolations from the present which we specially favour and to understand the range of possibilities, but in a significant sense it also opens up the past. It forces us to look into complexities of the past and reconsider lines of possible development which existed but might not have materialised, or towards which we may have been indifferent.

Samuel Huntington deserves credit for having restored at least one line of extrapolation in the study of world politics, the analysis of 'civilisations'. Clearly his thesis of a 'clash of civilisations' operating on a level different from the relations among sovereign states, remains hostage to a naturalised view of eternal strife modelled on Cold War realism. Also his identification of Islam as an antagonist of the liberal Christian West (with a Chinese threat thrown in for good measure) comes suspiciously close to the agenda of a resource-hungry civilisation intent on mobilising all possible forces to confront the currently most ambitious contender to Western primacy. Yet the argument is a reminder that the conquest of the globe by capital, interacting with the expansion of the West, has all along involved 'clashes of civilisation'; just as the resonance of Huntington's thesis may be an indication that the global reach of the West is faltering and the substantive reality of different traditions and types of society is becoming evident once again. But clearly this cannot rely on the imagery of an ethno-religious plate tectonics. The method of investigating cultural difference in its relation to world politics must radically break with the naturalisation of conflict, certainly now that the logic of a war without end, the 'War on Terror', threatens to engulf all political argument.

The approach to foreign relations proposed in this study is inspired by Marx's critique of liberal economics. Marx aimed to historicise and denaturalise the capitalist market economy coming of age in his lifetime by showing that there had been other forms of economy, which continued to play a role in the contemporary context; just as there was a possible new economy gestating inside the capitalist one, negating the capitalist form of economic life and mobilising the social forces to transcend it. Understanding the present as history goes to the heart of historical materialism, and I will take this method as my point of departure. This choice should not be mistaken for a sectarian commitment; on the contrary. The Marxist legacy as it exists has largely failed to develop its own method in the area of foreign relations, and politically it has run aground – for the time being. Still, its basic premise, that all existence is historical, the result of the exploitation of humanity's relationship with nature, and that social life is therefore destined to change towards novel forms just as it emerged from different relations in the past, in my view constitutes the beginning of all wisdom. In this sense historical materialism is not a method of lifeless academic observation, but a pedagogy of hope. There is no preordained goal to which history is moving; but humanity would do well to develop such goals in the light of present and future challenges and thus provide direction to what would otherwise be an aimless, vegetative existence. Of course these goals will always be contested themselves, but that is the stuff of history too.

That there did not emerge a Marxist analysis of foreign relations that is not derived from economics is due largely to the fact that the critique of liberal economics was Marx's preoccupying aim. Even so, the methodology of his writings is not 'economistic' in the sense that would make the economy the *deus ex machina* that explains everything else. After his death, however, the Marxist legacy became most influential in a series of countries (Germany, Austria, Russia) where a labour movement took shape in the context of catch-up industrialisation, and this tended to favour precisely such an economistic interpretation of history. It coincided with a return to the naturalistic materialism Marx had expressly discarded. As Gramsci put it in a letter from his prison cell (1989: 189), 'the so-called theoreticians of historical materialism have fallen into a philosophical position similar to mediaeval theology and have turned "economic structure" into a hidden god'. Indeed the leading lights of the Second International, and later, Soviet Marxism (in both its Stalinist and its Trotskyist lines of development) all tended to interpret politics and ideology as superstructures of economic relations. But understanding foreign relations in their own right is ruled out if we can only see them as epiphenomena of economics.

Taking the method by which Marx distinguished between several modes of production into the area of the relations between communities occupying separate spaces, I will develop the concept of *modes of foreign relations* to make a comparable historical distinction between different patterns of social relations in this specific domain. Like modes of production, modes of foreign relations combine, in a dynamic structure of determination, an evolving level of development of the productive forces with social relations – in this case, the relations involved in occupying a particular social and/or territorial space, protecting it, and organising exchange with others.

One will not find the argument in this form in the corpus of classical Marxist writing, not even in the debates on imperialism or national self-determination. Yet we may glean the elements for an analysis of modes of foreign relations from Marx's sketches for *Capital* (the *Grundrisse*), his and Engels' scattered writings on international politics, and his notes on ethnology that served as the basis for Engels' *The Origins of the Family, Private Property, and the State*, as well as from disparate passages in the work of Lenin, Bukharin, Gramsci, and others. Marxist anthropologists such as Eric Wolf, too, have sought 'to show that human societies and cultures would not be properly understood until we learned to visualize them in their mutual relationships and interdependencies in space and time' (1997: x). His *Europe and the People Without History* is testimony to how this works out in the hands of a great scholar. Yet with only 'modes of production' as a conceptual tool, the aspect of communities occupying separate spaces and considering each other as outsiders cannot be brought out fully.

Soviet ethnology likewise remained mortgaged by the limitations of the Marxist legacy, perhaps precisely because, in its own domain, the work of people like Bromley and Gumilev is highly original and not part of the self-congratulatory corruption that characterised so much of Soviet social science. The progenitor of this school of thought, S.M. Shirokogorov (who worked in China in the inter-war years and on that account was branded an émigré in the USSR), on the other hand, is not concerned with economic determination but with cultural adaptation in an 'interethnic milieu'. This opens the way into an investigation of the different ways of life that emerge from the exploitation of nature, on which both modes of production and modes of foreign relations are grafted.

'Foreign' is obviously a problematic concept. It must be opened up, specified, and broken down in its relationship to exploitation and class relations, and ultimately overcome. I use the term merely to avoid taking 'national' and the nation-state for granted and reach for more fundamental determinants of how communities relate to others whom they consider as outsiders, as *different* in the sense of not being part of the social whole. Today, (ethnic) difference is under attack from a homogenising cosmopolitan culture propagated by the West and backed up by capitalist market discipline; foreignness, paradoxically, is being reinforced as a result. The foreign has even come to articulate social dividing lines now that the Left is temporarily exhausted and it has become unfashionable to recognise the class dimension. Yet foreign relations are not just a cover for class relations, although in the relations between a globalising cosmopolitanism and those marginalised by it, it often comes close. They are an aspect of social relations in their own right, to be studied as such.

In the end, just as the contours of a mode of production beyond capitalism are in evidence in our globalised economy (an eco-managerialism reaching beyond class society is perhaps the best guess today), foreignness as a set of exploitative relations, imbricated with relations of production, is in a process of transition as well. Socialism, as a higher form of social relations developing under democratically set priorities and collective control of the means of production, cannot develop under a state of siege in less developed states; but neither can it be achieved by the coercive homogenisation of its human substratum. *It must include the overcoming of foreignness as a political and socio-economic condition and its replacement by reciprocity and dialogue.* Difference is a process, not a matter of essences; being different is not a fixed condition to be merely 'respected', although this is often a necessary first step. Overcoming exploitation will always have to be mediated by self-determination of communities of identity if it is to be a truly universal project, and not just that of a vanguard.

The book offered here to the reader is the first volume of a larger project. A second volume will deal with the treatment of foreign relations in myth, religion, and ethical philosophy; a third will provide an analysis of modern IR theories as an instance of English-speaking hegemony.

The plan for the present study is as follows. In Chapter 1, I argue how the concept of modes of foreign relations fits into the methodology of historical materialism, which itself must be rephrased to avoid the determinism of naturalistic materialism. Chapter 2 begins the journey through the historical development of foreign relations by an investigation of tribal relations and their specific forms of occupying space, protection and exchange. Chapter 3 takes the argument to the empire/nomad mode of foreign relations. The expanded reproduction of sedentary civilisations through conquest by 'marcher lords' on their perimeter prefigures the form of protection of developed empires, viz., the recruitment of nomad auxiliaries to keep others out. Exchange develops as tribute but also spawns ethnogenesis of specialist trading peoples who develop as quasi-nomadic diasporas. I will discuss at some length how and why the Chinese empire, after a pioneering experience of overseas exploration, turned inward again to deal with the challenge of the nomads on the Inner Asian frontier, leaving the terrain of future maritime supremacy to the English-speaking West.

In Chapter 4, I argue that the empire of Western Christianity, in the specific configuration that produced the Crusades, can be analysed profitably in terms of the empire/nomad mode too. Seeing how the popes in Rome recruited Viking sea-nomads and their Norman descendants as auxiliaries to fight off the Arabs avoids an economistic interpretation of European expansion. Since the imperial centre was embodied in a religious sovereignty, frontier lords eager for independence, merchants seeking to explore inroads into Asian trade, and urban dwellers, tended to cast their emerging collective identities in terms of religion too, as Protestantism. This contributed to the ascent and eventual global pre-eminence of an intercontinental, Anglophone West in which imperialism and nomad mobility have been synthesised.

The liberal culture of the West offered a hospitable environment to the capitalist mode of production, which developed in the interstices between separate state sovereignties. Such a fortuitous combination was not available for the land-based remnants of the empire of Western Christianity. As I argue in Chapter 5, here too Protestantism worked as a dissolvent of empire, but it led to religious wars within and between language areas controlled by rival absolute

xii   Nomads, Empires, States

monarchies. Formal sovereignty became a key prop for state classes emerging in revolutions pushing beyond royal absolutism, as contenders to Anglophone hegemony; only thus could they hold their own against the ascendant West, which operates on a distinct plane, that of global liberalism, and in tandem with capital. These twin forces have worked to undermine these states, forcing them on the defensive all along. The weakest states in the global order have actually collapsed into quasi-tribal fragments again, triggering migratory flows that feed into the West's inner cities. Along these tracks a global underclass has formed that is literally foreign to the abundance enjoyed by privileged minorities, but yet present among them. Mocking the idea that a homogenous West can still ward off the influx of those fleeing the effects of global capitalist exploitation, the current world has entered a phase of imperial retrenchment, with quasi-nomadic forces such as NGOs and the alternative anti-globalisation movement operating on its frontier as intermediaries with supposed 'barbarians'.

Acknowledgements

In December 2005 I was awarded a Major Research Fellowship by the Leverhulme Trust to work on a project 'Tribal and Imperial Antecedents of Contemporary Foreign Relations' from May 2006 to 2009. I thank Thomas Ferguson, Andrew Linklater, and Jan Nederveen Pieterse, as well as the anonymous referees for the Leverhulme Trust, for their support in obtaining this grant.

Others to whom I owe a debt include Benno Teschke, who invited me to a conference on Systemic Transformations and International Relations at Gregynog in Wales in April 2001, from which I took home the idea of modes of foreign relations; and Klaus-Gerd Giesen, who arranged for me to give a guest lecture on the topic at the University of Leipzig and who published a first sketch (cf. my 2004). Both Benno and Klaus wrote detailed comments on initial drafts. Chris Brown, Robert Cox, Earl Gammon, Jean-Christophe Graz, Clemens Hoffmann, Samuel Knafo, Kamran Matin, Ronen Palan, Magnus Ryner, and Jan Selby at various stages encouraged me to take the argument further and commented on its problems and implications. At least one lucky break occurred when materials I gathered early on were miraculously recovered from a crashed hard disk by Or Raviv, after other experts had given up hope. In May 2006, I had the opportunity to present a draft of Chapter 1 in Kassel, Germany, at a seminar organised by Ulrich Brand on my book *Global Rivalries from the Cold War to Iraq*. I thank Christoph Scherrer and Joscha Wullweber, the discussants in that session, for their critical comments. I also owe a specific debt to Ajit Roy, Marxist scholar and activist, who many years ago pointed out the importance of the Soviet ethnology school to me. Johnna Montgomerie and Renk Özdemir compiled bibliographies on this and other areas. Anatoly Kuznetsov, of Far Eastern University in Vladivostok, the leading specialist on Shirokogorov, kindly made available some of his work (in Russian, and translated for me by Ekaterina Korotayeva) when I was writing the final draft of the book.

I thank Anthony Winder for his thoughtful and constructive editing of the manuscript and Robert Webb and the team at Pluto for producing the book with professional skill.

Finally let me acknowledge my debt to the successive generations of students I have taught in Amsterdam, Sussex, and more recently during my visiting professorships at the University of Auvergne at Clermont-Ferrand. They, like my own children who are now students too, have always been and remain a source of inspiration, a source of optimism against all the odds. If none of those mentioned earlier bears any responsibility for what follows, they in a way do.

1
Foreign Relations and the Marxist Legacy

Foreign relations take shape in the encounter between communities occupying separate spaces and dealing with each other as outsiders. In these relations, the definition of social space and the nature of the sovereign claim to it, the conditions of its protection, and the ways in which communities organise exchanges with others, evolve through historical structures that I call modes of foreign relations. These comprise, like modes of production, a dynamic combination of a level and pattern of development of the productive forces (that is, the forces of nature mobilised as means of power, including the community itself) with a specific pattern of social relations; in this case, relations with foreign communities. Before addressing these issues in greater detail, let me first introduce the ontology on which this study is based.

'AN ABSOLUTE HUMANISM OF HISTORY'

Historical materialism assumes that history is the result of the conscious exploitation of the human relationship with nature, including the species' inner nature. As people train their physical and mental capacities in order to respond adequately to the world around them, communities change their environment and their own human substance, physically and mentally. Thus emerge the characteristics of their habitat, their way of life and their identity, as well as their attitudes to *order* – in the community and with other communities, in nature and in their imagination of eternity.

The initial means at the disposal of human groups are obviously minimal, and they are guided mainly by their instinctual apparatus and biological bonds. Surrounded by a vast, hostile environment in which their actions count for little, the best they can hope for is to blunt or neutralise some of the forces facing them, in order to sustain their life. Once they begin shaping their own lives actively, they also enter, involuntarily, into a different class of relations from the natural heritage, *social* relations. These relations – among people within the group, and with other groups – appear to those involved as equally alien and in need of appeasement and negotiation as the natural environment at large. This is why, for humans, the awareness of their capacity to act tends to be mortgaged by deference to other, metaphysical agencies – from spirits, the totem, and God, to 'matter', 'History' with a capital II, national destiny, and, today, 'the market'. In every community and society, there are mediators with the realm of the supernatural, from shamans to neoclassical economists. This is the pivot of social power. Without the intellectual, 'explanatory' function, no social structure will hold. With the growth of social complexity, the aspect of ideological cohesion may escape the hands-on management by those whose power is legitimated by it, and be entrusted to specialists; but the connection remains.

The concepts of order, through which social structures seek to perpetuate themselves in time and space, are subject to continuous change. No world-view survives the growing hold communities acquire, over time, on themselves and on their surroundings. Every ideology at some point unravels in the face of changing circumstances. Exposed as a concept of control by which a ruling class exercises power, it loses its grip, first on those whose fate is least dependent on it; the structure of society it seeks to naturalise in the process loses its self-evident rationality and becomes unstable. Indeed, in our present epoch, the exploitative relation with nature itself, the biosphere on which life depends, is becoming unstable too. But no god, invisible hand, or law of history will rush to humanity's aid to set this right. Only in struggles to overcome the specific limitations of the prevailing world-view and the structures of power upholding it can human self-determination prevail and the conditions of survival be secured. In this sense Marxism is *absolute historicism*, or to use Gramsci's phrase (1971: 465), 'the absolute secularisation and earthliness of thought, an absolute humanism of history'. This will be our starting point too.

Exploitation of Nature, Adaptive Choices, Ethnicity

Historical humanity emerged as a multiplicity of small groups of a single species, each exploiting its natural substratum in particular ways, beginning with gathering and scavenging. Thus units relatively separate from others were formed, albeit in constant interaction with others from the start. Let me first answer the question, What is it that allows us to speak of *exploitation* of the human relationship with nature?

The metabolism of human communities with nature takes place within a comprehensive energy economy in which all matter is ultimately involved. The warmth and light of the sun, their meta-morphosed instances such as the life functions of organisms and their energy content when consumed as force or food, the soil as a sediment of life containing the irreplaceable sources for its renewal, frozen or fossil carbon stocks, and so on, all are part of this cycle (Ponting 1991: 12–5).

Now, as the first law of thermodynamics states, energy cannot be created or destroyed, it can only change from one form to another. All living organisms partake in energy transformation as much as is necessary for their reproduction. Simple metabolism becomes exploitation, however, once groups of humans, by transforming the natural foundations of their existence, rise above their biological station in the earth's energy economy due to changes that give them a critical advantage over their competitors and limit their exposure to natural hazards. Walking upright, relative brain size, the discovery of making fire, instrumental intelligence and intra-group communi-cation: all these lifted human communities onto a plane where they established an order different from the one they emerged from as natural beings, but also different from other groups. Thus every unit sets out, irreversibly, on a trajectory no longer contained within that of biological reproduction and evolution – that is, not immediately.

To the degree a community or society exploits its metabolism with nature at a rate not covered by the reproductive cycles of the energy sources it consumes, it contributes to entropy. Here the *second* law of thermodynamics applies. It states that the transformation of energy always tends towards entropy – disordered, dissipated forms of energy no longer of use. A living organism apparently contradicts this law; in the words of the physicist, Erwin Schrödinger (as in Wright 2001: 245), 'the organism succeeds in freeing itself from all the entropy it cannot help producing when alive'. The ability of protein molecules to 'recognise' others and stick together, discovered by Jacques Monod, is at the root of this paradox. Organisms can thus maintain structure over their limited life-span, before decom-posing again. Human communities have exploited this ability to the full – under conditions, it should be remembered, of exceptional geophysical stability. The historical phase of human existence has so far proceeded in what is best understood as a pause following on more turbulent, far less hospitable conditions – extreme climate, tectonic and volcanic activity, and meteor impact. This pause will in all probability end at some point, and turbulence will return (Davis 1995: 232).

This takes us to the units in which humanity has evolved and developed historically. Each human community in its own particular way (its 'way of life') appropriates what Marx (1973: 485) calls 'the natural conditions of labour, of the *earth* as the original instrument of labour as well as its workshop and repository of raw materials'. This is how processes of *ethnogenesis*, from the root *ethnos*, come about.

An ethnos, in the definition of Shirokogorov (1970: 9), is the unit of social cohesion in which the evolutionary adaptation of the human species takes place. Thus it progressively differentiates itself from others. The concept was developed to capture the common element that runs through specific terms such as 'people', nation, 'national grouping'/nationality (Russian *narodnost*), and tribe, in a multi-ethnic society like the USSR and the tsarist empire that preceded it (Shanin 1986; Kuznetsov 2006). Adaptation is primarily cultural; collective identity overrides all other constitutive elements. An ethnos is 'an aggregate of people which recognises itself as such, distinguishing itself from other similar communities' (*Authors' Collective* 1982: 9–10).

To the extent that there is a biological aspect to an ethnos, it resides first of all in endogamy. Among Australian aborigines, no more than 15 per cent of marriages are outside the tribe; in the USSR of 1925, no more than 10 per cent were married to other nationalities either. Even in former Yugoslavia on the eve of the dissolution, the number of children from mixed marriages between the constitutive nationalities was around that percentage. Hence, 'the boundaries of endogamy form a sort of genetic barrier for the ethnos concerned' (Bromley, 1974a: 65; cf. Samary, 1995: 19). The biological–genetic aspect and the aspect of conscious desire to belong to a community and find one's partner there are distinct, although in practice they are of course mutually reinforcing (Smaje 2000: 127). An ethnos is not itself a biological entity, a view sometimes attributed to Gumilev (Bromley 1977: 142 note; cf. *evrazia* 2006); it is a historical, not a natural category.

As communication intensifies across ever greater distances, and migration brings large populations into the living space of others, difference becomes more complex and diffuse. With *ethno-transformation*, traits inherited from natural adaptation and from early ethnogenesis become increasingly intermingled; directly by intermarriage and indirectly by exposure to ways of life different from one's own, emulation, and social synthesis. History itself works as a powerful generator of mutations in collective mentality here. There are, for instance, few traces in contemporary Germany of the militarism that accompanied Prussia's rise and wreaked havoc on humanity in two world wars. Indeed, as Bromley reminds us (1977: 61), the interaction between societies turns the ethnic particularity of a people into an ever more relative aspect. But the adaptive choices made in the earlier phases of differential ethnogenesis remain crucial determinants of social development.

Today we face a situation in which the Western way of life has crowded out all others, or almost. The very idea that this way of life is rooted in the exploitation of nature is being eclipsed by the scale of the built environment and by ubiquitous mechanisation (each with its ever growing fuel requirements). Experimentation with the forces of life itself seems to mock natural limits. What else to make of the image, flashed around the world in January 2007, of a 67-year-old woman holding her newborn baby? The cloning of animals, *in vitro* fertilisation of humans, and genetic manipulation of plants, all herald further breakthroughs as they open up new terrains on which human ingenuity can be put to work. Certainly, as Lévi-Strauss observes (1987: 46–7), this triumphant distancing from natural constraints is also the greatest weakness of the Western way of life, and the mental illness indexes in the countries where it prevails point to fundamental imbalances. Thinking and feeling, Giedion writes in *Mechanization Takes Command* (1987: 13), have in the modern age become separated entirely.

Now there is no doubt that in the short run, the adaptive package that gave the edge to humans over the remaining animal world, and to Western society over others, has been extremely successful. Sometime in the Palaeolithic, the threshold of 1 million humans was reached, from an initial natural population which if measured by the number of other mammals of the same size and occupying the same position in the food chain, must have been very much smaller (de Vries and Goudsblom 2002: 26–7). Now there are six billion people, and growing fast. That this is not the even growth of a species, but is modulated by differential ethnogenesis and ethnotransformation, transpires in the fact that the population share of Europeans in the world total has risen from around 18 per cent in 1650 to more than one-third today (Spellman 2002: 6–7).

The hegemony of the Western lifestyle meanwhile reaches into the remotest corners of the planet. It affects the attitudes and aspirations of all of contemporary humanity, even of those diametrically opposed to it politically. However, as a process rooted in differential ethnogenesis, it remains a result of evolutionary adaptation; hence the way of life of the West will come more 'naturally' to some societies than to others. In this connection Ogburn's claim (1964b: 22) that there have been no biological mutations in humanity over the last 25,000 years overlooks the fact that cultural ethnogenesis has physical effects too, just as skin pigmentation adapts to sunlight or heart and lung capacity to altitude. It has been established that culture affects body chemistry as well as the functions, and possibly even the matter of the brain (Shirokogorov 1970: 9; Lorenz 1971: 246; Vroon 1994: 366–8). Thus centuries of mechanically regulated living environments have generated a level of rapid interactive abilities, control of bodily movement, and precision dexterity lacking in peasant societies (as are some of the nervous illnesses that come with them). Communist sympathisers delivering lathes to aid Soviet industrialisation in the 1920s and modern development workers alike have found that complex equipment may have a very short life in the hands of somebody for whom a pair of scissors or a water tap is a high-tech implement. Of course modern urbanites have in turn lost the capacity to find their way in the jungle and survive on wild plants, something which poses few problems for an indigenous forest dweller in Amazonia; that is no longer part of their evolutionary toolkit. To quote Bromley again (1978: 11), 'throughout its history any ethnos is subject to a practically permanent process of ethno-evolutionary changes whose reproduction is ensured by the functioning of some inherent informational bonds within it'. This also means that if the Western way of life is hegemonic in our contemporary world, the ability to assimilate it is unevenly distributed across the globe. What is pleasure and fun, honourable and rewarding in a North American suburb may be awkward and painful, the stuff of nightmares in a South Asian community – and vice versa.

Over the many millennia of their historical existence, humans have not only exponentially raised their own number. They have also removed certain favourite animals from the immediate constraints of natural selection. These include, notably, billions of cattle, pigs, sheep, and poultry, not to mention pets and vermin. Repeatedly struck by epidemics and itself a source of mass destruction for other species, this murderous column forces its way through the biosphere to devastating effect. Our closest relatives, the great apes, survive only in dwindling numbers and are in danger of extinction through the reduction of their habitat, or even through being eaten as 'bushmeat'. Plants such as grain or rice, too, have increased far out of proportion; biodiversity has been reduced to the lowest point in perhaps 65 million years (Megarry 1995: 14; Monbiot 2003: 18).

By removing itself from the systemic, self-equilibrating cycle of life for fear of death, then, the Western way of life has created a universe in which life itself hangs in the balance, even if the favourable geophysical state of exception were to endure. The deep exploitation of the human–nature nexus and the larger-than-natural demand people make of their environment have become positively life-threatening in our epoch. Exhaustion of the biosphere by pollution and other forms of destruction (one bumper sticker against genetic manipulation denounces it for 'giving pollution a life of its own') is today coupled with the social ravages of the dominant mode of production that emerged in the West, capitalism. Rampant exploitation on a global scale creates death – not the regenerative decomposition on which new life builds, but its actual disappearance, terminal consumption (Brennan 2000: 190; Dickens 1996: 34). There will have to occur, therefore, a transformation towards a culture that somehow re-equilibrates the relationship with the biosphere, or humanity too will be wiped out.

However, there is no way billions of people living the Western way of life can turn round and take up the more carefully calibrated approaches by which other cultures deal with their natural substrata. With yoga and tofu alone, overpopulation and the crisis of the biosphere will not be managed and overcome. This takes us to the concept of the productive forces.

Productive Forces and Power

Labour, the exploitation of nature, turns its elements (including the human brain, physical dexterity, longevity) into what Marx terms the forces of production. As instruments for human activity, these are then socialised, objectified for social use (Rupert 1993). Productive forces enable a community to raise itself to what Braudel terms 'the limits of the possible'. Every ethnos will select particular possibilities over others, and deal with imported innovations from the particular cultural perspective it thus generates. When the Papago Amerindians were given cattle to tend by the Spaniards, they set them free and hunted them, because that was how they related to animals of that size and shape (Bliss 1965). Indeed as Braudel puts it (1981: 396), 'What mattered on a world scale was not only technology itself but the way it was used', and this is still true today.

The concept 'relations of production' for the social relations through which the exploitation of nature take place followed on from an earlier, broader term used by Marx and Engels in the *German Ideology* (*MEW*, iii: 23), 'format of social intercourse' (*Verkehrsform*). Social relations not only comprise the exploitative relations within a community; they also include, from the very moment we may speak of relations no longer entirely contained in natural cycles, *foreign* relations. In Marx's words in the *Grundrisse* (1973: 491),

The only barrier which the community can encounter in relating to the natural conditions of production – the earth – is *another community*, which already claims it as its own inorganic body. *Warfare* is therefore one of the earliest occupations of each of these naturally arisen communities, both for the defence of their property and for obtaining new property.

Whether 'warfare' is an appropriate term at this stage will concern us later. Here it is sufficient to see that a productive force, that is, an element of nature mobilised by society as 'power', will always be applied on different dimensions of its existence, including the relations with other communities. In ancient Greek, Marx reminds us (1976: 310), *hoplon* means 'tool' as well as 'armour'; but also, the male sexual organ by which the community is literally reproduced. Gunpowder can be used for mining or road building, i.e. in relations of production, as well as for firearms, i.e. in foreign relations – just as nuclear fission can be applied either as a source of energy or as a weapon of mass destruction. How then are these applications related to each other? To answer this we must investigate the separate dimensions of socialisation.

Socialisation (from the German *Vergesellschaftung*, literally, 'societisation') denotes the process through which the elements of nature (humanity itself, soil, plants and animals, space and time, etc.) become components of a historical order. In the hands of Max Weber and Talcott Parsons it became a synonym for 'modernisation' (cf. Wolf 1997: 12), but *all* human societies in history are instances of socialised nature in this sense. Ethnogenesis constitutes the central axis of socialisation, because it is through a particular community that humans exploit nature and in the process create a particular social structure, including a pattern of dealing with other communities. This includes 'willed' structures and relations (say, the division of labour in a factory, or a framework for arms control negotiations) as well as structures and relations into which people enter 'involuntarily' and over which they have only limited control, or none at all. In those cases, socialisation is subject to *alienation* (*Entfremdung*), the reification and renaturalisation of social relations and practices. Alienated socialisation remains the overarching, determining form in all hitherto known societies; willed structures are embedded in them.

The condition of foreignness, too, is a form of alienated socialisation – we are aware of communities different from ourselves but see that as something beyond our will, immutable, 'natural'. The historical circumstance that communities occupy different spaces and consider each other as outsiders thus becomes a natural order of things, like geology and climate, or the animal world. Often the denial of the (full) humanity of others, 'pseudo-speciation' (Tiger 1970: 213), will be based on the unintelligibility of their language. Many communities whose name for themselves is a variety of 'the (real) humans', call neighbouring groups 'the stammerers' or 'stutterers'; 'barbarian' is just the Greek version of this. Designating them 'slaves' is another way of denying full human status – Slavs (from which 'slave' was derived), Serbs (from the Latin *servus*), or *dasa*, the Aryan word for the Dravidians in India, are examples (Enzensberger 1994: 109–10; Ostler 2006: 197 note). Clearly what is proper for and due to us as the civilised 'humans', and for them as stammering slaves, must be radically different. There is variable assignment of rights of place, different entitlements, including even the right to life – one is friend or foe before having spoken or acted. Inequality, both as domination/subordination and as exploitation, thus follows from the acceptance of 'difference' as natural, on a different plane of existence (Inayatullah and Blaney 2004: 7, 9; Mann 1986: 43).

The perception of difference, and the degree of foreignness attributed to any group of outsiders, is an aspect of the ability of the community to deal with its environment more generally; it constitutes one of the productive forces at its disposal. The socialisation of nature into cultural difference according to Shirokogorov (1970: 15) comes about on three different axes of adaptation:

conditions beyond the control of man, which may be called *primary milieu;* conditions created by man, which are essentially a product of culture, or *secondary milieu*; and conditions which are formed by other ethnical units in the midst of which the unit is living, called here *tertiary*, or *interethnical*, *milieu*.

A comparable threefold distinction is given by Habermas (1973: 19–20). In the interaction with its environment, he argues, a community socialises nature, first, by the appropriation of *external* nature (i.e. through production); secondly, by the appropriation of *internal* nature, our mental substratum; and finally by dealing with other communities. 'The environment of social systems can be divided into three segments: external nature or the material resources of the non-human surroundings; *the remaining social systems, with which one's own society is in contact*; [and] the inner nature or the organic substratum of the members of society' (emphasis added). The mobilisation of productive forces thus takes place internally, from 'nature', or by exchange with other communities – we may obtain the secret of nuclear fission by research or by obtaining it abroad, dig up uranium in our own soil or import it, and so on.

The consciousness of the environment as an object of exploitation, however, cannot simply be assumed. The community engaging in the socialisation of the natural substratum of its existence first of all mobilises *itself* as a force of nature. As Marx puts it in the *Grundrisse* (1973: 495),

The original unity between a particular form of community (clan) and the corresponding property in nature, or relation to the objective conditions of production as a natural being, as an objective being of the individual mediated by the commune ... has its living reality in a specific mode of production itself, a mode which appears both as a relation between the individuals, and as their specific active relation to inorganic nature, a specific mode of working (which is always family labour, often communal labour). *The community itself appears as the first great force of production.* (Emphasis added.)

In other words, the first 'tool' a community has at its disposal is not a stone axe, or a domestic animal, but the human collective as such, the unit in which it finds itself as it emerges from natural existence. This is what ethnogenesis refers to – the mobilisation of a community through socialising its own and surrounding nature into a source of power placed at the disposal of itself. Thus a complex of productive forces is made available, providing the community with the means to engage in a variety of relations, into which they enter as 'power', the power to exploit and dominate, wielded by those with preferential access to it.

Power is a key concept in all social science, and in IR in particular. But as Engels argues in his diatribe against Eugen Dühring, it should not be objectified. 'Power is determined by the economic condition, which provides it with *the means* to equip and maintain its instruments.' It is obtained through 'the appropriation of alien products of labour and alien labour power' (*MEW*, xx: 586, 588, emphasis added). This obviously covers the relations of production aspect in particular. In a separate fragment on 'power theory', however, Engels also notes that men mobilised for war, as human material, *change* along with other productive forces ('the change in the men of whom soldiers are made', ibid.: 155). The same point is made in Bukharin's *Economics of the Transition Period* when he writes (1976: 63) that states wage war by 'disposing of the live force of peoples on the battlefield just as they utilise it in the factories and mines'. War in this perspective is a means of enforcing and enlarging particular relations of production, expanding the rule of certain classes over others, in patterns that themselves have an ethnic imprint. Indeed as Bukharin observes in the same passage,

The entire social structure is characterized by *a peculiar monism of its architecture*: all of its parts have one and the same 'style'. In production relations men are arranged according to a specific hierarchical scale, corresponding to class groupings; in the same way this social hierarchy is apparent in the state apparatus itself and particularly, in the army. (Emphasis added.)

The social power obtained by mobilising the productive forces enters into various types of social relations simultaneously. Classes crystallise in a compound pattern synthesising productive and foreign relations; the state, too, 'is not an expression of the technical relationship of man to nature', but an outgrowth of social relations as a totality (Bukharin 1976: 61). As Kaldor notes in this connection (1982: 268), warfare is dependent 'upon the productive possibilities of society as a whole'. Power therefore should be interpreted, not as an extension of the *relations* of production, but as the productive *forces* placed in the hands of the community, first of all in the hands of its directive element or ruling class. This includes (and is premised on) the mobilisation of the community itself in the process of ethnogenesis, along with all the other natural forces over which it has secured a measure of control.

The fact that the community constitutes the foundational productive force may explain why there exists, in mainstream IR, a remarkable conflation of what constitutes *power* and what constitutes the
nation, the 'nation-state' on which the discipline hinges. In the
definition of the nation(-state), the focus is on what turns a particular society into a unit (territory, ethnic composition of a people,
language, community of fate); in the definition of power in foreign
policy, these objective attributes are then understood in their
quantitative aspect (*how large* a territory, *how many* people, *which*
resources), with the means of violence added to the list. So when
Aron (1968: 54) discusses the definitions of power of IR classics such
as N. Spykman, H.J. Morgenthau, and others, he distinguishes three
classes of elements: (1) 'the *space* occupied by the political units';
(2) 'the *available materials* and the techniques by which they can be
transformed into weapons, the *number of men* and the art of transforming them into soldiers'; and (3) 'the *collective capacity for action*'.
Clearly, this enumeration can be easily matched by classical definitions of the *nation*: (1) territory and its geographical attributes;
(2) common economy and resources; and (3) joint culture, language, means of communication, a state of its own, and a shared
sense of destiny (cf. Deutsch 1966: 17–28).

In the final analysis, the nation-in-action and power in the
process of its being applied are thus made indistinguishable.
Socialisation of internal and external nature, normative–ideological
cohesion and production and armaments statistics, all are mixed in
the brew. The result of this in realist common sense, I would argue,
is the naturalisation of conflict.

EPISTEMOLOGY AND PRACTICAL METHOD

The Marxist method is practical in the sense that all knowledge is
understood as an aspect of social practice. Hence there is no verifi-
cation of any claim about the world other than through practical
application; but historical processes occur on a scale disproportion-
ate to the experiences of individuals. Not everybody is in the position
to claim, as Lenin did in a later edition of his *Imperialism*, after the
Russian revolution, that events (in which he had himself played a
decisive role) had proved him right. We will always require a
methodology, an investigative procedure, properly speaking.

The study of society is an aspect of the productive forces which
that society has mobilised. It is a form of introspection that seeks to

establish the grounds for social development in the context of its environment – past, present and future. As Therborn writes (1976: 70–1):

the problem of the social disciplines as sciences can fruitfully be analysed in terms of a search for patterns of societal determination ... If there exist any sciences of society ... they will by definition be centrally concerned with the discovery of social determinants and the study of their operation.

The Marxist method of investigation is about choosing paths that lead to isolating such social determinants, their self-conscious abstraction from the world as it is. They are then put back into an operational context to the point where they can be recognised as being at work in the complex reality facing us 'empirically'.

In the (naturalistic) materialist tradition of Bacon, Holbach, and Feuerbach, with which historical materialism is often confused, it is assumed that what is the case is given by nature ('matter'); our capacity to study the world, too, is material in this sense. Hence materialism is the silent assumption of empiricism, which claims that we can only know what we observe as objective reality. Indeed as Hegel writes (1923: 87), empiricism 'ignores the autonomy of the thinking principle and a spiritual world which develops within it.' Hence, 'materialism, naturalism is the consequent system of empiricism'.

Marx criticised Hegel's rationalism because 'the autonomy of the thinking principle' in that philosophical system is turned into a quasi-religious world spirit encompassing everything in existence. Yet in elaborating his own method, he expressly incorporates the Hegelian emphasis on creative intellectual labour. In Marx this is no longer a functional mechanism in the discovery of a preordained, divine universe, but a historical force. Thinking is seen as an aspect of historical socialisation, by which the human mind is, so to speak, always trying to get ahead of things-as-they-are. This puts Marxism on a different plane from naturalistic materialism and its empiricist method. For all the superficial similarities (which in no small way contributed to the slide back into materialism and economism of Second and Third International Marxism), 'the fundamental tenet of materialism that the spiritual is determined by the material world means something completely different in the two doctrines' (Pannekoek n.d.: 25).

To bourgeois materialism it means that ideas are the product of the brain, to be explained from the structure and the transformations of brain matter, and hence, ultimately, from the dynamics of the atoms in the brain. To historical materialism, it means that the ideas of man are determined by social circumstances; *society is the environment which through his senses impresses itself on him.* (Emphasis added.)

In the process of exploiting nature, each society thus deepens its understanding of the world around it, for purposes determined by the power structures in that society and by the interethnic milieu in which it finds itself. Hence the relative truth of all advances in science and philosophy, and the continuities between them. But how do we proceed practically in an investigation?

To understand Marx's method, we must again go back to Hegel, whom he almost paraphrases in one of the few places where he speaks out on this issue. Hegel uses 'negation', i.e. the critique of an idea by contrasting it with its opposite, as a way of capturing that idea in its dialectical development to a higher, more complex unity which contains the 'negative' within itself. Kant had earlier claimed that fundamental questions such as whether humanity is free or acts according to external forces determining it can be convincingly argued either way. In other words, they lead into contradiction, 'antinomy', and are therefore best left to moral or religious disputation. Hegel replies to this argument that if one instead sees contradiction as a principle of movement, it becomes possible to understand (in this example) that freedom and necessity *develop* in an evolving combination, the one aspect negating and transcending the other. So an initially complete but aimless freedom 'takes in' certain impossibilities negating it, a more mature and rewarding sense of freedom is the result, and so on. Through an ever higher level of 'recognised necessity', developed freedom then acquires its true quality as the enjoyment of the possible. Hence, as he puts it in his *Encyclopaedia* (1923: 106),

the dialectic [i.e. of negation] has a positive result because it has a *determined* content, or because its result is really not the empty, abstract nothing, but the negation of *definite determinations* ... The rational, although it is something in thought and [hence] abstract, is therefore simultaneously *concrete*, because it is not a simple, formal unity [of ideas], but the unity of different determinations. (Emphasis added.)

Marx gives this, as always, a materialist twist. In the Introduction to the *Grundrisse* (1973: 100), he argues that one might begin the study of society by taking *population* as the starting point. But 'population' is an empty abstraction as long as its internal structure, its relation to the economy, is not further identified.

Thus, if I were to begin with the population, this would be a chaotic conception of the whole, and I would then, by means of further determination, move analytically towards ever more simple concepts, from the imagined concrete towards ever thinner abstractions until I had arrived at the simplest determinations. From there the journey would have to be retraced until I had finally arrived at the population again, but this time not as the chaotic conception of a whole, but as a rich totality of many determinations and relations.

This method is operative on the assumption that science is a product of mental labour, the exploitation of our inner nature at a given level of development. Therefore, the method of abstraction from the surface to the 'depths' (the exploitation of nature) does not *yield* anything, as a materialist–empiricist position would assume. We *choose* our path from the 'chaotic conception of the whole' into the depths of abstraction ourselves; on grounds which are ultimately social although refracted through our individual talents and motivations. Nothing is more telling in this respect than the fact that Marx in the *Grundrisse* takes the population as the starting point, whereas in *Capital*, which dates from roughly ten years later, he has exchanged this for the *commodity* as the key surface phenomenon traced to more fundamental determinations, and back again to complex understanding.

Yet the original thought experiment with 'population' and its determinants is of particular relevance if we want to escape the gravitational field of economic analysis. In *Capital*, the contradictory aspects of the commodity, exchange value and use value, are the starting point. They later return as the contradictory unity of, for instance, valorisation process (of capital) and technical labour process. But in reconstructing the real complexity of development from an abstract starting point, Marx's method, unlike Hegel's, takes into account historical developments which are *not* logically preordained, such as the expropriation of direct producers; a precondition of the universal commodity economy, but not itself an aspect of the commodity's dual nature. So if there is a 'logic of development' that begins with the commodity, Ritsert argues (1973: 14–7), it is one in which the commodity is itself transformed and turned into qualitatively different entities, such as money and capital. These cannot be reduced to the first element in the succession; they add *new* qualities with each step. The result is the 'thought-concrete', the

totality understood in combination with the process of its becoming. Below I will apply this to foreign relations, which does not
begin with the commodity, but with the community.

The relationship between the abstract determination and the
thought-concrete in its relation to the 'real concrete' is perhaps best
captured by the concept of 'overdetermination', a term from
psychoanalysis which refers to a deep structure operating behind
'what is at first glance but a simple pattern' (Lasswell 1960: 253).
Applied to social analysis, overdetermination allows us to see the
connections between a range of social activities and institutionally
objectified frameworks for action which would not otherwise appear
as related, because of the distances between them in time and space.
This is different from multi-causality. As Laffey and Dean observe
(2002: 100), multi-causality ('a multiplicity of externally related
causal factors') would require that each link in a series of intercon-
nected phenomena is empirically verified, since all connections are
at the same level of concreteness. Overdetermination instead refers
to 'a complex process of causality which functions in a contradictory
social whole, composed of a multiplicity of distinct, but internally
related and mutually constitutive, practices having a tendency –
because of their spatio-temporal separation within complex social
formations – to drift apart'. The 'contradictory whole' is anchored in
the abstract–general deep structure of historical development
(humanity emancipates itself from its natural constraints by exploiting its metabolism with nature, and yet ultimately cannot transcend
its own naturalness); the 'drifting apart' refers to the open-ended
quality of the course of history. What is 'internally related and
mutually constitutive', finally, points to the idea of *modes* – of production and of foreign relations.

THE ANALYSIS OF MODES OF FOREIGN RELATIONS

Let me now sum up the conceptual framework that I will develop
concretely in the chapters that follow. Foreign relations are overde-
termined by the relationship between humanity and nature; in the
process of socialisation they crystallise into more or less stable
patterns or modes, determined by the level of development of the
productive forces. Like modes of production, modes of foreign
relations originate in, reproduce and develop specific 'limits of the
possible'. Thus they determine the concrete flow of the historical
process as a whole, which in the end retains contingent, unforeseen

aspects as well. The last mile in social analysis, in other words, may have to be covered without actual theory.

The human group emerges from its natural environment as a biological–zoological entity mutating into historical existence. Between it and all other nature (including other human groups), there thus arises a contradiction: the group is part of it, and yet in its practical experience finds itself separate/different, facing a complex of alien forces which it seeks to exploit to survive. This determines its way of life and a consciousness of itself in its relations with the outside world, its subjectivity and sense of identity. 'Community' as the assertion of the particular existence of a unit of social cohesion, contradicting its submersion in nature (including the natural unity of the species, the 'human community'), thus constitutes the most abstract determination of foreign relations. It is this contradiction within which its further development will take place. Just as the wealth of the world appears to us under capitalist conditions as an ocean of commodities, so humankind is made up of a sea of communities.

In the process of ethnogenesis, the community as it arises from nature transforms its contradictory relationship to its environment into historical difference and foreign relations. Bromley (1974a: 55–6) speaks of the ethnos in this initial, formative stage as an 'ethnikos', which later develops into an 'ethnosocial organism' once it obtains a state to consolidate it (cf. Masanov 2002: 7). I will limit myself to the terms ethnos and ethnogenesis (and ethno-transformation) in order not to overburden the analysis with terminology unnecessarily; 'community' is used here as a synonym for ethnos, 'society' as a composite entity.

A 'mode', then, denotes the structure of determination by which we may recognise the particular coherence of a pattern of social relations. As a concept, it is conceived at a level in between the selected endpoint of abstraction (also the starting point of reconcretisation) and the thought-concrete; in practice, it is the evident presence of certain structural features of the social order. These will usually not be evident in their totality, but rather will transpire and reveal themselves, in the way the existence of a skeleton can be deduced from the shape and movement of the body it supports. A 'mode' is therefore simultaneously a structure of socialisation (in terms of its actuality in social development) and of determination (as an analytical structure facilitating systematic understanding). Concrete historical change always reproduces aspects of prior modes alongside the dominant one, in a fluid process of gestation, enfolding, atrophy, and sedimentation.

A mode of *production* refers to the 'complex unity of the forces and relations of production, specifies how labour appropriates from nature, how the means of production and social product are distributed in society and how the labour process is organised' (Megarry 1995: 217; cf. Balibar 1975: 98). Over time, successive modes of production develop, enfolding prior ones in often contingent combinations. Any given society, Poulantzas writes (1971, i: 72), will therefore comprise 'an entire series of phenomena of fractioning of classes, dissolution of classes, fusion of classes ... specific categories, etc. These cannot always be located by an investigation of the pure modes of production that have entered into the combination.'

Modes of foreign relations become entwined in the same way. A mode of foreign relations combines definite patterns of occupying space, protecting it, and organising exchange. These too are grafted onto a given level of development of the productive forces, mobilised for the encounter with others and geared to the spatial domain where it occurs. The contradiction between the productive forces and foreign relations, which at some point will generate a new mode of foreign relations and dislodge or marginalise the old, can be traced back to the contradiction between the initial separate individuality of the community and its immersion in the environment. Through ethnogenesis, the key productive force that is the community itself is created and reproduced. In it the limits of the possible are centrally embodied. In later development, ethno-transformation on the basis of new possibilities created by new productive forces (obtained by exchange, through migration, or otherwise), may compound the ethnic identity, along with the socialising effect of a form of state. At each stage, pressures will build up to transcend the particularities of the given mode of foreign relations to adjust to new limits of the possible.

In Figure 1.1, I have depicted the 'journey retraced' from the most abstract determination to concrete social change, for foreign and productive relations. Of course all the limitations of a schematic representation are acknowledged. The figure aims to show how the real complexity of foreign relations is (over-)determined by the productive forces as they develop in given productive and foreign relations. The productive forces provide the means (M) for the conduct of each (P and F, respectively). At a further level of concretisation

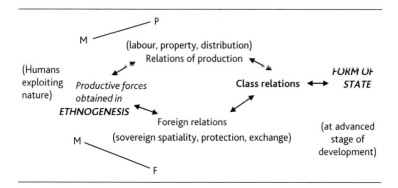

Figure 1.1 From the Abstract to the Concrete: Productive Forces, Relations of Production, and Foreign Relations

and development, ethnic identity and class relations are condensed into a particular form of state.

The line M—P in the figure denotes the mode of production (the relations of production within which the productive forces develop); M—F, the mode of foreign relations. Note than no lines have been drawn between foreign and production relations. Their mutual connection resides in the productive forces, on which each set of relations relies, and in class relations, which likewise rest on each, and which in the case of foreign relations, include the interethnic milieu and the imperial and inter-state contexts enveloping it at a higher level of development.

Let me conclude this chapter by briefly addressing a few general aspects of the foreign encounter.

Space and the Interethnic Milieu

Occupying space is the first element of every pattern of foreign relations. In Marx's phrase (1973: 474), it is 'the great communal labour which is required ... to occupy the objective conditions of being there alive'. By the appropriation of space and establishing sovereignty over it (not necessarily as a strictly demarcated, exclusive territory), ethnogenesis develops its initial momentum; 'ethnocultural differences, which lie at the basis of interethnic relations ... are the result of asynchronous adaptation of various groups to the natural, anthropogenic, technogenic, and civilizational conditions of mankind's development in time-space' (Masanov, 2002: 9).

Geography plays a role here, not as territory per se, but in terms of the natural milieu more generally.

In the shaping of a community, Shirokogorov writes (1970: 12), the primary milieu and interethnic pressure are the most important ones. Once a unit emerges, it 'transmits its experience of adaptation to the local conditions through tradition, and its physical adaptation through the complex mechanism of inheritance; accumulating, in this way, the work of previous generations.' Ecological conditions – topography, climate, vegetation, and animals – are varied, so the interethnic milieu will always be different too. Borochov makes the same point. 'The state of the forces of production and their development,' he claims (1972: 137), 'are primarily dependent on the natural conditions which man must face in his struggle for existence. The condition of the forces of production is therefore dependent on the geographic environment, and the latter is, of course, *different* in *different* places.' This is not geographical determinism: as Gumilev puts it (1987: 26), 'the historical fate of a people [ethnos], being the result of their economic activity, is not determined by, but is linked with, the dynamic condition of the landscape they occupy'.

Sovereignty over a spatial domain, then, is the pivot on which the foreign encounter is premised; whether we are speaking of a stretch of land, a street, a particular professional environment, or any other. Only its sovereign claim to space entitles an ethnos to enter into relations of competition, emulation, and exchange with others in foreign relations (Linklater 1990: 64; cf. *Authors' Collective*, 1982: 9). The 'competitive' aspect is not to be mistaken for the 'anarchy' of realist IR; division of labour between ethnoi is one obvious option open to every community, and whether foreign relations develop along conflictual or cooperative lines is itself an aspect of ethnogenesis.

The interethnic milieu has to be assumed as an aspect of historical humanity from the start, on a par with relations of production within the community. If not, we are assuming that societies develop on their own, engaging in foreign relations only *after* they have effectively constituted themselves – what may be called the 'comparative politics fallacy'. The idea of international relations in fact is based on this assumption. It presumes that the foreign has been exteriorised, and that a homogeneous community has been established as a result. Usually this homogeneity is then projected back into history, and what Benedict Anderson (1991) calls the 'imagined community', with hindsight endowed with a capacity to develop on its own.

Protection and the Dialectic of Change

'To protect and perpetuate the occupation' according to Marx (1973: 474) is the second task facing the commune once it has secured a living space. This refers to a range of protective activities to main tain its way of life and hold on a thoroughfare, territory, or sector, over which the community establishes its sovereignty. These activities include violence and war, but involve non-violent activities too, and are inevitably entwined with magic and ritual. Protection too evolves as the limits of the possible are widened. Indeed this aspect may be taken to illustrate how the dialectic between forces of production and foreign relations develops as a general principle.

When the productive forces available to the community, and the cultural level and political efficacy allowing it to wield them effectively, outgrow the conditions under which they have developed, the nature and measure of social space and the modalities of its protection (and exchange) have to be recast, too. Borochov, who does not explicitly identify foreign relations, sees the dialectic of change in ethnic terms as the outcome of a contradiction between productive forces and conditions of production. Thus (1972: 140) 'the nationality problem … arises when the development of the forces of production of a nationality conflicts with the state of the conditions of production'.

It is however perfectly possible to analyse the dynamic interaction between the productive forces and foreign relations in its own right. As with forces and relations of production, the former will develop to the point where the prevailing relations, which have congealed into a particular mode, can no longer accommodate them, and turn into an obstacle to further development – or in Braudel's terms, when the possible outstrips the actual. If we think of *revolution* as the shock-like adjustment of the relations of production to productive forces and possibilities that an existing social order can no longer accommodate, *war* operates as the synchronising force in foreign relations. Just as accumulated tensions on a tectonic fault line explode in an earthquake, war (and revolution) acts as a valve for the release of hidden energies generated by a growing disparity between the actual and the potential. By mobilising all the means a society has available for a supreme test, war raises and in the course of the struggle equalises the levels of material possibility and mental ability among the belligerents. Even the retreating/defeated party in war is brought closer to the general level of development by exposure to the actions of the advancing/victorious side (cf. Kolko 1994: 65, 78–9).

There have been few revolutions that did not arise from or entail war, and vice versa. The growing scale of socialisation would suggest that these wars, too, involve ever larger belligerent formations and turn into world wars. But the same development drives towards political integration, inducing further ethno-transformation; thus war is exteriorised and protection eventually made part of routine policing.

Exchange and Language

Exchange, finally, should not only be understood as trade. It includes the provision of spouses, exchange of gifts, and the dissemination of culture that is inevitably involved in being exposed to foreign communities. Neither is it something which belongs to the mode of production on which foreign relations are then grafted as a superstructure. Exchange is of all ages and according to Marx (1973: 103) appears first 'in the connection of the different communities with one another, not in the relations between the different members of a single community'. Since I will elaborate the typical patterns of exchange of each mode of foreign relations in later chapters, let me here briefly mention an aspect that also runs through all of them, language.

All ethnogenesis evolves along 'frontiers of contiguity' with others. Proximity, including demographic dynamics along the boundary line, obviously influences the distribution of space (*Authors' Collective*, 1982: 18–19). The combined reproduction of an endogamous population conscious of its identity, merging with others through intermarriage and passing on genetic material that way, may then contribute to ethno-transformation, the change into a new ethnos. Here language plays a role, because a medium of communication is a crucial element in defining an ethnos. But it is not itself a sufficient criterion. There are multilingual societies which have maintained themselves over time (Bromley 1977: 53). Indeed, as Shirokogorov writes (1970: 61), 'when the language does not obstruct the influx of other ethnographical elements transmitted through language, the ethnographic complexes blend together, or some better adapted elements of one complex substitute the elements of another'.

Language is the repository of the collective experiences of an ethnos. It therefore necessarily records the presence of others, their habits and actions, and the words for them; just as it contains the central storyline of the ethnos itself (Ostler 2006: 7). All languages will show a tendency to absorb elements of speech from across the frontier of contiguity. Languages with a common origin,

Lévi-Strauss notes (1987: 15), 'have a tendency to differentiate themselves from each other (such as Russian, French and English), whereas languages with different origins but spoken in contiguous territories, [may] develop a common character'. The example he gives is Russian, which has differentiated itself from other Slav languages by adopting certain phonetic traits of Finno-Ugrian and Turkic languages spoken on the country's frontiers.

Words will be assimilated across borders through direct contact. There may be a phonetic basis for their adoption; otherwise, tones, flexions, suffixes and prefixes will be used. Single words may be distributed across languages whilst their meanings may shift. 'Zaun' in German is the fence around a garden; in Dutch, it is the garden itself ('tuin'); in the English 'town', it is the settlement as a whole. Sometimes assimilation happens by logical selection. Shirokogorov (1970: 105, 176) gives the example of the Siberian Tungus word for 'pit dwelling', the semi-underground house of Chinese origin, which in the dialect of a group not using this type of house means 'the bear's haunt'. Sometimes word spreads by what is called spontaneous etymology, as with children. The German word for mobile phone, 'handy' (as in English) is an example of that. The French on the other hand are wont to develop alternatives for English terms by tapping into their own vocabulary in an attempt to resist the prevailing language hierarchy. 'Courriel', e-mail, combines 'courrier', message, with 'el' from electronic. However, as outlined by de Swaan (2001: ch. 1; cf. Ostler 2006: 517), in today's hierarchical order of languages, English appears solidly entrenched as the 'hypercentral' language associated with the globalisation of the Western way of life.

Summing up, a mode of foreign relations comprises three aspects (sovereign spatiality, protection, and exchange) that crystallise into a definite pattern enabled by a certain level of development of the productive forces. The community itself is the key productive force, the subject disposing of the means ('power') to conduct foreign relations; although at a higher stage of development, states claim that prerogative from/for the community(-ies). As a structure of socialisation and determination, a mode of foreign relations is also a constitutive force in the shaping of class relations. It would be hard to imagine a 'ruling' class which did not, from the start, assume key tasks in making the sovereign claim to space, organising protection, and regulating exchange. All class formation, it would follow, is refracted through the lens of ethnogenesis, lending a particular

Table 1.1 Modes of Foreign Relations and their Defining Characteristics

Mode of Foreign Relations	Sovereign Occupation of Space	Organisation of Protection	Patterns of Exchange
Tribal Relations	status in shared space, ancestral claims	symbolic rituals, feud, threats	barter, gifts, exchange of women, raiding
Empire/ nomad Relations	sedentary versus mobile occupation, incorporation	recruitment of nomad warriors on frontier	tribute, frontier trade trade diasporas
Sovereign Equality	exclusive territorial jurisdiction	popular armies, natural boundaries, power balance	mercantilism, dissemination of national cultures
Global Governance	functional multiplication of sovereign spheres	rapid deployment police forces, collective security	homogenisation/ differentiation, globally integrated production chains

'ethnicity' to each class as it forms in the process of exploitation of nature through society. Not only as the ethnicity of a ruling class but also, say, as a willingness to work for one's 'own' employer, for instance in order to maintain the distance from other employable ethnic groups.

On the basis of the foregoing, then, I distinguish four modes of foreign relations (Table 1.1).

Clearly these modes should be taken for what they are: structures of socialisation and determination understood in relative isolation. They cannot be seen as straightforward historical stages. The earlier patterns re-emerge in 'postmodernity' as part of the extreme inequalities characterising our contemporary world: 'empire' is all around us, as is, paradoxically, the 'tribal' (or, for that matter, 'nomads'). Let us begin with the original tribal form in the next chapter.

2
Tribal Encounters

There is no founding date like 1648 for foreign relations; the origins of difference among human communities must be traced to how we assume they began to socialise their relationship to external and internal nature and to each other from the very dawn of humanity. Humans evolved first in Africa as opportunistic gatherers and scavengers, broadening the limits of the possible by walking upright, developing tools and weapons. Thus they branched out, adapting to their environment and to the proximity of others. In the process of ethnogenesis, a shared culture and subjectivity arise from this process, shaping the ethnos as a unit separate from others; common physical traits are then a matter of lineage and the passing on of genetic material and habits from parents to children. This is not to say, of course, that skin colour and other signifiers of difference that result from the adaptation to natural conditions do not play a role in how others are perceived. Race and racism have been and remain major forces in politics, and as such contribute to foreign relations; but not biologically.

In this chapter I look at foreign relations in the earliest form we can assume they existed, which I label tribal. I begin with the question of the differential socialisation of nature, turning next to the Marxist legacy, notably Marx's ethnographic notebooks and Engels' *The Origins of the Family, Private Property, and the State*. These works identify the issue of endogamy/exogamy as the bedrock of ethnogenesis and foreign relations; for all their other limitations, they prefigure Lévi-Strauss's theory in this domain. The three aspects of the tribal mode are then developed in more detail.

DIFFERENCE, COMMUNICATION, FOREIGN RELATIONS

The exploitation of nature by human communities mobilises the material forces at their disposal. It moulds the human collective as such, its capacity for action and reflection, as well as the overall view of the world through which it validates the actions of its own community and of others. Initial ethnogenesis consists of the community's creative response to the challenges and opportunities posed by the geography and climatic conditions in which it finds itself – on the seashore, in forests, on the steppe, and so on. In the words of A. Bell-Fialkoff (as in de Vries and Goudsblom 2002: 83), 'if the core European areas bordered on a wide expanse of the steppe or if China faced a densely forested zone in the north, their histories might have been very different'.

The presence of others is a crucial determinant in the process. It provides the spur to reflect on how to develop the community in an ordered way, however elementary; further development is premised on it. As Gledhill argues (1994: 46),

forms of human social and political organization cannot be seen simply as the unconstrained exploration by 'people' of a series of logical possibilities, as if every human community sat isolated on an island in the midst of a limitless ocean. Other societies are part of any human group's environment.

Difference at a low level of development is obviously still limited. The means at the disposal of the community allow little fundamental variation. This also holds for the elementary mode of production, the domestic mode (alternatively labelled lineage or kinship mode – Rey 1983; Meillassoux 1981). Braudel (1981: 176–8) notes how the 'people of the hoe' (the planting tool of early agriculture) on different continents, who cannot have had an inkling of each other's existence, nevertheless do many things in strikingly similar ways. However, since ethnogenesis builds on initial adaptive choices, small variations may produce huge differences within a fairly short time.

Tools and Consciousness

Ethnogenesis begins with anthropogenesis, the evolution of hominids into the human species (Megarry 1995). Beginning some 5 million years ago, lower temperatures and changes in precipitation made tropical forests shrink, and the onset of glacial conditions may have gradually led to the extinction of many primate varieties in Eurasia. In Africa, hominid populations were also under pressure, and the unstable environment created rapid evolutionary change. The initial transformation towards the human form, still entirely through natural selection, notably includes walking upright. This posture frees the upper part of the body from the functions of locomotion, so that arms and hands can be used for lifting, carrying, and handling objects. It entailed physiological changes that made childbirth more difficult, however, and strong group bonds were needed to rear and protect vulnerable offspring.

Around 2 million years ago, as many as seven hominid species may have lived in Africa, but not all had equal chances of survival. Omnivores had an advantage over vegetarians, who were outcompeted by more efficient herbivores in the expanding savannahs; those walking upright and using their hands for manipulation outperformed those who did not; whilst those who used pieces of rock for cutting and scraping branches or hides did better than those relying only on their teeth. *Homo habilis*, four feet tall but with a large brain, earned its name by combining these advantages. They and other hominids are assumed to have migrated already into Asia Minor, spreading further into Eurasia very early on; traces of this early migration have been found as far away as China. A second wave of communities migrating out of Africa was made up of the later evolved *Homo sapiens*. It began around 200,000 years ago, taking the same route (de Vries and Goudsblom 2002: 24–5). Once the making of fire had been mastered (estimates vary about when this happened), its use for cooking, heating, and protection greatly enhanced the life chances of the groups to whom it was available.

The term 'Stone Age' is usually reserved for the epoch in which the tools of Homo sapiens were stone implements obtained by cutting and carving. Thus it coincides with the second wave of migrations and their aftermath. But the use by hominids of pebbles and flints as tools goes back much further (Barber 1999: 99, cf. 182–3). Already in the middle Pleistocene, 500,000 thousand years ago, there are traces of differential socialisation, with distinct regional patterns of tool-making. One, concentrated in central and east Asia, consists of flint choppers and, less frequently, hand cutters, apparently developed to exploit food supplies available on the seashore, on grassland, or in river valleys. The other, the so-called Acheulean tools, in addition include hand axes, especially hand axes chipped on both faces. These were found notably in what were heavily forested areas, in Africa, Europe, western Asia, and India (cf. overview in Megarry 1995: 162–3, table 6.1).

With the longer range of territorial displacement made possible by bipedal walking, hominids cultivated memory, knowledge, and learning, passing it on to offspring during extended child-rearing intervals. Distant sources of stone used in tools suggest that hominids already had a mental map, an image of the finished product, and other indications of planned activity (Ponting 2001: 37–8). Exogamy, a hallmark of human society, would have been a cultural attribute of contact with outsiders, probably building on an instinctual substratum; with time it became embedded in ritual greetings, exchange of gifts and various other early forms of dealing with foreign communities. All of this (not least the need to avoid a fight) presupposes the ability to communicate more complex messages through a system of starters (signs, sounds) and reflexes which lays the groundwork for the later development of language (Shirokogorov, 1970: 39–43).

Speech and language are premised on the ability to break up the total vision that animals have of the world around them. The objectification of things by words (initially, words denoting an act conjoined with the thing) makes possible their discrete observation and identification; relations between them, such as the distinction between means and ends, can then be postulated 'abstractly', through a mental activity which distances itself from the immediate time/space constraints of the objectified world. Indeed as A. Leroi-Gourhan puts it, 'the domestication of time and space is the most important factor in hominisation' (as in Attali, 2003: 42). Words then mutate and language expands in contact with other groups, possibly strangers, with whom new items may by exchanged and experiences communicated in ways that avoided conflict. The contradictory separation of an ethnos from the species obtains its express form in the mosaic of languages.

The evolutionary mutation of the shape of the human mouth and throat that made rapid speech possible occurred between 150,000 and 100,000 years ago (Barber 1999: 183). It distinguishes *Homo sapiens sapiens* from *H. sapiens neanderthalensis*, the last rival subspecies. Neanderthals lived between 130,000 and 24,000 years ago in western Asia and Europe and combined large brain size, fire, clothing and tool making with primitive features. They also buried their dead, which suggests a sense of an after-life, something of which no evidence exists in other proto-humans. But Neanderthal anatomy lacked the physical preconditions for speech, and tooth-wear patterns suggest that they still used their mouth where humans use their hands (Diamond 1998: 37–40). Aleksejev (1974: 289) claims that the Australoid human type has certain Neanderthal features. It is more likely, given the archaeological record, that interbreeding occurred with Europeans, if at all. According to a recent hypothesis (as in Foucart 2006: 7), a 5 per cent share of Neanderthal DNA would explain the genetic difference of Europeans compared to west Africans, who by that measure would have been the 'purer' humans.

A major cultural leap occurred around 35,000 years ago. This resulted in bone-tipped harpoons, spears, eyed needles, and eventually the bow and arrow, the high-tech implement of its age. Communities able to obtain these implements spread from the Middle East into Europe, along the southern limits of the ice sheets. Cromagnon man (named after the cave in France where signs of their existence were first discovered) apparently settled in relatively large numbers in what was then the taiga of the Dordogne and northern Spain (Ponting 1991: 28–9). Figurative art dating from this era and found in south-west France and in Altamira in Spain (as well as in South Africa and Australia) is indicative of communities' capacity to understand their condition and express it in specific cultural terms. After a visit to the Lascaux caves, with their dazzling murals of prehistoric bulls and reindeer, Picasso made the oft-quoted remark (here in Graff 2006: 36) that he and his fellow modern artists had invented nothing that was not already there.

In contrast to our contemporary self-consciousness and aesthetics, however, the elementary cosmology of early communities articulated the extremely limited control of the forces of nature, including their own mental world. They were conscious of their precarious existence, given their dependence on muscle power, including a radius of action limited by walking distance. The idea that there was a separate world of the spirits, and that each person and object in the temporary world has a spiritual 'double' animating it, guided them. Not only was one bound to return to it, but dreams and hallucinations allowed glimpses of this other world during one's lifetime (Barber 1999: 161). Orally transmitted myths – interpretive, sacred narratives about ancestors, eternity and temporal existence, darkness and light – sought to rationalise this condition. If these myths are often remarkably similar, this is partly because people had not yet progressed much beyond the mental substratum inherited from nature, and their experiences, whilst differently articulated in speech and in the imagery employed (few canoes in the savannah), tend to be limited to broadly identical classes of events. Myths also provide a common normative structure to separate but affiliated groups (Buzan and Little 2000: 132; Bromley 1977: 121).

The role of myths and those able to transmit and interpret them, and hence of custom and ritual, is as important as the ability to obtain food and shelter. Since the community is the paramount productive force, its sense of identity, the presence of others, and the internal structure of the unit all depend on the power of 'explanation' that ideas provide at any prevailing level of material and mental development (Mann 1986: 21). Power is articulated by the command over the sphere of ideas coupled with the capacity to enforce compliance; it is not a mechanical reflection of a prior exploitative relation in the sense of productive relations. As al-Khafaji writes (2004: 204), 'political authority is the first embryo of class division, rather than being a medium to regulate existing class conflicts'.

Let us now investigate more closely how differential socialisation occurs in relation to the natural and interethnic environments.

Differential Socialisation and Ethnogenesis

After the last glaciation (Alpine and Scandinavian ice sheets were growing until 18,000 years ago), bands of humans living in various parts of Eurasia migrated further to Oceania and Australia, and across the Bering land bridge to the Americas. By the end of the ice age, 12,000 years ago, all ice-free parts of the globe had been settled, very sparsely of course. This spread in itself produced further cultural variation. 'The conditions of the primary milieu, which on the surface of this planet form thousands of distinct regions ... imply a special local adaptation', writes Shirokogorov (1970: 20). *'The better the unit is adapted, the more distinct it is*, as compared with other neighbouring groups living in different conditions of milieu' (emphasis added). Institutions such as the ceremonial burial of the dead, the incest taboo and various concepts of (extended) family associated with it, gifts and sacrifice, are testimony to the fact that human communities at an early stage saw themselves as units and identified others as foreign (Kelly 2000: 125–7).

Nevertheless contact must have been eagerly sought to avoid being enclosed in too small a unit. To survive and procreate communities of a few hundred would have needed to find mates from neighbouring bands, voluntarily or by force (Buzan and Little 2000: 116–18). In the words of L.T. Hobhouse and his associates (as in Vincent 1990: 122), 'Culture contact, direct or indirect, [was] ... the normal, not exceptional, process throughout human history.' This made it possible to draw resources, human and cultural, from others; widening the community's mental horizon and opportunities for survival. 'The contactable world', Mann notes (1986: 46), 'was always larger than could be organised practically into one group.' Stone, bone, and antler artefacts served as signifiers in these contacts, as means of visual communication to facilitate interaction and make it more predictable. Distinctive styles of common art forms carried a message of separateness within a larger, shared territory or community; they may also have served to signify exchange or mating networks. Like piercings and tattoos today, 'the sudden appearance and spread of various modes of personal adornment could also have had this function' (Megarry 1995: 278).

Interactive socialisation is in turn determined by the natural milieu, so that it proceeds differentially. In mountainous regions near the sea, especially in the lower latitudes, a great many ecological niches may allow a large number of small ethnoi to maintain relatively separate existences, Shirokogorov claims (1970: 25); a large territory with uniform climatic conditions and identical flora and fauna on the other hand will favour the formation of larger units early on. But whilst a community 'always tends to avoid interethnical pressure, it cannot successfully survive without this pressure' (ibid.: 18). This sums up the contradictory dynamic of ethnic separation and common humanity in which foreign relations evolve.

All along, the community changes itself as it transforms its environment. Thus it appears in a different shape, and differentially equipped, in the encounter with other groups. This includes physical changes. The bludgeoning of prey animals with clubs places a premium on pure muscle power and weight, which also can be brought to bear on human neighbours. Compact bodies help preserve heat; tall, slender postures make running at greater speed possible; on horseback, a stocky athlete can become one with his riding animal more easily, and so on and so forth (cf. Megarry 1995: 209–10). Obviously, with the increasing role played by artefacts, bodily qualifications recede into the background, but they are reproduced genetically, and mental differentiations remain, too.

Communities specialising in hunting among other things will socialise the characteristics of prey animals. 'For the hunter, animal wildness is the essential "other", the ontologically and morally opposite condition against which he defines his own humanity', Zulaika writes (1993: 24, referring to G. H. Mead's concept of the 'generalised other').

The hunter's self emerged in intimate confrontation with that wild quality – with all its trance-like ferocity, yet also with all its symbolic limitations and conceptual indeterminacy. The categorical 'man' that emerges from such a close encounter with the savage beast partakes of the semantic uncertainties of his antagonist.

By using techniques such as lying in wait, surprise, and speed, human hunting parties had to beat their quarry on its own terrain. Eskimos do not just mimic the seals they hunt by the shape of the kayak, their paddles (the seal's flippers), and so on; they also must 'think like' the seal if they want to catch one (Toynbee 1935, iii: 87). It was not everywhere, however, that hunting was a matter of 'trance-like ferocity'. In the harsher climate of ice-age Europe, it had to be confined to culling the sick and the old from herds of larger animals to avoid scaring them out of range entirely, so that in the area stretching between Hungary and the Black Sea, what developed was a matter of carefully following the animals' seasonal movements, herding rather than hunting (Ponting 1991: 27).

Collective hunting and the capacity for strategic violence it entails had important consequences for the social organisation within groups, especially gender relations. The male hunting/raiding party raised the profile of men on account of their physical strength and granted them freedom from nurturing tasks. Tiger's concept of 'male bonding', which he sees as 'the spinal column of a community' (1970: 78), may be an over-generalisation. Yet for communities shifting from trapping and gathering and scavenging to confronting larger game in an armed encounter, it seems safe to assume that they indeed 'derive their intra-dependence, their structure, their social coherence, and in good part their continuity through the past to the future, from a hierarchical linkage of significant males'. Earlier, the capacity to give birth had privileged 'significant females' in this sense; now, in Mumford's words (1961: 21), 'the masculine contribution, curbed and tamed, if not rejected, by the earlier acts of domestication, suddenly returned with redoubled vigour, bringing with it a new dynamism, expressing itself as a desire to tame and control nature, to dominate and master strong and mettlesome animals'. Engels (*MEW*, xxi: 61) famously described this as the 'historic defeat of the female sex'.

The reason people shifted from gathering wild fruits and hunting animals (always a gamble) to planting seeds differs for different places. Communities living in the monsoonal forests of south-east Asia could not clear and work the land until they obtained sufficient quantities of iron tools, which only happened somewhere halfway through the first millennium BC. In south-west Asia on the other hand, forms of agriculture emerged as far back as the eleventh millennium. As a cooler climate dried up the 'Garden of Eden' in the upper reaches of the Euphrates and Tigris rivers, with its abundance of game and fruits and berries, people migrated to the Jordan valley lakes and the alluvial plains of the south which then had plentiful wild cereals. They survived by domesticating goats and sheep (de

Vries and Goudblom 2002: 83–4, 97). From harvesting wild varieties, people took to sowing their seeds; first, according to Engels (*MEW*, xxi: 33; cf. Ponting 1991: 44), to provide fodder for the animals, only later for human nutrition.

Southern Mesopotamia, the river basins of Egypt and west Asia, and of the Don and Dnepr in today's Russia, all offered suitable grasslands and arable fields. Hence they became the poles of attraction for further migration. 'To those regions they gravitated naturally', Marx writes (1973: 472). 'There the distant Aryan ancestors are found, where they encountered similar Semitic pastoral tribes'.[1] Thus they obtained land that was fertile enough, he notes elsewhere (1976: 178), to suspend 'the migratory form of life … the first form of the mode of existence'.

Given their limited means, however, the number of people that early agricultural settlements could support was limited too, so that those on the margins of settled areas would be forced to wander off to find grass for the animals. At some point they would drop agriculture altogether and become full-time pastoralists again. This is how, according to Lattimore (1962: 24–5), actual nomadism developed as a counterpoint to sedentary life. It might include taking up an exchange role: as still happens in Iran and Aghanistan, traders may be part-time pastoralists, part-time merchants travelling round to trade with sedentary communities (Rosman and Rubel 1976: 548). For coastal and river peoples, waterways always offered an escape route from the dull compulsions of agriculture, both for trade and for piracy. 'Water … thus became a crucial element in another aspect of human development … *exchange*, in the form of trade, raid and conquest' (de Vries and Goudsblom 2002: 80, emphasis added).

The return to a free life on the steppe, with the periodic migrations within a specific cycle that gives it its specific character, exposed the nomads to the vacillations of climate. Dry spells would trigger incursions by pastoralists into the arable land of sedentary neighbours. From tooth marks on horse skulls found in the Caspian steppe, it has been inferred that around 4000 BC the animal was harnessed by herders; this also enabled them to undertake surprise raids on settled communities. How the connection between climate and nomad raiding must be understood remains contested (as we shall

[1] The term 'Aryan', meaning 'noble' (as in the Greek 'aristos'; the words Iran and Eire come from the same root, M. Wood 2005: 50–1), obtained a racist connotation in Hitler Germany, and I will speak of Indo-European (or Indo-Iranian for the eastern branches), reserving 'Aryan' for the peoples invading India in the second millennium BC.

see in Chapter 3), but not the connection itself. 'Since the dawn of nomadism', Barber writes (1999: 36, cf. 192), 'perturbation any-where on the steppe seems to have sent ripples of upheaval across the grasslands from one end to another – from Hungary to China and back again.'

To protect themselves against their nomadic neighbours, the earliest settled communities organised their defences by erecting palisades or walls of sun-dried brick. Thus actual proto-cities, such as Jericho in the Jordan river valley and Çatal Hüyük in central Anatolia, developed as early as 7000 BC. Çatal Hüyük was a compact urban area without streets and with an estimated 5,000 inhabitants (Soja 2003: 30). Whether rising productivity on the land enabled urban-isation (the position of Mumford 1961) or the other way around (Jane Jacobs' claim, as in Soja 2003: 32 and Diamond 1998: 111, 284) cannot be answered in general. The sequence is dependent on particular opportunities for exploiting nature in each case. Çatal Hüyük had obsidian deposits, and may have been one of the first places where people dug up small globules of copper which they hammered into tools or ornaments. Two or three thousand years later, the practice of smelting mineral ore into copper was developed in eastern Turkey, and spread from there across the Fertile Crescent by the mid fourth millennium BC (Ponting 1991: 46, 66).

The transition to agriculture was obviously tortuous and often hard to accept. The human instinctual apparatus is not pre-programmed for observing seasonal patterns of precipitation and cycles of growth, or for maintaining an infrastructure of flood protection and irrigation. Neither will a community by nature be mentally equipped to store some of its foodstuffs as reserves, and have the discipline to gear to a lower intake to overcome scarcity and preserve stores. To observe these rules, new dispositions must be developed and some form of rank society is required to enforce them (Diamond 1998: 86–9). Priestly intervention to reconcile agricultural communi-ties to their fate has left us with circles of megaliths which, by their layout and the rituals presumably performed in them, record the effort to assimilate a new, precarious dependence on the sun and on water. Such monuments have been found on the shores of a former lake in what is now the Sahara, and later appeared also in Europe, most famously at Stonehenge (de Vries and Goudsblom 2002: 56). Rank society and elaborate ritual and monuments thus differentiate agricultural communities from more loosely organised, egalitarian, and independent-minded pastoralists.

In turn, river delta agriculture dependent on irrigation, with its extensive layout and cereal monoculture, must be distinguished from the forest-edge agriculture on the mountain slopes of the Iranian Plateau, northern China and Central America, which exploits high biodiversity instead (de Vries and Goudsblom 2002: 76). In monocultures, the choice of cereal is a vector of differentiation too. Braudel (1981: ch. 2) expounds at length on the differential effects of a particular type of staple food in ethnogenesis – wheat in Europe, rice in Asia, and maize in the Americas; each has specific implications for the use and organisation of space and time, as well as requiring different forms of social organisation. Even dry-field and wet-field rice cultivation have different requirements and consequences. Dry-field rice growing was unattractive to the stone age Japanese gatherers and fishermen of the Jomon culture; only when the high-yield wet-field pattern became available was the turn to agriculture worth taking (de Vries and Goudsblom 2002: 93).

The river plains of southern Mesopotamia gave rise to the first truly urban civilisation, Sumer. Occupying space in the form of a city entails a greater population density, and hence, to quote Mumford (1961: 31), 'an enormous expansion of human capabilities in every direction'. The largest Sumerian cities, such as Uruk and Lagash, developed to a size of tens of thousands of inhabitants; their achievements are all the more impressive because so many were entirely indigenous, such as writing. The cities were still independent, ruled by priesthoods in the name of their respective deities. Feuds between them erupted regularly as they 'learned to prey on each other' (ibid. 1961: 43). Sumerian civilisation developed propitiously because the 'unsettling' proximity of nomadic tribes required constant adaptations and innovations. Pastoral nomads are described as 'dangerous and disruptive' in contemporary texts as early as the third millennium (Buzan and Little 2000: 184). Semitic pastoralists may have migrated from east Africa to the Middle East to evade the expanding Sahara; the similarities between Ethiopic and Akkadian, the Semitic master language which replaced Sumerian whilst adopting its script, would speak for this (Ostler 2006: 36–7, 54).

Sumer exerted a cultural influence along trade routes reaching as far as Syria, Arabia, and the Indus valley. Its form of urban settlement spread with it, but with the temporary exception of the ruler of Umma in the twenty-fourth century BC, the city-state form was not truly transcended until the Akkadian conquest to which we turn in Chapter 3 (McNeill 1991: 44–5). Overgrazing by goats, desertification, and the salinisation of the low-lying Mesopotamian floodplains at some point triggered migration pressures towards the north again, resulting in bitter wars with those who had meanwhile taken up residence there (Diamond 1998: 110, 411; de Vries and Goudsblom 2002: 85).

The Indus valley (covering modern Pakistan, Kashmir, and the Punjab) was also home to an urban civilisation, created by what may have been a branch of the pre-Aryan, Elamite ethnos of Iran. Judging from common terms in Elamite and ancient Dravidian (from which the Tamil language of south India and northern Sri Lanka derives), the Elamites–Dravidians were already agriculturalists before they migrated to the south-east. Unlike Sumer's cities (which were often within sight of each other), Indus settlements were spread over an area stretching from Afghanistan to the Himalayan foothills. The largest cities, Harappa and Mohenjo-Daro, by the mid third millennium were each inhabited by up to 80,000 people. They were in regular contact with Sumer; the coastal seas between them were navigated as early as 2000 BC (M. Wood 2005: 53–7, 122–9).

One effect of the urban way of life is the homogenisation of language. Writing, initially to maintain records, in addition enables a community to develop a collective memory, carefully watched over by those in power – this is a key aspect of social discipline. A lingua franca to communicate with foreigners is also an urban phenomenon (Ostler 2006: 10–11; cf. Buzan and Little 2000: 141). If city life entailed a notable decline in human health as well, this was because the freedom, excitement and physical exertions of migratory existence in small groups had gone; people now shared cramped quarters by their thousands, with diseases easily jumping from domestic animals in daily proximity to them. Towns took measures to improve sanitation early on (fresh water tanks and public baths already existed in the Indus cities), but frequent epidemics are a feature of urbanised existence (cf. Ponting 1991: 225–7; 348).

Thus with each mutation – from scavengers and gatherers to big-game hunters, from forest tribes and steppe pastoralists to agriculture and urban settlement – the range of differently socialised communities increases. Their mutual relations become more diversified with the greater variation; they are truly *foreign* relations in the sense of a naturalised, alienated perception of difference. Geography is the initial differentiator, eliciting different methods of occupying space, protection, and exchange. As Michael Wood puts it (2005: 14), 'Hill peoples against peoples of the plain, nomads against sedentary farmers: these are two of the most ancient confrontations in human history.' This leaves the choice of conflict or cooperation open. We return to the nomads in the next chapter; as to the hill peoples, Braudel observes (1981: 64) that in Europe, mountain dwellers were integrated into wider society, whereas in the East, difference was not overcome. 'The Chinese waged an unceasing war against their wild mountain population ... It was the same in India.' Another geographical peculiarity of world-historic importance was the proximity to water routes all along the perimeter of Europe. This would stimulate, in due course, the conquest of the Atlantic and the creation of an English-speaking heartland at the centre of the modern world.

Differential ethnogenesis gives rise to different sets of values. A comparative study undertaken by Hobhouse and his associates (as in Vincent 1990: 97, table 2.2) showed that hunting communities typically respond to injury by seeking violent retaliation, whereas agricultural societies tend to opt for atonement and compensation to satisfy their sense of justice. Regular exchange developed as differently socialised communities were pressed together more closely. As Shirokogorov writes (1970: 21), 'specialisation opens a new possibility for a further increase in population; for along with the establishment of close relations, intercourse becomes frequent, the individuals who belong to the distinct ethnoi have no more negative reactions when meeting each other, and cultural phenomena are freely borrowed'. In west Africa, nomadism developed because different peoples sharing a rich but regionally varied resource base adopted the habit of meeting temporary shortages in one category by exchange with others (de Vries and Goudsblom 2002: 81). Likewise, the !Kung hunting people of the Kalahari desert lived in peace with pastoral neighbours for more than a century, exchanging iron working technology, intermarrying, trading and even employing them (Megarry 1995: 212).

If exchange relations nevertheless slip into conflict, the different means at the disposal of communities for their economic activities also provide them with different weapons, attitudes, and strategies. In the words of Mann (1986: 48),

The weaponry and organization of early fighters derived from their economic techniques – hunters threw projectiles and shot arrows; agriculturalists wielded sharpened, modified hoes; herders eventually rode horses and camels. All used tactics consonant with their forms of economic organisation. In turn these military differences increased their sense of general cultural distinctiveness.

It is the level of possibilities, 'productive forces', mobilised for the encounter in the interethnic milieu on both sides, that demarcates a particular class of foreign relations as 'tribal'; not the quality of the unit engaging in them, which can be any unit ranging from the primary group to early aristocratic formations (see, for four alternative taxonomies, Vincent 1990: 326–7). As a rule of thumb, we may say that the typical community engaging in tribal foreign relations has not yet developed to the point where it can afford to set free a special class of people for tasks associated with a 'state' (Clastres 1972). In our contemporary world, tribal patterns of dealing with foreigners may therefore return as an aspect of cultural regression and state collapse, or otherwise loss of contact with state authority.

THE MARXIST LEGACY IN ETHNOGRAPHY

'The more deeply we go back into history, the more does the individual ... appear as dependent, as belonging to a greater whole', Marx writes in the *Grundrisse* (1973: 84). The reference here, Linklater comments (1990: 36), is to 'the family, clan, tribe etc. which then in a historic process of intermixture and antithesis with others acquires its particular shape and identity'. Thus 'the estrangement from neighbouring communities and the perception of nature as an alien and mysterious force were the two phenomena imprinted on the structure of the earliest societies'.

This led Marx to the recognition that humanity develops along a variety of lineages in response to differing geographical and climatic conditions. His main source of inspiration was the nineteenth-century American anthropologist Lewis Morgan, who in turn relied on the English jurist Henry Maine. For Morgan, the control of nature is the measure of human progress; of all living beings, humanity alone has achieved control over the production of its foodstuffs (Engels in *MEW*, xxi: 30; Krader in Marx 1976: 21–3, 46). Rejecting the biological or racial analysis of difference, Morgan moved from a historical analysis to an evolutionary one in the course of his career. In his ethnographic notes, Marx tended to follow Maine's lead and the historical Morgan, whilst Engels rather adopted an evolutionism in the spirit of Morgan's later work (Vincent 1990: 65, 229). The important point, Linklater writes (1990: 45), is 'that Marx's later thought recognised that the world system consisted of very different societies with their individual historical dynamics'.

The notion of modes of foreign relations as developed in this study seeks to articulate what in these late writings as it were floats just under the surface. Thus Marx (and with his usual positive–didactic twist, Engels) identified *intermarriage* as the key determinant in the ethnogenetic transformation of the small human group as it emerges from nature. This central insight is certainly obscured by misunderstandings and misinterpretations of other aspects – in the hands of a Lévi-Strauss, who founded his anthropology on it, the subject is obviously dealt with much more competently. But the link with exploiting nature lends its treatment by the Marxist classics its particular quality. Only an approach that anchors particular modes of foreign relations in the productive forces mobilised by this exploitation can properly historicise them – otherwise we will not be able to go beyond an anthropology of early communities, however brilliantly conceived and executed. Let us look at how Marx and Engels approached this.

Endogamy/Exogamy as the Bedrock of Foreign Relations

The first longer-term, 'political' problem that arises among early human groups is to ensure survival through reproduction. This goes to the heart of the contradictory nature of the separation into an entity distinct from others, ethnogenesis. Finding mates outside the small initial unit, perhaps best understood as an extended family, is paramount. It is this quest out of which emerges the ethnos, the unit of identity and (preferential) intermarriage. Mating as a social process interacts with internal structure in various ways. Marx and Engels, following Morgan, argued that the clan (or, in Graeco-Roman antiquity, the *gens*), develops as the unit of exogamy (one marries outside the clan/*gens*). The selection of particular groups as providers of marriage partners (other clans/*gentes*) thus lays the foundations of the formation of a tribe. This is a dialectical process. Kin-groups obtaining partners from groups on their frontier of contiguity coalesce into a larger ethnos by intermarriage; the ethnos in the process emerges as an objectification, a structure of socialisation regulating the reproductive aspect of the community authoritatively.

Myth and ritual provide legitimacy to these rules. They fixate clan and tribal demarcations as principles of identity and order deriving from a universal cosmology. With the real 'outside', those with an entirely different culture and unintelligible language, there is no ordered communication yet because they are not part of this cosmos. Everything that is outside the tribe is outlawed. In Engels' words

(*MEW*, xxi: 97), 'the tribe, the [clan] and its institutions, were holy and unquestionable, they constituted a higher power descending from nature, to which the individual was unconditionally subordinate in feeling, thinking and acting'.

Morgan studied the Iroquois Amerindian confederacy with the help of the concepts of tribe and nation; in his later work he developed a concept of the clan/*gens* as the constitutive unit of tribes. He indiscriminately lumped together the clan of the Iroquois, the *genos* of the Greeks, and the *gens* of the Romans, overlooking important differences, and Marx and Engels, lacking a specific competence in this area, took this on board wholesale (Khazanov 1974: 135; Vincent 1990: 38). Another insight they did not question was Morgan's assumption that inbreeding was prohibited because it was seen to produce less viable offspring; today, this eugenic understanding of the incest taboo has been abandoned. As we shall see below, exogamy is now recognised as part of strategies 'to fix the economic or social bonds between neighbouring collectives' (Pershits 1974: 127). The core argument, however, is not affected by these errors.

The clan descends from the totem, the mythical ancestor. In the Seneca tribe of the Iroquois, Morgan counted eight clans, each named after an animal (wolf, bear, and so on). Because of the mandatory exogamy, the procreative bond always straddles two clans. Here, in the socialisation of ancestry, kin and sexuality, resides the elementary sense of identity, which may explain its enduring emotional content. The clan could also adopt strangers as members; as Engels notes (*MEW*, xxi: 87–8), captives who were not killed were welcomed into the clan and enjoyed all the rights.

The exogamy rules anchored in the clan structure may be considered universal. Thus the Mount Gambier aborigines in Southern Australia were divided into two units equivalent to clan-like entities (Engels speaks of 'classes'; the current anthropological term is 'moiety', from the French *moitié*, half). Sexual relations within a moiety were forbidden. Rules of intermarriage extended to relations with communities who were literally foreign, unknown to each other, but who yet 'knew' of the dividing lines between legitimate and illegitimate sexual partners. A 'foreigner' straying far from his own group would be welcomed in a community whose language would be unintelligible to him, and enjoy the sexual partnership of a wife offered him for the night; but the woman would be of the proper moiety. This rule would even be observed when women had been abducted (ibid.: 49–50).

From their reading of Morgan, Marx and Engels identified exogamy rules as crucial determinants of how communities defined their identity. Lévi-Strauss (1962: 172–3) goes further, because for him these rules (connected with other aspects of a way of life, notably rules concerning food) are what makes a natural kin-group a community in the cultural sense to begin with. They give it, in Smaje's words (2000: 45), 'a consciousness of a differentiated and thus an organized unity or "self", which the incest prohibition achieves by preventing arbitrary relationships'. The key feature of culture for Lévi-Strauss, Smaje notes, 'is the fact that it *creates* difference'. Lévi-Strauss thus challenges the central assumption of historical materialism, viz., that it is labour, the exploitative socialisation of its natural substratum, that defines humanity as historical. Instead he claims that the incest taboo and its corollaries perform that function; thus he seeks to emphasise the horizontal differentiation among human groups as compared to the vertical, class dimension. The incest taboo is the 'social construction' that creates the barrier with undifferentiated 'nature', identifying the ethnos as different from others at the same time.

Marx and Engels, however, whilst recognising the importance of this aspect, situate it within the broader context of a particular *Verkehrsform*, a mode of social intercourse. It is coupled to a particular level of development of the productive forces obtained from nature; foreign as well as production relations are aspects of it. Morgan's insights allowed them to modify their earlier understanding of exploitative socialisation in general, by the real diversity of human groups undertaking it. Already in the *Grundrisse*, Marx writes (1973: 472) that 'this naturally arisen clan community is the first presupposition – the communality of blood, language, customs – for the appropriation of the objective conditions of their life, and of their life's reproducing and objectifying activity (activity as herdsmen, hunters, tillers etc.)'. Each unit participating in these relations, derives its identity, in Engels' words (*MEW*, xix: 317), from 'two circumstances carried over from nature, which determine the earliest history of all or almost all peoples: the structuring of a people by kin relations, and communal property of the soil.' As Engels puts it in a footnote to the first volume of *Capital* (*MEW*, xxiii: 372 n.), Marx concluded from his ethnographical studies that

originally, it was not the family which developed into the tribe, but the tribe that was the original form, inherited from nature, of kin-based human socialisation;

and that only later, the various different forms of family developed from the incipient dissolution of the tribal bond.

The rules governing exogamy grafted onto the clan/*gens* structure served as a path along which family connections developed within the larger unit. They knitted together distinct clans or gentile equivalents into a larger community, the tribe, which then (as were the clans) was naturalised again, and seen as descending from a common ancestry.

Feud in the Gentile Structure

The second aspect of the Marxist legacy that gives us the contours of a tribal mode of foreign relations also builds on inner differentiations which then contribute to defining the relations with foreign communities at a higher level of integration. Clan membership included the obligation to provide help and protection, especially in the case of the revenge of an injury caused by foreigners. 'The individual relies for his security on the protection of the *gens* and could do so; whoever hurts him, hurts the entire *gens*', Engels writes (*MEW*, xxi: 87), taking his clue from Morgan again.

On this, the bonds of kinship in the *gens*, rested the obligation of *blood feud*, which was recognised by the Iroquois unconditionally. If a non-member of the *gens* killed a member of one's own, the entire *gens* of the slain individual was committed to blood feud. (Emphasis added.)

In the process of settling feuds with foreign communities, however, the clan was usually not large enough to mount the war party required. Here the *phratry* or the actual tribe had to step in (Marx 1976: 291). Phratries, brotherhoods, combined several clans; among the Seneca, clans 1–4 formed one phratry, 5–8 the other. They were also found among the Greeks of antiquity, and there too they functioned as vectors of ethnogenesis. Thus in the *Iliad*, Engels notes (*MEW*, xxi: 102–4), Agamemnon, the leader of the Greeks before Troy, is advised to deploy the men according to tribes and phratries, so that they will fight *for their own* – which was clearly more relevant than the fact they were all Greeks.

The principle of feud in due course migrates from within the tribe, where it is practised as a gentile institution, to the sphere of the foreign relations of the larger community. Here too the separation into distinct entities goes together with an ecumenical, shared set of attitudes concerning retribution for injury or death. The power to hurt or kill is a force of nature, but once wielded by outsiders occupying a separate space must be controlled through foreign relations. Domestically, feud eventually becomes penal law; in foreign relations it mutates to 'international' law (from the original *ius gentium*, literally, inter-clan law).

Because organised violence usually requires a unit larger than the clan, the peacetime chief (the *sachem*) of the Amerindians holds a hereditary office within the clan, but the war leader is elected, and can be of a different clan. Again the same figure can be seen among the ancient Greeks: Agamemnon is not a monarch, but an 'official' confirmed in office by peer consent. When it comes to dividing booty, on the other hand, it is not Agamemnon who decides, but 'the sons of the Achaeans'. 'Monarchy', Marx writes in this connection (1976: 230), 'is incompatible with the gentile organisation'. This changes when a hierarchy among clans emerges and aristocratic lineages begin to be recognised. Thus the Seneca believed that the Bear and the Deer clans were the original, and hence, the senior clans (although the Iroquois never moved beyond a tribal confederacy as far as state formation was concerned, and aristocratic rule of the confederacy did not materialise). The gentile structure may actually play a role in this stagnation. Marx notes that among the Kutchin Amerindians in north-west Canada, who were divided into three exogamous clans in a rank order, the kin connection prevented the development of a full-blown aristocratic order, congealing instead as a caste system (cf. Krader, in Marx 1976: 48).

The connection of the clan with feud and its development towards foreign relations also transpires in the evolution of *peace*. In foreign relations (that is, with units outside the tribe), peace, which is associated with feud (and is obtained by arbitration, revenge or settlement by some form of retribution), is still absent. War can end with the destruction of the tribe, but never with a settlement that would imply its submission, Engels writes (*MEW*, xxi: 155). Only in later history, peace, originally associated with the settlement of feud in the gentile set-up, also appears in the relations among tribes. But this requires a minimal 'diplomacy' and quasi-juridical structure, as with feud; something for which a tribal council was the designated institution. It dispatched and received diplomatic missions, declared war, and concluded peace. According to Engels (ibid.: 92), in the relations with those tribes with which it had not concluded an express peace treaty, a tribe was considered to be in a permanent state of war. Peace in other words is something that is superimposed on the state of war; whereas in the gentile organisation, between clans, peace is the starting position and violence constitutes a breach of the peace that must be settled. In this sense, there is no original state of war, or original state of peace, but a contradictory mixture of both, albeit at different levels of socialisation and ethnogenesis.

Summing up, the legacy of Marx's ethnographical notebooks and Engels' *Origins of the Family, Private Property, and the State* for the analysis of early foreign relations consists in identifying, in the area of reproductive exchange and feud, the internal practices of the gentile structure that crystallise within the tribe (which itself is constituted in the same process). These practices provide social structure to the definition of insider and outsider, and to the use of violence. On the real 'outside', these issues remain unregulated. Over time, however, the internally developed rules spread beyond the original relations to which they pertain, demarcating and regulating new boundaries; so that here too, a measure of regularity obtains.

SPACE, PROTECTION, AND EXCHANGE IN THE TRIBAL MODE

Let us now investigate the three aspects of tribal foreign relations as they have been observed among indigenous peoples in Australasia, the Americas, and sub-Saharan Africa. The reason for this geographical selection is that rising sea levels in the fourth millennium BC and the spread of the Sahara desert, the result of the heating up of the planet at the time, cut off these peoples from their regions of origin. Ethnogenesis of those who had crossed the Bering land bridge and the island chains into Australasia and Polynesia, and those fleeing the desertification of middle Africa southwards, continued in a less challenging interethnic milieu. A few communities would rise to imperial civilisation; yet without horses, wheels, and metallurgy, even they remained pedestrians, liable to subjugation and extermination once 'discovered' (Attali 2003: 127–9).

Ancestry, Tribal Spaces and Neutral Zones

The sovereign right of 'being there alive' in tribal relations, to use Marx's aforementioned phrase, has it origin in ancestry. The totem, the mythical, life-giving progenitor of a community, entitles the community to assert its presence in the encounter with others. Usually symbolised by a sacred animal, the totem marks the entry point from the world of the spirits onto earth and serves as a tutelary spirit on the way; it is simultaneously a focal point of prohibitions and taboos, of which the exogamy rules are paramount (Freud 1938: 25).

Fixed, mutually exclusive territories are not part of tribal foreign relations. The totem only exceptionally has a territorial reference, such as a particular cave among Australian aborigines. For certain Amerindian groups, totem animals may themselves represent the elements: the bear refers to land, the eagle to the sky, and the tortoise to water (Lévi-Strauss 1962: 90; cf. 78). Otherwise, Freud notes (1938: 17), the totem is 'not limited to district or to locality'. The community bond anchored in ancestry is the source of identity and at the root of the group's claim to sovereign presence. Even a man who has been excluded from the tribe may still be allowed access to land; the real punishment is the exclusion from the social space that is the community (Meillassoux 1981: 35).

Hospitality is a routine form of broadening the limits of the possible by bringing outsiders in. If a less numerous group is invited to join the host community and 'live as brothers', this is often a way of obtaining the consent of other groups' chiefs to the occupation of a particular area of residence. A chief may actually try to bring new-comers in as a way of increasing his own status, although he has to be careful to secure his position by redistribution when he does (Wolf 1997: 94). In west African villages, there are foreigners' quar-ters, in which reside immigrants aspiring to become members of a tribe. Even if they are admitted, however, their rights will be limited; in the case of land use it is always clear who uses land on grounds of ancestral rights and who does so on a special dispensation from the chief. The latter category will never acquire land rights because these have been bestowed by the ancestors, who can only be those of the tribe (Apter 1968: 52–3; 85).

Attachment to a particular stretch of terrain in tribal relations develops between two poles, the sacred connection with ancestry and practical occupation and use. Once the dead are no longer eaten by the survivors or left to scavenging animals, burial mounds or graves are obvious places of return and significant connection. They may become an 'estate' with magical/sacral connotations, of which a community makes itself the custodian (Buzan and Little 2000: 117). At this level of control of the environment, Maiguashca writes (1994: 368), the land 'takes on a sacred quality that is absent in Western thinking, and this spiritual bond with the earth is one of the crucial markers that distinguish indigenous societies from others'. Whether a particular spot becomes the object of that bond, however, is a variable. Lévi-Strauss (1962: 112) describes Amerindian groups who consider the ancestral land as having only a temporary quality, on the assumption that a spirit renews itself in the community but loses its attachment to a particular locality after completing a cycle. On the other hand, there are cases where the lack of an area associated with ancestry diminishes a community's status: among native peoples in north-west Canada, migrating tribes unable to find suitable land may be taunted as 'people without origin' (Sterritt et al. 1998: 26).

Occupying land involves presence and naming it, imprinting it with the identity of the community in its particular language. Thus the Gitskan and Nisga'a peoples of Canada's Pacific coast take possession of a particular tract of land by 'walking the land' and giving names to its mountains, rivers and streams, and lakes. 'I have taken this river to be mine alone', it is said in the Gitskan (oral) record (Sterritt et al. 1998: 27). European discoverers would of course do the same. But then, as Nietzsche writes in the *Genealogy of Morals* (as in Ovalle-Bahamón 2003: 148), 'The origin of language itself [is] an expression of power on the part of the rulers … they seal every thing and event with a sound and, as it were, take possession of it.'

The need to gather, fish, or hunt obviously provides the material counterpoint to the sacred concept of occupying space in the tribal mode. But the two are always related. Thus the Miwok Amerindians of California had hamlets near water, in a neutral zone in which the right of all groups to hunt and gather was recognised; in summertime, however, they went up into the mountains to their own ancestral village (Vincent 1990: 178). Different spaces serve different purposes; when the Canadian government in the 1920s attempted to settle the definitive territories of the north-west native peoples, these turned out to include, besides their actual area of residence, trails, trap-lines, berry-gathering tracks, and fishing stations along rivers all strung out around it. 'The land was divided into stream drainages which, along with specific fishing sites, were the units owned by [kin-] groups', S. McNeary writes (as in Sterritt et al. 1998: 185). 'The spawning grounds on the creeks often belonged to the [kin-group] which owned the rest of the creek, while fish sites along the river were sometimes not contiguous to other property of the owner'.

Territory may have a complex spatial infrastructure depending on its use. The Cape York peninsula of Australia is divided, for the aboriginal communities there, into thousands of named small tracks which are clan 'property', and which are clustered into larger, unnamed tracks; boundaries between these clusters are exactly known (Jones 1959: 242). What is 'their' territory for one activity, may be different from the territory they require for another, be it hunting, watering domestic animals, gathering, or ritual. Whether others may enter that area depends on its momentary use, and is premised on respecting the primacy of the main residents, their occupation and its purpose. Fried (1967: 95–6) quotes M.J. Meggitt, an authority on the Walbiri aboriginal people, who claims that

The older Walbiri men ... have no difficulty in defining the limits of their own [territory] fairly precisely ... The positions of the boundaries are fixed, validated and remembered through the agency of religious myths. These stories not only plot the totemic tracks and centres but also specify the points at which the custody of the songs, rituals and decorations associated with them should change hands as the tracks pass from one [territory] to another.

To deny others access may endanger their survival, so if proper respect is paid to the sacral coordinates of a community's land, foreign groups may pass through and share the terrain and its resources. The Nuer people of the upper Nile, famously investigated by E.E. Evans-Pritchard, rely on a limited number of waterholes on their seasonal migration and hence must allow and be allowed peaceful passage (Vincent 1990: 266). Among native Australians, conflict can flare up easily and hence 'the formalities of crossing territorial boundaries could involve delicate negotiations and specially appointed heralds complete with appropriate body paint and carved message sticks who acted as officials' (Megarry 1995: 212). As long as walking is the main form of displacement, space is not quickly occupied outside the core residential area; to contest it means putting survival at risk. This only changes with the development of the productive forces, with the wheel and the drawn cart or horses.

Clearly the ability to communicate is essential. On the Andaman islands in the Indian Ocean, tribal territories changed constantly, but only in the case of one tribe speaking a completely different language did this involve conflict (Kelly 2000: 90–1). Among Canadian Amerindians, being hospitable to others even makes the claim to occupy land more valid. *Not* exploiting the earth on the other hand can delegitimise it: in the example of the Gitskan, the arrival of certain powerful newcomers was resented as intrusion, 'as they had no hunting, fishing, or berry tracts of their own exclusive property', but relied on those of others (Sterritt et al, 1998: 29–30).

Like ethnogenesis generally, concepts and practical use of space also vary according to the socialising effect exerted by geographical conditions, or the particular quarry of hunting communities. Distinct hunting territories among Amerindian tribes in Canada thus were typically found in the boreal forest ecosystem towards the south; further north and east in the Quebec–Labrador peninsula, conditions are different. Here migrating caribou is the principal game animal and this itself ruled out a system of sedentary land tenure. But even in the James Bay area,

the hunting territory system existed alongside other, entirely different, patterns of resource distribution, such as the use of resources in the summer, with fishing camps, berry-picking areas and goose hunting territories which utilize overlapping systems of land use to that of the winter hunting territories. (Tanner 1983: 317, cf. 313)

The requirement of really using the land, its meaning as a thoroughfare to the other world (burial place, sacred spot, etc.), all point to the primacy of the community as a sovereign kin-group over other determinations. Hence the idea of conquering more territory for territory's sake is usually absent from foreign relations under the tribal mode. When the Iroquois in 1651 defeated the Erie and the 'Neutral nation' (another tribe), they were only driven from their lands when they declined the membership of the Iroquois war confederacy (Engels in *MEW*, xxi: 96). But here we must recognise that by then the intrusion of European settlers had triggered a competitive quest for land, as traditional horticulture gave way to hunting beavers for the fur trade. Since beaver was rare in Iroquois country, the confederacy, with Dutch and English support, attacked the French-backed Hurons to gain access to beavers, before finishing off the Erie and the Neutral nation (Wolf 1997: 165).

To the extent there exists a particular spatial layout that we may see as territorial in the modern sense, it consists of a zonal structure, with a core area bounded by neutral zones as a buffer. In the Luzon mountains of the Philippines, R.F. Barton (as in Vincent 1990: 136–46) found that although community bonds are anchored in kin connections, certain kin-groups were organised into distinctly territorial units. Where this was most pronounced, as in the case of the Kalingas, boundaries tended to be well-defined too. The Ifugaos on the other hand had the zonal concept. A home zone was surrounded by a neutral zone, inhabited by groups with which the Ifugaos were at peace and with whom they intermarried; then a feuding zone with more conflict and less marriage; finally a war zone where hostility was the normal expectation (Jones 1959: 242). Engels (*MEW*, xxi: 91) also gives examples of such depopulated neutral zones (with the width depending on whether tribes with identical languages or familiar dialects were on the other side or not). They existed in the border forests of the Germanic tribes, in the wasteland which the Suevians created around their territory, on the *limes Danicus* between Germans and Danish tribes, as well as in the Saxon Forest and the *branibor* (Slavic term for a protective forest, later bastardised into 'Brandenburg') that separated German and Slavic tribes. Only when population grew would these boundary zones become contested terrain. This takes us to the aspect of protection.

Shouting Matches in the Jungle

Protection in the tribal mode is about perpetuating the occupation of space. It is constructed around the initial perception of a single, overawing universe of potentially threatening forces; all are animate, and hence open to 'negotiation'. The totem, which the community honours in the hope of receiving protection from it in return, is the key mediating instance between the vulnerable early community and the vastness confronting it. Obtaining protection in encounters with others is therefore always primarily ritual, a matter of observing rites and taboos that surround the totem. In the New Guinea highlands, the totem decides whether a stranger is a foreigner. Papua men on a chance encounter may avoid fighting by sitting down and trying to identify a common ancestor. The same practice was found among Amerindian Chippewa (Diamond 1998: 271; Lévi-Strauss 1962: 221). This is less exotic than it seems if we think of how people meeting at a party may wish to check out possible common acquaintances as a means of removing distrust – even though they no longer have to fear cannibalism if they don't find one.

Given the very limited means at the disposal of the early community, life is valuable and cannot be risked in a fight unless one is an implacable enemy. 'Human labour power at this stage does not yet provide anything like a surplus beyond its maintenance costs', Engels writes (*MEW*, xxi: 58). This is not to say that originally violence is non-existent – as Kelly reminds us (2000: 42), warless societies may have staggering homicide rates, and are not typically characterised by internal peacefulness at all. But they do observe 'intrinsic limitations on the extent to which one act of lethal violence leads to another'. Communities may be separate, but they share a respect for life which prohibits killing without a clear reason and without atonement for it. An overview by R. Holsti of the ethnographic corpus on organised violence early in the twentieth century yielded 'a lack of indiscriminate slaughter, low death rates from war, the killing only of adult males directly involved in combat, institutionalised inviolability of go-betweens or messengers between potentially hostile groups, and the prevalence of peace making and treaty keeping' (Vincent 1990: 91). Let us first look at feud, which as we saw lays the groundwork for a rule-based, structured pattern of protective foreign relations (besides engendering domestic 'penal law').

Feud is a means of protecting the community from the threat posed to its viability by violence. But to bring this under control by means of *organised* violence also poses a threat to the community's viability, because of the low level of productive forces and the need to avoid unnecessary loss of life. Violence can always run out of hand – a killing over a marital infidelity among the Amerindians studied by Sterritt and his associates (1998: 29–33) led to a revenge raid by the relatives of the victim, then to the massacre of an entire village. The 'war' by then had so much weakened the group originally victimised that it had to migrate and seek its fortune elsewhere. Hence 'while the ideology of honour and group dominance spurs people to retaliate', Boehm concludes (1984: 202), 'rational decision making keeps them from ruining the quality of life – or possibly their very adaptive viability – in the process of trying to maintain respect. It is indigenous common sense that limits escalation in these volatile conflicts'. An entire history of protecting the community from violence is therefore contained in the notion of 'respect' (and honour as its counterpoint), from the distant past to the contemporary inner-city encounter.

In principle, feud works best within the community. Barton (as in Vincent 1990: 144–5) considered that among the Ifugao of the Philippines, 'war, murder, and the death penalty' were almost synonymous terms; feud on the other hand was confined to the sphere delineated by 'ties of blood and marriage'. Only at this level can the socialisation of 'internal nature', the normative system that Habermas refers to, be assumed to operate and to impose the rules of feud around an ever-tighter set of limitations, 'law'. Initially there is no law outside the community. Those removed from the ancient Germanic community became 'outlaws', foreigners, and hence enemies (van der Heijden 1958: 25). Yet the principles of feud early on spill over into relations with foreign communities through interactive socialisation. In their research on tribal relations in Iran and Afghanistan, Rosman and Rubel (1976: 554) found that the rules governing the settlement of feuds (such as that the woman given in compensation for a killing of a man, must have the same social rank as the deceased) applied both in cases of settlement within a community and between different communities. It is on the basis of the spread of such rules and their wider acceptance that *peace* becomes meaningful; a breach of the peace then can become the occasion for feud with the community that has committed it, be settled, and so on. So already in the tribal mode, rules binding different ethnoi into a common normative structure begin to emerge.

Since the community at this level cannot afford to embark on organised violence, however, war is not part of protection in the tribal mode. War differs from feud in that revenge is no longer 'private', directed at a particular member or family group of a community, but at all its members via social substitutability (Kelly 2000: 6; Rosenberg 1994: 65). 'If we insist that war is a fight between two independent and politically organised groups', Malinowski writes (as in Vincent 1990: 214), 'war does not occur at the primitive level.' A survey of 14 kin-group societies by L.T. Hobhouse (as in Fried 1967: 100) records that 'seven had prolonged feuds and four others indulged in hit-and-run ambushes and attacks'. 'Protracted attacks and sieges do not occur', Fried concludes (ibid.: 102).

The typical action is a raid involving few attackers; the appropriate word for what occurs seems to be *clash* – there is a sudden violent set-to and most of the participants return hoarse from screaming threats and insults but are otherwise unscathed.

This may produce fatalities, but there is due respect for death and enough abhorrence of killing to act as a brake. The association of fighting with retribution, too, is inconsistent with mass slaughter. Among Australian aborigines, 'the first blood that flows puts an end to the fight' (G.C. Wheeler as in Vincent 1990: 124).

Fighting among early communities may even serve to maintain the dispersal of groups whose survival would be threatened by merger and state formation, as documented by Clastres (1972) for the Guayaki Amerindians of Paraguay. The Swazi and Zulu peoples in Africa, too, lacked the means to develop a comprehensive political entity and this 'necessitated widespread dispersal of the population' (Vincent 1990: 253). As a result, there could not emerge a specialist political authority and/or a warrior caste sustained by the larger ethnos to devote itself to fighting until the advent of the Dutch and British forced them to defend themselves. As long as the means for sustained military campaigns are lacking, one would therefore expect that violence would stop short of all-out war; Kelly (2000: 133–4) indeed found that poor tribes are peaceful by necessity and that wealth translates into increased bellicosity. Malinowski on the other hand (as in Mumford 1961: 25) characterised his Trobriand islanders 'pacifists of the Neolithic state', in spite of the fact that they had complex political structures and extensive organisation.

Given that there is no specialised warrior caste, it is always a volunteer army that undertakes raids or punitive expeditions. The war dance of the North American Amerindians served to assemble those willing to join, and both the departure and the return of the tribal war party were celebrated by such festivities. Demonstrating one's readiness to fight, in the war dance or otherwise, also served to reaffirm the community bond and to bolster maleness in the 'perpetual struggle to assert its domination over femaleness' (Gledhill 1994: 29; cf. Kelly 2000: 107). The claim that the early community on these issues would have been formally egalitarian, the thesis of 'military democracy' that Marx and Engels took from Morgan, has been challenged by later research. The need to obtain consent from the community to go out to fight is more limited; thus in Polynesia tribal chiefs have to seek the consent of lesser chiefs, but not of commoners (Khazanov 1974: 138).

For chiefs, raiding is the one way of enlarging their grip on resources without the immediate need for redistribution (Wolf 1997: 94). Prominent warriors relying on a following of their own could undertake 'private' raids and dispense with tribal approval altogether. It is this type of private war party, Engels observes (*MEW*, xxi: 93), which already assumed a more permanent status among Germanic tribes like the Alemannians in Roman imperial times. Feudal retinues can sometimes be traced to such war bands, which were occasionally made up of slaves. In the next chapter we shall see that in Asia men like Genghis Khan and Timur Lenk, too, began their careers as private warriors on the margins of their respective tribal societies.

To give a sense of a potentially violent encounter, we may rely on Lévi-Strauss' detailed account (1989: 396–7) of a confrontation between two groups of indigenous Brazilians – with a peaceful outcome in this case. The event unfolds as follows:

The men had come alone, and almost immediately a lengthy conversation began between their respective chiefs. It might be more accurately termed a series of alternating monologues, uttered in plaintive, nasal tones ... 'We are extremely annoyed. You are our enemies!' moaned one group, whereupon the others replied more or less, 'We are not annoyed. We are your brothers. We are friends – friends! We can get along together! etc.'

A communal camp is set up, and the two groups begin to sing and dance, comparing the quality of each other's performances in sometimes unflattering ways. As a result, the quarrel flares up amidst continued singing and dancing. As night falls, threats multiply, whilst some men intervene to mediate. Threatening gestures are directed at the male sexual organs, and fighting takes the form of trying to pull off the flimsy straw tuft which covers the opponent's genitals. But while the confrontation continues to raise emotions, the men shift to a sort of negotiation that forms the prelude to barter.

Throughout these actions, the natives remain extremely tense, as if they were in a state of violent and pent-up anger. The scuffles may sometimes degenerate into a free-for-all, but on this occasion the fighting subsided at dawn. Still in the same state of visible irritation and with gestures that were anything but gentle, the two sets of opponents then set about examining each other, fingering their ear-pendants, cotton bracelets and little feather ornaments, and muttering a series of rapid comments, such as 'Give it ... give it ... see, that's pretty,' while the owner would protest, 'It's ugly ... old ... damaged!'.

After this 'reconciliatory inspection', the quarrel is terminated and a sort of barter ensues, pottery for necklaces, and so on. This exploration to find out whether the others are potentially willing to engage in peaceful exchange and avoid a fight highlights how exchange is just round the corner of an antagonistic foreign encounter. Indeed, as Polanyi writes (1957: 59), 'external trade is, originally, more in the nature of adventure, exploration, hunting, piracy and war than of barter ... A tribal expedition may have to comply ... with the conditions set by the powers on the spot, who may exact some kind of counterpart from the strangers'. Market-like exchange may, but does not necessarily follow. 'This type of relationship, though not entirely peaceful, may give rise to barter – one-sided carrying will be transformed into two-sided carrying.' The resolution of feud also inevitably involves exchange, e.g. when settled by payment of blood money or by giving away a woman (Rosman and Rubel, 1976: 548). I shall come back to this below.

The readiness to avoid an all-out fight and sublimate the animosity in a shouting match has travelled through the ages to our present world. In his account of military engagements on the Arabian peninsula during the First World War, T.E. Lawrence writes (1997: 81) how

to my ears they sounded like oddly primitive battles, with torrents of words on both sides in a preliminary match of wits. After the foulest insults of the languages they knew would come the climax, when the Turks in frenzy called the Arabs 'English', and the Arabs screamed back 'Germans' at them.

George Orwell's record of the Spanish Civil War, *Homage to Catalonia*, includes comparable scenes of soldiers shouting '*¡maricones!*' (homosexuals) at each other from their trenches. And didn't French and German soldiers, on Christmas Day 1914, actually leave their positions and engage in a reconciliatory football match, abandoning animosity altogether?

Of course the modern war machine has developed ways of restoring military discipline in such situations. Already under the tribal mode however, war-proneness was routinised through internal differentiation and the growth of a warrior aristocracy. This obviously fosters the aspect of exploitation as the outlines of a class society become evident within the community, along with new ways of dealing with foreigners. Hobhouse and his associates (as in Vincent 1990: 101) found that slavery replaced the killing (or adoption) of vanquished enemies as the productive forces increase; a warrior class can impose itself in its own society if it procures the labour necessary for its maintenance, or vice versa, if there is an increase in the wealth of the community to begin with. 'On all sides social and economic differentiation replace the comparative equality of the hunting peoples. The extension of order is also, upon the whole, an extension of subordination.' According to Malinowski (as in Vincent 1990: 214), slavery was 'perhaps the first really constructive advantage derived from inter-tribal war'. Very often this process was influenced, or even entirely overtaken, by the appearance of conquerors, warrior peoples of nomadic origin establishing their rule over sedentary agriculturalists. This will concern us in the next chapter.

The advent of Westerners, who had vastly greater means at their disposal but did not merge into the local communities, was of a different order. It produced dislocations and migrations, and in many cases was the reason why tribal warfare became endemic in the societies affected (Fried 1967: 103; cf. Meillassoux 1981: part II). The Dakota Amerindians, who had been pedestrian horticulturalists and hunters, were given guns by the French to assist in warding off the advance of English traders and settlers; once they obtained horses, too, in the mid eighteenth century, they began to raid the villages of neighbouring horticulturalists. 'By 1775 the Dakota were the horse-riding and gun-toting lords of the northeastern plains' (Wolf 1997: 177). The idea of the ferocious, bloodthirsty tribal warrior could thus become a motif in colonial history, certainly when locals resisted Western rule. However, Holsti's research already referred to, which covers the ethnographic record of supposedly warlike communities such as the Maoris, Fijians, Tongans, Dayaks, Galla, Masai, and others, found that in practically all cases it was the intrusion of Western influences such as property rights and the actual presence of a colonising power, the spread of firearms as well as newly imported codes of behaviour, which produced, among many other ills, the new bellicosity. V. G. Childe, too (as in Vincent 1990: 92), concluded that war is a perversion accompanying 'civilisation'.

Every step forward in armament is always a step towards broadening the limits of the possible. In Engels' words (*MEW*, xxi: 31), 'the bow and arrow were to savagery what the iron sword was to barbarity and the rifle to civilisation: the decisive weapon'. Of course there is more than a hint of the 'noble savage' in the pronouncements on the tribal abhorrence of war quoted earlier. But there is no question that when the rifle landed in the tribal context, it decided more than just the chances in battle.

Exchange in the Tribal Mode

Early foraging communities were usually too small to survive on their own. Given short lifespans, they had to be constantly on the lookout for reinforcement, find mates or trade food. At the same time, these groups lived such precarious existences that babies were often killed; infanticide of girls especially was widespread (Megarry 1995: 221). A shortage of females might then later create an acute need to roam around for sexual partners, and so on. Exchange in other words originates at the dawn of human history, for reasons of survival. It is a key channel for overcoming the contradictory nature of the separation from the wider world and the human and material resources it holds.

The aforementioned encounter between two parties of Brazilian Amerindians, recorded by Lévi-Strauss, is probably a good indication of how contact in this sense was originally established – nervous, loud, with a distinct threat of violence, but ultimately open to exchange and accepting its associations of mutuality and reciprocity.

Once such encounters became more regular, exogamy, too, could begin to acquire the pattern of moieties within a larger ethnos, the gentile structure around which tribes are formed. Obviously this is not always a peaceful process. On their raids in the interior of Ecuador and Peru, Jivaro headhunters kill everybody except the women, who are taken as prizes (the male heads captured are displayed to provide mythical strength and protection). At some point, however, violent capture is replaced by peaceful ways to procure mates, because other purposes are served by it as well. New Guinea offers examples of clans which are hostile to each other and yet supply each other with wives peacefully (Lind 1969: 39; on the Jivaro, cf. Boehm 1984). An active marriage policy aims at securing kinship ties with other groups, and thus provides protection through exchange; one reason why it survived as a tool of diplomacy well into the era of actual inter-dynastic relations. Marriage connections serve to guarantee support of other communities in times of war, integrating units over time and creating durable systems of reciprocity (Lévi-Strauss 1983: 655–6, 665; Meillassoux 1981: 87).

The ability to keep track and interpret complex kinship ties and develop rules based on them, is a result of considerable historical development and civilisation. Strategies to reinforce or restore kinship connections within communities (e.g. by encouraging cross-cousin marriages, to get the offspring of aunts and uncles, dispersed under exogamy rules, back into one's own community) are therefore evidence of advanced social organisation and consciousness (Megarry 1995: 214, 218). In the earliest communities, such insight was still lacking. Because levels of sexual equality were higher and marital ties weaker, women could not be bartered away either. But with the rise of sedentary, agricultural communities, the exchange of mates acquires a quality that goes beyond securing the physical existence of the group; it now enables the regulation of the relations with other communities. The exchange of women demarcates 'matrimonial areas' of allied communities supplying each other with girls. On the other hand, 'absence of exchange of women is one of the ways in which ethnic boundaries are maintained' (Rosman and Rubel 1976: 548).

Control over marriages, and hence of marriageable women, thus becomes a crucial asset. It defines in turn who in the community holds a position of relevance in external relations: they are, in the words of Meillassoux (1981: 44–5), 'those individuals who are in a position to return a woman in the foreseeable future'.

To maintain their power to negotiate, elders must assure that the girls of their community are available for exchange and hence must maintain control over the latter's fate ... When the [productive] cell, in order to reproduce itself, must open itself to the outside world in order to secure wives, the elders' power tends to shift from control over subsistence to control over women – from the management of material goods to political control over people.

Sexual taboos proliferate as more and more rules are developed. There emerges in this way a kin system of such complexity that the number of categories with whom sexual relations are prohibited comes close to our contemporary understanding of monogamous matrimony. But this continues to be driven by the need to control the rules of reproduction, the ground rules of the mobilisation of the community as a productive force. All exchange in the tribal mode remains anchored in this vital connection, all power in the community has its roots here. The 'bride price' paid by the relatives of the male partner to the relatives (the kin on the mother's side) of the bride, and dowry, the price paid by the family of the bride upon marriage, develop as aspects of this exchange, just as exchange may serve to settle a conflict, as we saw earlier. They illustrate the 'commercial' implications of exogamy, although we are looking at practices closer to slavery than to free exchange. Purchasing wives is a form of obtaining bonded household labour, and can itself be substituted by slavery. It is in fact the position of women in the community which 'determines to some extent whether or not slaves are wanted' (H.J. Nieboer, as in Vincent 1990: 89).

Another example from the ethnographic record given by Vincent (1990: 237, citing O. Lewis), describes how certain Amerindian tribes in the United States developed an extensive horse trade once Europeans had introduced the animal. This was not straightforward modernisation; the horse trade led to an increase in polygamy because men with large herds were able to exchange horses for wives and thus 'transform idle capital (surplus horses) into productive capital (women)'. As the bride price in horses went up, Wolf writes (1997: 181), horse raiding and rustling became necessary to pay for more wives to employ in preparing pemmican, the dried bison mix eaten on long trips to steal more horses, and so on.

Trade as the exchange of equivalents goes back far into prehistory. Upper Palaeolithic communities traded stone, amber and shells over distances of hundreds of kilometres (Megarry 1995: 268, 277; Curtin 1984: 2). On closer inspection, trade is always imbricated with other aspects of exchange, first of all the exchange of marriageable women, but also rules of hospitality and sharing with strangers. Polanyi (1957) in this connection speaks of the 'embeddedness' of the economy in society. However, investigating the ways in which tribal patterns of exchange operated, not unlike the measurement of subatomic particles in physics, is itself an invasive act that distorts what goes on. Thus rituals such as the potlatch, the competitive giving away of blankets or other goods practised by North American Amerindians, can be seen as a sign of egalitarianism rooted in the native idea that owning something while others don't is illegitimate. An alternative explanation is that the political reorganisation triggered by the appearance of Westerners upset traditional ranking principles, so that potlatching became a way of establishing hierarchy (Wolf 1997: 190–1; cf. M. Douglas, in Mauss 2002). In addition, tribal exchange is always imbricated with other aspects of foreign relations, notably protection. The Brazilian encounter recorded by Lévi-Strauss again should be taken as the most probable sequence of events. So the question is, how did people carrying tradable items deal with the threat of violence?

The first is to avoid direct contact altogether. Thus groups with different occupations may make 'gifts' to each other, which in effect are exchanges establishing a division of labour – as between the agricultural tribes of the Trobriand Islands in the western Pacific and fishing tribes on the coast, who leave part of the harvest, and part of the catch, respectively, near each other's villages (Mauss 2002: 38). This ritual, backed up by magic and myth, deals with the fear that physical proximity may lead to violence if things go wrong. The same practice, called 'silent trade', was recorded by Herodotus as taking place on the coasts of Africa (Curtin 1984: 12). It is a phenomenon not confined to the tribal encounter either. In Defoe's novel (1992: 23–4), based on the author's own seafaring experiences, Robinson Crusoe is not willing to forego the safety of his ship for much needed food. An equally frightened group of natives on the beach is willing to supply it, but how to exchange?

[They] came back and brought with them two pieces of dry flesh and some corn, such as is the produce of their country, but we neither knew what the one or the other was; however, we were willing to accept it, but how to come at it was our next dispute, for I was not for venturing on shore to them, and they were as much afraid of us; but they took a safe way for us all, for they brought it to the shore and laid it down, and went and stood a great way off till we fetch'd it on board, and then came close to us again.

The second form of ensuring that exchange and the possibility of conflict over 'value' remains peaceful is to separate it from normal dealings with foreigners. For trade to take place, the foreign in other words must be suspended. Even the ferocious Jivaros already referred to will honour those with whom they exchange as having a special status for the time being. A 'friend', i.e. a trading partner (who is usually a stranger), does not have to fear that his head will end up on a pole to dry and shrink. The reciprocal obligations incurred in the exchange even dictate that if a 'friend' is killed while visiting to trade he will be avenged by his host (Boehm, 1984: 209). Making the exchange part of a festive occasion is a further development of this. Fairs and festivals were usually religious in origin and often associated with pilgrimage, if only to provide a measure of immunity to those on their way to the market. Overcoming the foreign to facilitate trade has a long history. In India, Braudel writes (1983: 129), 'a country of separate races, tongues and religions', primitive fairs were held 'along the borders of its hostile regions'. They were 'placed under the protection of tutelary divinities and religious pilgrimages and thus rescued from constant neighbourhood feuding'.

In all these cases, mutual relations are broadly predictable. Such a shared normative structure is absent in the case of exchange with people representing a totally different life-world. Thus, after the famous 'sale' of Manhattan by the Amerindians to the Dutch, the 'buyers' rejoiced about the bargain they had struck. But the indigenous party only accepted the payment because they did not consider their rights of residence impaired in any way. 'The tribal groups in the region of New Amsterdam', writes Shorto (2005: 162),

were far from simple in their understanding of the land transactions they had made with the Europeans. The armful of goods mentioned in each title transfer was not, in their eyes, an outright purchase price, but a token that represented the arrangement to which they were agreeing. Under that arrangement they shared the land with the 'purchaser', and at the same time entered into a defensive alliance.

Such encounters of the 'third kind' no longer belong to the tribal mode. The means that brought the foreigners on these distant shores and allowed them to prevail would soon also land in the hands of the 'primitives', guiding them into a different world of foreign relations as well.

Summing up the three aspects of this mode, occupying space, protection, and exchange, we get the following.

Space is occupied for reasons of practical livelihood, often temporarily, but in the final analysis is shared; it is part of the generally respectful attitude of early human communities towards their natural surroundings. Since ethnogenesis at this stage revolves mostly around ancestry and kin, sovereignty resides in surviving as a unit independent from outside control in a sacred bond with one's origins. Once people begin to bury their dead, ancestry also acquires a territorial reference, laying the groundwork for future 'fatherlands'.

Protection is likewise anchored in the sacred nature of the bond with ancestors, the totem. Nothing compares with the protection gained by paying respect to this bond, within and outside the group. Violence is a threat in itself, and feud serves to minimise the killing that may be the consequence of an initial injury. It also introduces the concept of peace into the relations with foreign communities, and war as a feud-like, collective response to a breach of the peace.

Exchange, finally, is about finding mates outside the primary group; the kin-structure and its evolution into a larger, endogamous formation determine ethnogenesis at this stage. The subordination of women to the community, governed by the male elders, is therefore the central axis of class formation. Trade as barter evolves through rituals such as gifts and fairs.

These then are the defining characteristics of the tribal mode. They rest on a particular level of development of the productive forces, on limits of the possible which, if transcended induce transformations that at some point will converge on a different mode. In the process, Smaje argues (2000: 65), the sacred will be secularised (e.g. common ancestry and kinship become citizenship); and this, paradoxically, calls forth the sacralisation of the secular (say, nationality as a 'sacred' bond with the soil). As with all modes of social relations, tribal relations may persist or return in more complex societies as an enfolded, subordinate form. When the political structures by which the tribal has been overcome unravel again, the affected communities may also regress towards tribal patterns in their relations with others occupying separate spaces and considered as outsiders. In the chapters that follow, I shall provide examples of this.

3
Imperial Universalism and the Nomad Counterpoint

In the evolution of the historic land empires, foreign relations assume a new form, transcending the tribal mode. Communities occupying separate spaces and considering each other as outsiders now do so hierarchically, within a single jurisdiction. Usually this comes about when warriors impose themselves on agricultural communities as a ruling stratum, attracted by the surplus generated by the sedentary way of life. Seizing control of the levers of this wealth, the warrior aristocracy must then negotiate further pressure from new outsiders and recruit some of these communities on the frontier for protection. The latter in turn may be tempted to reverse the hierarchy and become rulers themselves, and so on, in what Mann calls (1986: 82) 'the dialectic between empires and marcher lords'.

Imperial sovereignty is usually proclaimed over the world as a whole. This is implied in the divine status or mandate of the emperor. In practice, of course, the empire's occupation of space remains tied to a geographical core suitable to agriculture; every land empire therefore will reach a saturation point beyond which no further expansion occurs. Drawing in resources from outside its domain will then primarily depend on trade, dressed as tribute and often entrusted to foreigners granted residence for the purpose. This is how commercial diasporas, implanted across a wider space, come into being.

Foreign relations with communities *not* incorporated are also hierarchical in nature. This derives from pseudo-speciation and the assignment of barbarian status by the empire, and its definition of trade as tribute. But roles may be reversed if the empire weakens; especially since pastoral nomads, too, tend to claim space as if it were infinite. In Marx's phrase (1973: 491), 'Among nomadic pastoral tribes ... the earth appears like other natural conditions, in its elemental limitlessness, e.g. in the Asiatic steppes and the high plateau.' These constitute the settings of nomad ethnogenesis – as did the oceanic expanses across which ventured mariners from the coastlines of Europe and Asia. In the words of Toynbee (1935, iii: 7–8), there is no difference in terms of motive forces, therefore,

between those explosive movements of population which impel Norsemen or Minoans or Crusaders to take to their ships and to break like tidal waves upon the coasts of Europe or the Levant, and those other movements which impel Imoshagh or Arabs or Scyths or Turks or Mongols to swing out of their annual orbit on the steppe and to break, with equal violence and equal suddenness, upon the settled lands of Egypt or Iraq or Russia or India or China. [Imoshagh is the name used for themselves by the Touaregs of the Sahara; cf. Attali 2003: 241.]

On account of their mobility, nomads have been the key antagonists of sedentary empires throughout history. The nomad role on the fringes of the empire consists, in the phrase of Deleuze and Guattari (1986: 21), 'in being distributed by turbulence across a smooth space'. How sedentary and tribal nomadic social forms are articulated into an empire, and how the imperial formation then deals with nomadic mobility within its own structure and on its frontier, determine the further course of development to a considerable extent.

In this chapter, I will first develop the general characteristics of the empire/nomad mode from a historical overview. Then I look at the Chinese empire, which by its development as an integral, political–economic and cultural centre absorbing all frontier development back into itself provides the starkest contrast with the empire of Western Christianity, to which we turn in Chapter 4.

SEDENTARY CIVILISATIONS AND SEMI-BARBARIAN NOMADS

The early civilisations, according to Mann (1986: 123), were composed of (1) 'an ecological niche with alluvial agriculture', and (2) a 'relatively bounded, *caged* core' (emphasis added). This applies to the floodplains of the Tigris and Euphrates in Mesopotamia, along the Nile in Egypt, and in the Indus valley. These areas had been in contact with each other since prehistoric times; the Shang civilisation along the Yellow River in China, which dates from the second millennium BC, was an unrelated development. Agriculture generates the social surplus necessary to support a ruling class; 'caging' occurs when the community mobilised to exploit the opportunities of the geographic and interethnic milieu then finds itself 'constrained to accept civilization, social stratification, and the state' (Mann 1986: 75).

Wittfogel's (1977) 'hydraulic society', the central organisation of irrigation of arable land, refers to a key complex of productive forces underlying this transformation, from Mesopotamia to China. Certainly his thesis has been powerfully challenged. Archaeological research suggests that large-scale hydraulic infrastructure was a *result* of imperial organisation, premised on a prior population concentration; hydraulic agriculture, too, is a form of socialisation of the geography, enabling the community to broaden the limits of the possible after it has first enabled itself to do so by its number and organisation (Diamond 1998: 283–4; Mann 1986: 92–8). There is no doubt however that there exists a powerful functional connection between imperial centralisation and an infrastructure of irrigation, from flood control to systems of canals and aqueducts.

No longer, then, are foreign relations a matter of randomly roaming communities occasionally encountering each other for mates or prey, or of villages or cities surviving precariously through intermittent contact. Empires now take their place in cumulative, chronological history. They demarcate, in Wolf's definition (1997: 82), 'cultural interaction zones pivoted upon a hegemonic tributary society central to each zone'.

The State Form of Empire

Empires are ruled by aristocracies, often of foreign origin. Aristocracies arise from tribal/clan society when control over women and juniors by elders shifts to control over junior lineages by senior ones. Senior lineages may bring forth a priestly class, writing and enforcing the rules for observing the seasonal discipline under which agriculture must operate as well as those governing redistribution; they may also assume tasks of protection and become a military aristocracy set on conquest. This latter form can equally emerge from the margins of tribal society, as warriors outside the clan rank order build up their own retainer force and conquer a sedentary settlement as a food base. Either way, the ruling stratum obtains a position in which it can centralise a social surplus, in exchange for which it provides ritual–administrative and/or protective tasks; the 'cage' ultimately is about a compromise (Godelier 1980). These changes obviously interact with the shift from the domestic mode of production to the tributary one.

The apparatus through which the aristocracy governs is a state. States are intermediary structures through which a ruling community, caste, or class, at a given level of development of the productive forces (including the level of cultural development), interacts with the wider society and with its environment. In a state, the attributes of the social basis are unified and crafted into a collective capacity to act, thus adding the condensed power of the totality, what Lenin calls (1975: 12) a 'bureaucratic and military machinery', to the social forces it unites. Once the limits that make communities resistant to supporting the specialised class operating this machinery have been overcome, those wielding state power will seek to consolidate and develop it, for their society's as much as for their own interest as a ruling class. The 'machinery' in which the capacity to think and act collectively is embodied thus develops from elementary hierarchy (literally, 'holy rule') to more complex forms. 'The' state is an abstraction; there are only concrete forms of state (Cox, 1987).

The imperial state brings together communities which as kin-groups were foreign to each other, under a single authority. But this is not the modern state that demands of its subjects that they place citizenship before everything else. The subjects of the empire relate to the state as members of bodies that have constituted themselves prior to it, and to which their primary allegiance pertains. They are individuals 'imprisoned within a certain definition, as feudal lord and vassal, landlord and serf, etc., or as member of a caste ... or as members of an estate' (Marx 1973: 163). An empire is a hierarchic conglomerate of ethnic or quasi-ethnic social bodies, and its internal structure will often resemble foreign relations of a tribal type. To maintain overall cohesion, complex arrangements and ritual between these communities have to accompany coercion and 'caging'.

Caste is always an aspect of empire, but when the formation of an empire remains incomplete the caste structure may crystallise into the dominant mode of social cohesion altogether. A caste system develops when '*kingship* attempts to assert itself against *kinship* but ultimately fails' (D. Quigley, as in Smaje 2000: 118, emphasis added). Of course India comes to mind here, but we are looking at a more general principle. Thus a Pashtun conqueror in late nineteenth-century Afghanistan gave Ahmadzai Pashtun nomads grazing rights on the lands of the sedentary Hazara people (a branch of Mongolians). The two communities traded but did not intermarry and so retained their ethnic identity, giving 'a caste-like appearance to their relationship' (Rosman and Rubel 1976: 560). This then is how tribal foreign relations may persist within a single, hierarchical social structure. In such situations, Shirokogorov writes (1970: 22 n. 2), 'the formation of distinct classes corresponds to the formation of ethnoi (e.g. special dialects, endogamy, complexes of customs, "class consciousness", etc.)'. Castes, he adds, may also result from 'the adaptation of ethnical units for special social functions in larger units'. This would apply to India's *jati*, the sub-castes loosely ordered in the ritual four-caste *varna* structure, of which there are several thousand. These specialise in particular trades or professions in a system of division of labour which also creates opportunities for emancipation (Marriott 1955). I come back to India's caste system below.

The discipline that we saw has to be imposed on an agricultural society, in the context of empire, is formalised by *law*. Law is obtained in written form (e.g., as in the Judaic or Mesopotamian cases, as stone tablets) and is of supposedly divine authorship. It designates the recipient(s) as the mediating force between the gods/God/heaven and worldly affairs, thus setting apart an emperor from a mere chief. Writing, developed to maintain records of harvests and the distribution/storage of produce before it served to spell out the law, likewise worked to create a common bond of civilisation; particular (ideographic) scripts in turn deepen the linguistic differentiations as they develop according to their own internal logic.

Since the empire rules over a collection of (quasi-)corporate entities, the law does not extend to all subjects, at least not in the same way. An empire can absorb foreign communities more easily than a national state because it relies on *incorporation*, the accommodation of the foreign leaving its ethnic identity intact. An incorporated community (traders, warriors, even administrators) may retain its own laws, its language, religion, dress, or any other particularity. This practice sets the empire apart from the indiscriminate mixing of tribal relations on the one hand, and from national states on the other, although the dividing lines are obviously not absolute.

Imperial Ethno-Transformations

The first land empires emerged in the urban civilisations of the Nile Valley and Mesopotamia. Egypt's imperial consolidation is the oldest: the south and the delta were unified by Menes in 3100 BC. The 'Old Kingdom' thus established owed much to the Nile geography with its fertile floodplains and to its relative security from external threats; this imparted an inward-looking, conservative strain to further development. When the Egyptians began building wooden ships for sailing the Nile waterway instead of vessels made of reeds, timber had to be obtained through the 'Peoples of the Sea', Minoans and later Phoenicians, from across the Mediterranean (Herman 1966: 19–20).

After taking to the seas themselves, Egyptian sailors crossed the entire length of the Red Sea to the mysterious land of Punt, where they purchased cosmetics from a people resembling Hottentots. Land expeditions to Nubian gold mines in the south have been documented from 2270 BC, and Nubian warriors at some point were incorporated for defence.

This takes us to Mann's 'dialectic of empires and marcher lords', the principle underlying foreign relations and ethno-transformation in the empire/nomad mode. Stored harvests and temples with their treasures inevitably attracted the interest of neighbouring pastoralists and roaming warriors, who needed cereals, salt, or metals. But settled society will not fall to any passing tribe. Only those close enough to the civilised zone to develop a sense of its workings, and able to monitor the possibilities for exchange and protection, can attempt conquest. They must therefore be part-civilised, 'semi-barbarian'. Of course, as Ibn Khaldun argued in the fourteenth century AD, yielding to the attractions of city life comes at the price of a loss of martial character (and, as noted, physical and mental fitness). Yet the nomad tribe needs just these qualities if, after conquering the settled region, it must defend it against rival predators again. Hence the actual conquerors, Lattimore claims (1951: 72) were typically those able to assimilate civilisation and yet retain a degree of fierceness – 'men from the lower strata of the ruling class', not the established nomad chiefs.

The first well-placed (and well-known) nomad maverick with talent and charisma and a capacity to adapt was Sargon, an Akkadian military commander of the Sumerian king of Kish in the twenty-fourth century BC. The Akkadians, recruited as military auxiliaries in the later phases of Sumerian civilisation, created the first empire in which we see the elements of empire/nomad foreign relations in operation. Sargon's grandson, Naramsin, proclaimed himself 'god of Akkad' and 'ruler of the world', thus unifying religious and (universal) worldly sovereignty into a single office. Two centuries after Sargon, history repeated itself when semi-nomadic military auxiliaries of the Akkadians threw the empire into disarray, from which emerged the so-called Third Dynasty of Ur as the next centralising force. By then, Akkadian, in which we already recognise the roots of Arabic, had become the lingua franca of the entire region (Ostler 2006: 38–40). Mutual intelligibility lubricated further imperial/ nomad incorporation and expansion; it is a productive force in its own right. Towards 2000 BC, another auxiliary nomadic people, the

Amorites, gained control, and the imperial centre would shift further north to Babylon in the centuries that followed (Ponting 2001: 84–5). We are looking, in other words, at a process with an obvious regularity that we also find elsewhere, and hence we may designate it as a 'mode'.

The empire/nomad mode came to characterise foreign relations over a much larger area as a result of the Indo-European, 'Aryan' conquests in the second millennium BC. These inaugurated the epoch in which the earlier forms of sedentary and urbanised civil-isation merged into a common imperial pattern and even a measure of inter-imperial sovereign equality emerged, involving both actual Indo-European and Semitic rulers. The Indo-Europeans originated in the areas north of the Black Sea and around the Caspian (cf. McNeill 1991: 169, 111, map). As migrating pastoralists, they were caught in a Mann cage too: they had lost the capacity to live in dense wooded land, where their flocks would go hungry. 'The Semites and Aryans', Engels writes in this connection (*MEW*, xxi: 33), 'found it impossible to enter the West Asian and European forest areas before they had enabled themselves, by the cultivation of grain, to feed their cattle on this poorer soil and more particularly, to hibernate.'

Conquest constitutes the high road of imperial synthesis because it incorporates foreign relations into a coercive, 'despotic' state structure without entirely overcoming internal foreignness. As Linklater writes (1990: 37), conquest

replaced the original condition of intersocietal estrangement with a new form of vertical estrangement in which the conquerors exercised class domination over a subject people which had become one of its 'conditions of production'. The possibility that a new 'synthesis' could arise indicated that the rise of empire was a major reason for the development of unequal yet more inclusive social formations which destroyed the symbols of an exclusive tribal unity.

Thus the foreign is partly metamorphosed into a hierarchy of class/caste, even though the ethnic association survives. In terms of their respective modes of production, the conquering people either subjugated the vanquished community under its way of life, other-wise it 'leaves the old mode intact and contents itself with a tribute', or else 'a reciprocal interaction takes place whereby something new, a synthesis, arises' (Marx 1973: 97, 141, cf. Linklater 1990: 37).

Why we speak of 'Indo-European' conquests is a matter of a common master language of which Sanskrit is a formalised version. Celtic,

Italic/Latin, Germanic and its offshoots, Albanian, Greek, Phrygian, Anatolian/Hittite, Armenian, Balto-Slavic and their branches, Iranian, Indic/Sanskrit, and Tokharian all derive from this common root (Barber 1999: 115, fig. 6.3; Shirokogorov's work cited in this study challenges the hypothesis that there would be a comparable master language for the Ural–Altaic language group too). Given that the conquests themselves entailed further ethnogenesis and ethno-transformation, the linguistic connection is the material one; the idea of a common Aryan 'race' is a Nazi fiction.

A more tenuous Indo-European legacy is the triadic pantheon of deities postulated by Dumézil (1952). This pantheon probably only emerged in the synthesis with settled civilisations, since for most nomad tribes the three functional areas of community life overseen by dedicated (groups of) gods – sovereignty, war, and fertility – were not yet differentiated to the degree that would warrant such an explicit division. Indeed when the Indo-Europeans split into different ethnoi in the migrations from their staging areas, they did so as pastoralists. As Engels notes (*MEW*, xxi: 33), words for cattle among European and Asian 'Aryans' are still identical, but plants have different names, suggesting they were cultivated later. The words for soft metals, gold, silver, and copper, are also identical in the daughter branches of the Indo-European master language, so these too were known before the break-up (Barber 1999: 184).

Common to all Indo-European pastoral peoples was their military prowess. Their ferocity and the fast horse-drawn war chariot with two six-spoke wheels provided them with an advantage to which the settled agriculturalists (who at best had oxen- or mule-drawn carts with solid wooden wheels) had no answer. The spoke wheel was an invention of Indo-Iranians in the southern Urals; it made its first appearance around 2000 BC; possibly it was a by-product of wood-bending techniques for bow-making (Barber 1999: 204). Bronze, obtained by mixing copper with tin, in addition provided a hardened metal used in battle axes.

In their heroic poetry (the *Mahabharata* epic, or Homer's *Iliad*), the Indo-European invaders appear as outspoken 'personalities'. They combined unique characters with a sense of honour stronger than their fear of death, although Vroon has argued (1994: 370–1) that this courage was possibly the result of an inability to conceive of themselves as autonomous agents; they thought that their hands, feet, and so on, were separately operated by divine forces. If so, this was only one more reason why the war god occupies such a prominent place in the religions of the empires established by the conquests.

Mesopotamia's experience with Indo-European invasion began when Mitannians and Hurrians descended from the southern shores of the Caspian in the sixteenth century BC. After destroying Babylon, the great centre of civilisation made famous two centuries before by its ruler and lawgiver, Hammurabi, they went on to establish the state of Mitanni to the north-east of today's Syria. Mitanni would in turn be overwhelmed by the Hittites, another Indo-European people, whose empire had its core in central Anatolia. The power of the Hittites was anchored in the royal monopoly of iron-making, the secrets of which were only revealed after their demise. They were a highly literate civilisation: their capital, Hattusas, west of Ankara, housed a library containing texts in Hittite and Akkadian and at least three other languages using cuneiform. Terms for horses and their handling leave no doubt about the common 'Aryan' connection with horse-drawn chariots (Ostler 2006: 41, 196). The Hittite conquerors subdued an aboriginal Hattian people, but their provincial governors in Anatolia had to respect a degree of autonomy of the Hattian city elders – an early instance of how foreign relations between conquerors and locals become constitutionally enfolded into an imperial state structure (cf. Gurney 1952: 68–9). However, the Hittite warrior aristocracy, as well as the nearby Hurrians, also intermarried with the local populations they subdued. The Hyksos who invaded Egypt were probably mixed Semitic and Hurrian (Mann 1986: 181).

The Old Kingdom of Egypt collapsed under the strains of the dry period from 2200 to 2100 BC. Unlike Sumer, however, Egypt recovered to a population of around 5 million under the 'Middle Kingdom' (de Vries and Goudsblom 2002: 194). The Hyksos incursions wreaked havoc, but were repulsed around 1500 BC, after which the Egyptian empire was reconstructed again under Tuthmosis. It reached a final period of splendour under Ramses II two centuries later. Egypt at that point was at the centre of a Middle Eastern diplomatic system, maintaining formal relations with Babylonia and Mitanni. When Mitanni was subdued by the expanding Hittite empire, the Hittites took its place in this inter-imperial system. Embassies went to and fro with gifts and messages of friendship (in Akkadian, the region's lingua franca); the emperors called each other 'brother', often underscoring this by marrying off relatives to each other. Hattusilis III of the Hittites had a royal dagger made of iron presented to the king of Assyria, of the type Tutanchamon had received from an earlier Hittite ruler (Barber 1999: 185; Ostler 2006: 62). With Ramses II, Hattusilis concluded a famous treaty that ruled out war between the Hittites and Egypt. The treaty provided for a defensive alliance against outside attack, and contained provisions guaranteeing the accession of the legitimate heir in each other's empires (Gurney 1952: 77–8). The Hittites soon after passed their peak; they were first displaced from Anatolia to Syria by the Phrygians, and then declined altogether.

In the ensuing centuries, the Scythians descended from the steppes between the Danube and the Don. They harassed neighbouring empires such as Persia from the seventh century BC onwards, and later also the Roman empire. The Scythians constituted one branch of a cluster of Indo-Iranian tribes migrating into southern Siberia and Turkestan, and across the Iranian plateau as far as western Ukraine; the Aryans who invaded India between 1800 and 1200 BC were another branch. They all spoke (a version of) Persian close to Vedic Sanskrit, as common words like *as(h)va-* (horse) as well as the names of gods in the triadic pantheon testify (Barber 1999: 185; Ostler 2006: 43, 187). The Scythian incursions continued to the third century AD, when they were overwhelmed by the Goths (Chaliand 2006: 39–43).

We saw earlier that if an established empire is conquered by invading warriors, this typically occurs only after the latter have first been recruited as frontier auxiliaries, 'marcher lords'. This is a key characteristic of the empire/nomad mode. Thus one target of the Scythians was the Semitic Assyrians, who had taken power in the Babylonian empire with the nomadic Medes as auxiliaries. The Assyrians had horse cavalry instead of chariots, whilst adopting iron and early steel (developed initially by the Hittites) for improved armament. Warding off the Scythians was therefore a task they could handle. The Medes, on the other hand, had been entrusted with the keys to the empire, as so many military auxiliaries before and after them. They brought down the Assyrians in the seventh century, only to be unseated in turn by Cyrus II, their Persian vassal, in 550 BC (Mann 1986: 231–7).

Mesopotamia by then had been culturally unified by the influx of Semitic warrior–pastoralists, the Aramaeans. One of their tribes, the Chaldaeans, rose to power as the last ruling dynasty of Babylonia; another, the Itu, were later employed by the Assyrians as a mobile military force to quell dissent. This contributed to the replacement, from the eighth century BC, of Akkadian by Aramaic as the lingua franca of the entire Fertile Crescent and direct precursor of Arabic. 'As once had Sumerian, so now Akkadian fell victim to a new language brought by nomads and newcomers', Ostler concludes (2006: 68).

The reordering of foreign populations within their realm earned the Assyrians their reputation as particularly despotic rulers. In over 300 years of rule they deported an estimated 4.5 million people from their original lands, including, notoriously, the Jews of Israel. In fact we are looking at a particular form of incorporation and deterritorialisation of the subjected peoples. Oriental despots did not typically mix with their foreign subjects, and their despotism was the result of that distance. Thus the expression, a 'law of the Medes and the Persians' evokes the idea of a forbidding, immutable instruction; in reality it was a despotic intervention, a decree that left the practices and habits of the subjected communities intact (Marx 1976: 495). The stationary village world was usually not much affected by the struggles among warrior factions or peoples at the centre. As Marx notes elsewhere (*MEW*, xv: 514), 'Oriental empires exhibit a permanent immobility in their social foundations, and restless change in the persons and tribes who seize control of the political superstructure.'

Of the ancient rival valley civilisations, only the Indus valley in the end was conquered by Indo-Europeans, the Aryans of the Indo-Iranian branch. This is the classic case of a caste system emerging from an incomplete empire. Coming from the cooler north, the Aryans were 'white', and their sacrificial officers were called Brahmins. However, the ideal of transcendence and renunciation associated with the later Brahmin caste was not germane to the invaders' warrior ethos (Smaje 2000: 109). The ethno-transformation in which the priestly and warrior castes took their places resulted from a protracted cultural and political synthesis. Marx (1976: 138; cf. Ostler 2006: 197, 223) notes that Hindi, Bengali, Marathi, and other north Indian languages are mostly Sanskrit in vocabulary, but take their grammatical structure from the Elamite Dravidian root. Politically, the Maurya (322–185 BC) and the Gupta (AD 300–600) empires of Bengal's Ganges plain crucially contributed to the dialectic of change. Inspired by spreading Buddhist and Jainist doctrines, Ashoka, the Maurya emperor, famously renounced armed conquest following an exceptionally bloody military campaign. Instead he professed to aspire henceforth only to right conduct, *dharma* (Sen 1961: 66). Following his death, the Aryan ruling strata were able to restore their power to a considerable extent, but Buddhism and ascetism left their traces in the varna caste hierarchy, a complex system of occupying social space roughly along the (colour) lines of the initial north–south divide.

Hinduism is an ethical-religious ecumene rather than a single religion (the term merely refers to the area beyond the river Indus). It easily incorporated local beliefs into its evolving pantheon. Brahmins claim supreme authority in the ritual domain, as a hereditary caste; the warrior aristocracy was congealed into the caste of Kshatryas, who claim worldly authority. The figure of the chief/king (*raja*) became submerged in the Kshatrya caste in the absence of an emperor unifying religious and secular supremacy in his person. As a result, the two castes acted as a double apex, each professing to encompass the other (Smaje 2000: 18, 110; Heesterman 1973: 105). Foreign relations are thus metamorphosed into a hierarchy of caste without losing the association of distance, from nature and from others. A Brahmin child from days immemorial learned to accept the responsibility for its bodily cleanliness in these terms. As Carstairs writes (1957: 67),

It was taught the importance of avoiding the invisible pollution conferred by the touch of members of the lowest castes. The mother or grandmother would call him in, and make him bathe and change his clothes if this should happen, until his repugnance for a low-caste person's touch became as involuntary as his disgust for the smell and touch of faeces.

Hinduism and Indian civilisation generally expanded 'by incorporating diverse populations through assigning them different positions in the larger network of caste' (Wolf 1997: 49); its script (actually a collection of related scripts) spread across all of south-east Asia (Ostler 2006: 203).

The furthest eastward extension of the Indo-European advance was the Tarim basin in what is today Xingjian (Sinkiang) in China. Mummies with Caucasian facial traits and wearing textiles made with weaving techniques used by Indo-Europeans provide testimony of this. The Chinese name for these foreigners was Yuezhi, and records describe them as 'hairy' and 'white'. The Yuezhi called themselves Kushan and spoke Tokharian, an extinct Indo-European language paradoxically closest to its relatives furthest to the west, Celtic and Italic (Barber 1999: 19–21, 60, 118; cf. Aleksejev 1974: 284). Stein (1984: 155) speaks of the 'homo Alpinus' and cites a Jesuit travelling in Tajikistan in 1602 who compared them to the Flemish in their appearance.

To the west, finally, the Indo-European migrations/invasions initially remained tribal in nature. The imperial synthesis would come
much later, compounded by barbarian egalitarianism in various
ways. The Celts, who probably migrated from the Caspian to southern
Germany in the second millennium BC, were the first 'westerners' to
adopt horse-riding, but not the steppe form of cavalry warfare, nor
the bow and arrow. In the Central European forests and marshlands,
the long sword was apparently more useful (McNeill 1991: 237).
Celtic culture developed on the basis of salt mining and trade; the
Hallstatt culture is named after one of their salt mines, *(g)hall* being
the old Celtic root for salt. The names of the areas where they settled
later all got their names from this connection – Gallia (Gaul), Wales
(in French, Pays de Galles), Galicia in Spain and in Poland, Galatia
in Anatolia, etc. (Barber 1999: 135–7). There was intensive exchange
between the Iberian Atlantic coast and Brittany, Cornwall (a source
of tin for bronze), Wales, and Ireland, which may have contributed
to the spread of Celtic as a lingua franca early on (Ostler 2006:
290–1; Marcus 1998: ch. 2).

The Graeco-Roman imperial lineage that eventually overwhelmed
the Celts can be traced to the conquest of the Greek peninsula by the
Indo-European Mycenaeans in the eighteenth century BC. Crete too
fell to them after the island's Minoan civilisation had been
destroyed by an earthquake in 1450 BC. Greek civilisation was built
on city-states; Athens had imperial ambitions, but its maritime
colonial network rather belongs to the Minoan tradition of sea-
nomadism. The role of the Greeks as military auxiliaries for Persia
and their trade diaspora would also speak for this nomadic aspect.
As a high civilisation, Athens was exposed to semi-barbarian
Macedonia, 'a tribal monarchy of the mountainous interior', as Perry
Anderson characterises it (1996: 45), 'a backward zone which had
preserved many of the social relations of post-Mycenaean Greece'.
Out of the synthesis between semi-barbarian Macedonia and Greek
culture emerged Hellenistic civilisation and empire on which Rome
would build in turn.

Before investigating the foreign relations of the classical land
empires more systematically, let me briefly reflect on the normative
unification on which they were premised as distinct civilisations.

Cosmologies of Empire and Nomadic Origins

The cosmologies and ethical–religious systems that we associate
with the major world civilisations originated around the seventh

century BC, the period that Karl Jaspers (as in M. Wood 2005: 64–5; cf. Buzan and Little 2000: 204) baptised the 'Axis Age'. At that juncture, processes of socialisation had apparently reached a stage where new codes of behaviour, valid for all members of a larger community and no longer based on tribal rules, required some form of articulation. Buddha, the early Greek philosophers, the prophets of the Old Testament, and the Chinese sages, all were engaged in this endeavour.

Already in the Mesopotamian setting, a shift occurred in which the scope of consciousness, at least of the ruling stratum, expands beyond the mythical imagination of the tribal way of life. 'Th[e] individualisation of Babylonian religious practice', McNeill writes (1991: 137), 'implies that at least some persons were conscious of serious defects in the older collective religion.'

In the megalopolitan environment of Babylon, individuals could no longer identify themselves entirely with the fate of the social groups to which they belonged: native city, occupational associations, and even family ceased to have unchallenged sway over men's affections ... [But] if the past and future welfare of a man's family and city ceased to serve as an adequate criterion of effective relationships with the gods, what consolation could a helpless mortal find in the doctrines of traditional Babylonian religion?

The sense that the old deities had abandoned humanity to its fate in many cases produced a pessimistic concept of the present and a quest for redemption. The Manicheism of abandonment and salvation thus stimulated epic–mythical history, as rulers harked back to a heroic golden age in the past from which they sought to draw inspiration to deal with contemporary challenges. Certainly these changes tended to be confined to fairly narrow circles at the apex of the imperial formation. It would take until the rise of Christianity in the Roman empire before subjectivity of this type assumed a wider, 'popular' dimension. This coincided with its transformation into an imperial doctrine laying down rules of citizenship. In Hegel's words (1961: 173), in the Roman–Christian context, 'the general [still] subordinates the individuals, they have to merge into it; but in exchange they obtain their own generality, that is, personality: they become legal persons in a private capacity'.

The ethical–religious departures of the Axis Age, however, were far from being imperial projects. They were associated with flight and exile, with wanderings in pursuit of truths that had yet to be discovered and often contradicted the established order. Ezrah, Isaiah, and the other biblical prophets rail against the kings of Assyria and

Egypt; large parts of the Old Testament were written in Babylonian exile (Friedman 1997). The young prince who became Buddha travelled among hermits and challenged the cruel ritual demanded by the local ruler (Beal 1884: 236–7). Socrates was condemned to death, and Confucius and Mencius, too, were distrusted by the authorities of their day, if only because their dialectical method of arriving at the truth did not rule out any question. Empire to all of them was a nearby or emergent reality, but there was an interstitial, nomadic quality to the teachings of these sages that pitted them against coercive monarchic rule.

In the imperial context, however, their reflections and meditations were codified into apodictic doctrines or state religions. In due course, Mann (1986: 341) argues, this led to 'a branching of the ways, the emergence of at least four different paths of future development'. Those treading in the footsteps of the prophets and sages were enlisted as priests or intellectual functionaries; their ideological role placed at the service of the state, incorporated into what Deleuze and Guattari call (1986: 41) 'the imperium of true thinking operating by magical capture'. This was always an incomplete process and even to the extent it worked cannot be dismissed as outright perversion. In the Roman empire, Christianity still served as an ecumene transcending tribal differences, softening hierarchical rigidities, and shifting military imperialism to an ethical concept of citizenry and collective life; (neo-)Confucianism, to which we return below, and Hinduism (partly absorbing its internal counterpoint, Buddhism) were likewise employed to overcome a spiritual crisis of empire (Mann 1986: chs 10–11).

The imperial capture of ethical–religious systems is never secure either. Certainly a 'church' may be 'a strictly dependent organ with an autonomy that is only imagined' (Deleuze and Guattari 1986: 30). But the roots of a doctrine in social critique cannot be entirely obliterated. Social development itself will reopen the dialogue, require answers that may depart from the codex, and produce 'nomadic' alternatives to the official, 'royal' version again. Islam in this connection occupies a special place. It emerged as a monotheism of nomad origin, like Judaism. But it did not, as Judaism did, spawn a separate religion (Christianity) to serve the spiritual needs of a stagnant sedentary empire (Rome); nor did it dissolve into separate denominations with the break-up of another empire (i.e. Western Christianity). Islam uniquely assigns a high status to merchants, and its teachings echo tribal egalitarianism, whereas imperial Christianity was hierarchical and persecuted its commercial diaspora, the Jews, when it broke up into nationalised versions.

The political and economic rise of the West constrained pastoral nomadism to the point of extinction, and Islam, having first risen to unparalleled cultural splendour, was pushed onto the defensive along with it. However, as Gramsci writes (1975, i: 247–8), the disjunction of Islam from the pace of change in Western Europe does not mean that the Muslim world would not at some point reinsert itself into the process. The Islamic world, he noted prophetically, would react to the pressures of modernity in the same way as Christianity had done before it, that is, by developing 'heretical', denominational departures from the mainstream as an expression of emergent national consciousness against theocratic cosmopolitanism, whilst presenting them as a *return* to the sources of its mode of existence. In that sense, the Wahabite sect of Saudi Arabia in Gramsci's view was not different from Atatürk – just as we may think of the Sunni–Shia divide today.

THE FRONTIER AS THE MAINSPRING OF EMPIRE

Once stabilised, an empire becomes bounded by a *frontier*. The frontier is 'a zone rather than a line' (Lamb 1968: 6), a geographical unit in its own right: the steppe gradient across Eurasia, or the coastline and river systems of Europe. In the Roman empire, the boundary was designated as the *limes*. The *limes*, Stein notes (1984: 178), 'served as the technical term for Roman military roads pushed forward from a base of operations on a frontier'.

It is on the frontier that the daily encounter between empire and (semi-)barbarians takes place and the social structures of each become enmeshed. The principles of sovereignty and bureaucratised authority of empire, heralding the territorial state, here mix with the notion of shared space reminiscent of tribal foreign relations. Different ways of life are pressed together, and the density and intensity of social interaction works to accelerate development. Throughout history, from Mesopotamia to the American Midwest, the frontier has therefore been a zone of experimentation and innovation; here adaptive practices are least constrained by established custom.

Toynbee (1935, ii: 212–13 and iii: 391) also highlights the 'conductivity' of the frontier, its role as a conveyor belt of both innovations and actual peoples. It facilitates the flow of cultural achievements far from their place of origin even if the inventors stay put. The Chinese invented woodblock printing in the ninth century, using moveable type by 1040–50; it reached Turkestan, westwards along the Inner Asian frontier, in the fourteenth century, and was in wide use when it was finally also 'invented' in Europe (Braudel 1981: 399). As a 'contact zone' (Inayatullah and Blaney 2004: 9, 17), the frontier also facilitates the flow of disease – bubonic plague carried by rats travelled west along the caravan routes of the Silk Road and reached the Mediterranean in the fourteenth century.

Trade Diasporas, Incorporation, and Tribute

One need not travel to the extremities of the empire to reach the actual frontier zone. Every city is a frontier formation in this sense, even if it is physically located in the heart of the empire. Indeed as Mumford writes (1961: 96), Toynbee's *Study of History*

has given our generation a fresh insight into the role that 'encounters' and 'challenges' play in the development of a civilization no less than in that of an individual. But what is curiously lacking in his otherwise almost too-exhaustive essay is a realization of the fact that it is in the city – and only there, on an effective scale, with sufficient continuity – that these interactions and transactions, these proposals and responses, take place.

This refers, obviously, to the aspect of exchange first of all. In the imperial setting, exchange cannot yet take place in a market in which identity is universally substitutable. The distance and 'anonymity' required for the free exchange of equivalents is incompatible with community, so ethnic difference is a precondition for it to take place at this stage (Rosman and Rubel 1976: 553; Buzan and Little 2000: 213). Ethnogenesis of commercial peoples is determined by professional specialisation, often the result of being excluded, as foreigners, from owning land (Engels in *MEW*, xxi: 108–9). Now as Curtin argues (1984: 8), specialisation allows people to take their distance from nature, but not from other people; traders will be attracted to places where crowds gather. Temples, public squares, or court houses are therefore the obvious places of exchange (just think of Jesus chasing the money changers from the temple), and they are also the constitutive spaces of cities.

Exchange specialists, then, will at some point be granted rights of residence in the imperial city. This represents an instance of incorporation, a key socio-spatial technique of empire. The right of residence includes maintaining their own customs, religion, and even law – something unthinkable in early national states, which invariably seek to exteriorise the foreign from the social body. Like other specialists in the service of empire, the incorporated communities will often become a caste or class in later development, without losing the original association with foreignness.

When trading communities move between several host cities, we may classify them as (quasi-)'nomads' too. Marx (1973: 858) in this connection emphasises their role as 'living money' in between sedentary societies:

The trading peoples of antiquity [lived] like the gods of Epicurus in the spaces between the worlds, or rather like the Jews in the pores of Polish society. Most of the independent trading peoples or cities attained the magnificent development of their independence through the carrying trade, which rested on the barbarity of the producing peoples, between whom they played the role of money (the mediators).

The empire is content to levy a tribute on these mediators. Tribute is in the nature of a tax, and even where it is indistinguishable from trade, the fact that it is conducted under the authority of the empire lends it a different quality. The tributary mode of *production*, too, can only evolve in the hierarchical structure of empire, be it full-fledged oriental despotism, or a form associated with imperial decay, such as feudalism (Amin 1973: 10–1). Tribute as a form of exchange in foreign relations likewise presupposes hierarchy, although there can be situations in which it is not the empire that taxes the nomads, but the other way around, depending on the actual relations of strength.

The incorporation of trading colonies and diasporas has been a feature of imperial formations throughout history. In Ur, the centre of Sumer's third dynasty, there was a colony of Indus merchants already in the third millennium BC (M. Wood 2005: 55). Assur in northern Mesopotamia, the centre of the later Assyrian empire, in the second millennium BC dispatched its representatives to faraway places to ensure supplies. Tin from Afghanistan was handled by merchants from Assur resident in Iran; they also had their own quarter in the city of Kanesh in central Anatolia. The Assur merchants were taxed by local authorities and faced restrictions as to the goods they could legitimately trade (Ponting 2001: 176–7).

On the frontier of the Assyrian empire, another trading people, the Phoenicians, became the principal carriers in the Mediterranean from the ninth century BC. They operated from the port cities of Lebanon and established famous colonies, such as Rome's early rival, Carthage, in North Africa. Herodotus records that the Phoenicians already sailed round the southern tip of Africa in the service of an Egyptian pharaoh (as in Neumark 1964: 11–2). Like the Minoans before them, the Phoenicians exploited waterways and the cost advantages they offer. 'The sea route, as the route which moves and is transformed under its own impetus, is that of trading peoples *par excellence*', Marx writes in the *Grundrisse* (1973: 525). Highways, on the other hand, 'originally fall to the community, later for a long period to the governments, as pure deductions from production'.

The role of mediator also encouraged the development of new means of communication. The Phoenicians perfected earlier scripts into an alphabet in order to record foreign languages by their sounds, unlike the ideographic scripts typical of empires. The hiero-glyphs of Egypt, of the Olmec and Maya cultures, or Chinese char-acters are examples of such imperial scripts; Mesopotamian cuneiform, a shorthand also developed from pictograms, stands midway between an ideographic and a phonetic script. Aramaic however could become the lingua franca of the Middle East by adopting the Phoenician alphabet of 22 signs instead of the more than 600 of cuneiform (Ostler 2006: 44, 76–7). The Greeks took the Phoenician alphabet and developed it further by adding vowels. Greek rather than Semitic Phoenician became the commercial lingua franca in the Mediterranean. The Vikings, nomad warrior–traders on the frontiers of Western Christianity, to whom we return in the next chapter, likewise exploited their runic alphabet (a simplified version of a Germanic script) to record foreign words by their sound as they explored rivers and coastlines beyond the horizon (Boyer 1992: 58–9).

The Arabs, too, developed a phonetic script. Their seafaring com-mercial activities, along with the Persians', expanded when Indian traders shifted their attention to south–east Asia in the second cen-tury AD (Wolf 1997: 44). With the rise of Islam, the influence of Arabic, and especially of its script, spread far and wide. Yet in con-trast to the Muslim religion, the only legacy of Arabic as a commer-cial lingua franca would be its imprint on Swahili in East Africa, which otherwise, according to Ostler (2006: 103), remains a basically Bantu language.

The Jews became a trade diaspora only when they had been dis-persed; they were not originally traders. As a nomadic frontier people of the Egyptian empire, the *Habiru* (Hebrews), migrated across the Sinai peninsula to the Jordan valley in the fourteenth century BC. Freud (1967; cf. Redmount 1998) claims this was because of a crisis following the death of pharaoh Achnaton and the priestly backlash against his experiment with monotheism. The tribes settling in the biblical 'land of milk and honey' were unified by King Saul around 1000 BC to fight the Philistines, who had come from the Greek islands. After the northern kingdom of Israel had been destroyed by the Assyrians in 722 BC, its population was forcibly resettled in Mesopotamia; the southern state of Judah survived another 100 years before it too was destroyed and its population dispersed across the Middle East. Often, the Jews moved on voluntarily to serve as mercenary soldiers and merchants. They actually flourished in the Roman empire, and until the mid third century AD were the foreign ethnos with the highest growth in numbers, despite ferociously fought Jewish insurrections in Palestine, Cyprus, and North Africa. They spoke Greek, the commercial lingua franca, until the end of the Western empire; the word 'Jew' by then had become synonymous with 'merchant'. After the collapse of the Roman empire and the money economy, 'living money' was once again in demand, and Jews and Lebanese (Syrian) traders took up that role (Toynbee 1976: 280–1). There were always instances of persecution of Jews, but the principle of tributary incorporation is premised on leaving them alone. Expulsion or worse typically occurs once a host community begins to urbanise and takes up a commercial role itself.

Trade diasporas often developed as quasi-tribal kin networks. 'Since the merchant profession could not do without a network of reliable go-betweens and associates', Braudel writes (1983: 150), 'the family offered the most natural and sought-after solution.' This held already for the Assur traders in the second millennium BC, referred to earlier. Extended families followed in the footsteps of the family son dispatched to a foreign port of trade, and as they intermarried within their own community, they evolved into actual diasporas. Networks of Chinese traders from Fujian province fanned out into Japan and south-east Asia, later enlarged by exported contract labour. In south-east Asia, commercially oriented 'harbour principalities', separate from the tributary inland states with their monuments and bonded labour, provided the nodal points for the spread of merchant colonies from the north. Thus Indians exported their culture and religion (Muslim and Hindu) to parts of Indonesia; their traders were often accompanied by Brahmins who bestowed the dignity of Kshatrya (warrior caste) on local rulers (Wolf 1997: 56). These trade diasporas always took care to avoid absorption into the host societies by cultivating their own language and religious practices, even proselytising. It is important to remember, however, as Buzan and Little underline (2000: 222), that the vast majority of any empire's population still lived off local produce, remote from the channels of long-distance trade.

In the Ottoman empire, Christian Armenians developed as a key commercial community. The Armenians established excellent relations with the Genoese from their entrepôt in the Crimea; in the Persian empire, they had their main centre at Isfahan, the capital of the Safavid rulers of the sixteenth and early seventeenth centuries, who relied also on Armenian bureaucrats converted to Islam. The Armenian traders 'made their presence felt practically throughout the trading world' – the major exceptions being China and Japan (Braudel 1983: 156; cf. Curtin 1984: 185–7). Their darkest hour came when the Ottoman empire became embroiled in imperialist conflict, and Turkish nationalism began to stir. In 1895, some 90,000 Armenians were killed and further massacres occurred in 1909. Finally during the First World War, the deportation of more than a million Armenians away from the boundary with Russia ended in genocide (Kloss 1969: 179–80).

A related form of incorporating a foreign element for economic purposes concerns labour – whether as slaves or otherwise as bonded labour. Conquest is again the starting point. 'If human beings themselves are conquered along with the land and soil as its organic accessories, then they are equally conquered as one of the conditions of production', Marx observes (1973: 491). The Roman empire developed through a mechanism of conquest fuelled by a slave-worked plantation economy; new conquests brought more slaves. When the wars of conquest came to a standstill, the Germanic tribes on the frontier, with whom the empire traded, according to Engels (*MEW,* xix: 453) were asked to begin supplying slaves too. The frontier continued to be a transit point of slaves from the barbarian periphery, but 'not in sufficient numbers to solve the supply problem in conditions of peace' (P. Anderson 1996: 76–7). In the tenth century, the eastern frontier of Western Christianity along the Elbe was still a collection zone for Slavs sold to Islam; Crimean Tatars provided Istanbul with Russian slaves as late as the sixteenth century (Braudel 1984: 436).

Frontier nomad or other semi-barbarian tribes, entrusted with tribute-collecting tasks for the empire and supplying it with exotic goods and slaves raided from neighbouring communities, tended to undergo a hierarchical mutation in the process. Thus, on the frontier of the Roman empire, forest barbarian middlemen with a role in the organisation of tribute and trade, often became local lords, prejudicing the relative equality of tribal society and prefiguring mediaeval feudalism (Gledhill 1994: 44–5). Engels makes the point (*MEW*, xxi: 139) that the retinues recruited by barbarian military chiefs, and originally made up of slaves, sometimes developed into a nobility later. This takes us to the aspect of protection.

Foreign Auxiliaries for Frontier Protection

The military abilities of nomads and other mobile warriors were always the nightmare and envy of settled agriculturalists and city dwellers. Appearing with chariots or on horseback, their form of warfare caused great problems for the infantry or otherwise static battle order fielded by the sedentary society. Fast manoeuvring and harassing with concentrated forces, withdrawing again quickly, and using methods of deception and ambush, their surprise and shock tactics often gave the nomads the advantage over numerically stronger but static opponents (Chaliand 2006: 23). Deleuze and Guattari (1986: 7) make the claim that the 'war machine' of an empire is actually imported from its nomad periphery; but to recruit military auxiliaries on the frontier, the empire of course had to exist already and be able to wage war itself. The Romans had their citizens' legions before they recruited Germanic tribesmen, to give but one example. It is true though that the war function, which is latent in the nomads' tribal organisation, becomes their primary role once enlisted by the empire (ibid.: 113). This is another route to frontier feudalism.

The principle of nomad auxiliaries has many early examples. Libyan troops served the Egyptian pharaohs to keep out other Libyan nomads in the fourteenth and thirteenth centuries BC. Another characteristic, their incorporation into the host society and the ability to seize power as a result, has also been documented for the Libyans in ancient Egypt (Ostler 2006: 126–7). Germanic tribes made themselves available as mercenaries to Macedonia in the second century BC, but their fame as auxiliaries dates from the Roman empire. As the population pressure on the *limes* mounted, entire peoples were recruited as *foederati*, allied auxiliaries. They inevitably acquired the military abilities and organisational capacities of the imperial state, as the Romans were to find out in the campaigns to hold the Danube frontier against the Germanic Marcomanni between AD 167 and 180. Not all frontier warriors were nomads; the

Germanic forest tribes were not even horse riders at first. They only acquired equestrian skills (and according to Engels, 'morbid sexual perversions', *MEW*, xxi: 71, 89) on their visits to the steppe nomads on the Black Sea. As Mann notes (1986: 286), 'they were aware of the enduring Roman weakness in cavalry, and they consciously exploited their own superior mobility'.

Incorporating frontier warriors was itself a contribution to the consolidation of empire. The Romans, like the Chinese and other rulers of classical empires, were not inclined to accept a limit to their sovereignty, and when the Rhine and the Euphrates were suggested as a *limes* for the Roman empire, it was an idea not of the Romans, but of barbarian chiefs (Jones 1959: 246). Indeed as Engels argues (*MEW*, xix: 448), with an army largely composed of foreign auxiliaries, no further wars of conquest are possible. But then, auxiliaries not only defend the empire against barbarian attack; they also prevent it from overextending itself (Lattimore 1951: 245). In the case of the Roman empire, this stage was reached by AD 200.

A particular form of recruiting foreign auxiliaries was military slavery. The Abbasid caliphs employed Turkish warrior–slaves, the Umayyad caliphs in Spain, Slavs. Chaliand (2006: 83–5) gives the example of the Samanid dynasty of Iran in the ninth and tenth centuries, which employed Turkish-speaking military slaves, Ghulams. Towards the turn of the millennium the Ghulams of Afghanistan rose to great power under a dynasty of their own, the Ghaznevids, who had to be solicited by the Samanid emperors for protection, as if they were a foreign power. Eventually, the Ghaznevids were driven into the Punjab by the Seljuk Turks who displaced the Samanids. More familiar are the Mamluks protecting Egypt (they seized power in the mid thirteenth century). They too were Turkish-speaking military slaves, who fought the Mongols and the Crusaders. The Ottoman Turks, finally, had their military slaves too, the Janissaries. Janissaries were forcibly recruited Christian boys, mostly from the Balkans, who were converted to Islam (under a system called child tribute, *devşirme*, Toynbee 1935: iii: 79). They were an elite corps, their internal cohesion cemented by iron discipline and widespread homosexuality. In all cases, foreign communities were incorporated as military auxiliaries with their ethnic identity left intact, just as happened with the exchange specialists resident in the empire. But we should not think of ethnic identity as 'national'; once the national aspect rose to prominence, incorporation and recognised difference were suspended with it, often with ethnic cleansing as the result.

The Inner Asian frontier, the steppe gradient that runs from Manchuria to Hungary, until the fifteenth century remained a seemingly inexhaustible reservoir of nomad tribes, auxiliaries and conquerors alike. Small wonder it produced some of the greatest military geniuses of history. Barber (1999: 192, fig. 9.9) identifies four successive epicentres of nomadic expansion, each one further to the east: first the Indo-Europeans spreading from the area between the Black Sea and the Caspian; a millennium later, the Indo-Iranian branch, from the area north of the Caspian and Aral seas and the Urals; then the Turkic speakers west of Lake Baikal; and finally the Mongols. To the Mongols and Genghis Khan I return in the next section. The Turkic-speaking tribes in the late fourteenth century produced another chief of world-historic renown, Timur Lenk ('the lame', 'Tamerlane' in the West). Like Genghis before him, Timur as a young man was a 'marginal' of his tribal society before rising to become a conqueror. The conversion to Islam of part of the Chagadai Mongol khanate of Central Asia and the refusal to convert of another part provided the setting for Timur's ascent (Hattstein 2000: 408; Chagadai was the second son of Genghis Khan). When the future conqueror in 1360 joined forces with the Islamic rulers to fight off the 'infidel' Mongols, his ability not only as a military leader but also as a ruthless operator, changing sides whenever he saw a chance to increase his own following, led to the whirlwind conquests that made him notorious. Timur's cavalry were armed with long sabres of damask steel, an Asian secret producing a blade of unrivalled sharpness. As Braudel notes (1981: 377), European blacksmiths only succeeded in forging such steel in the early nineteenth century.

The Timurid 'empire' at one point extended from western Xingjian to Anatolia, with Persia as the central node. This explains why Islam's eastward expansion along the frontier was accompanied by the spread of the Persian language, rather than Arabic (Ostler 2006: 98–9). Unlike Genghis Khan, however, Timur was thoroughly familiar with the sedentary societies he conquered; the aspect of the frontier as the launch pad of conquest was receding. Timur's wars against the Golden Horde in the north, and Byzantium in the west, were already more in the nature of the inter-state relations of a new age. That the Timurid experience had its origins in tribal society transpired after his death in 1404/5, en route to subdue China. Nomad empires or confederations generally do not leave behind an urban infrastructure and can disappear as quickly as they have arisen (Buzan and Little 2000: 187);

Timur's successors, unlike Genghis' descendants, could not even uphold the semblance of unity. Only Babur, who conquered India in the early sixteenth century, escaped this trap. His Mughal realm ('Mongol', actually Islamic Turkic speakers with a Persian-speaking elite) was an empire proper and already relied on its own frontier auxiliaries, the Rajput warriors of the desert fastnesses of Rajasthan, to control the Hindu hinterland (Spear 1970: 34–5).

Whether the Maya, who succeeded the Olmec empire in the Yucatan lowlands of central America, were a frontier formation of the powerful but obscure empire of Teotihuacan in the Mexico valley, is unclear. Maya civilisation did enter two centuries of great splendour after the demise of Teotihuacan in the sixth century AD, however, before it collapsed into internecine war over diminishing resources as a result of deforestation (Ponting 2001: 119–21; 1991: 78–83). In central Mexico, on the other hand, events very much fit into the general framework of the empire/nomad mode. Here it took until around AD 1000 before Toltec military clans initiated a process of empire formation that culminated in the rule of the Mexica, or Aztec. The Aztecs were also a military clan confederation; in the 1420s, as frontier warriors for the ruler of the city of Tenochtitlán in central Mexico, they seized power to establish an empire of their own, just as Sargon had conquered Sumer 4,000 years before (M. Wood 2005: 153–60; Slicher van Bath 1989: 16–7, 121). The Inca did not follow this path. They expanded northwards from the region of Lake Titicaca on the border of modern Peru and Bolivia, and when they came into conflict with the Chincha around modern Lima, a peaceful solution through dynastic marriage avoided full-scale war.

The development of a new mode of foreign relations heralded by Timur's conquests is even more pronounced in the case of the two last classical empires apart from China – the Ottoman empire and Russia. In important respects they were frontier formations themselves, combining aspects of nomadism with territorial state formation.

The Ottomans (named after their legendary chief Osman) were frontier warriors of nomadic origin, known as *gazis*, for the Seljuk Turks – the opponents of the Christian Crusaders. The Seljuk sultan already took steps towards a modern state by separating his authority from that of the caliph who was notionally under his protection; the Seljuk army was Turkish, although the language of administration was still Persian. When the Seljuk empire disintegrated, the Ottomans rose, first defeating Timur Lenk in 1402 and then pushing into the Balkans. Byzantium, Chaliand notes (2006: 26), was 'their' empire and model for state formation (as it would be for Russia). Until the fall of Constantinople in 1453, the Ottomans were a frontier threat to Byzantium, and then took over its imperial status themselves. However, the practical attitude and adaptability characteristic of the frontier continued to characterise Ottoman rule. They typically 'learned many useful techniques from their enemies'.

The Ottoman fleet that came into being in the sixteenth century copied Venetian models; European renegades contributed knowledge of firearms and helped to make Ottoman siege and field artillery invincible ... [Indeed, when Constantinople fell], the Ottoman realm was still largely in an embryonic state, retaining many features of the original marcher principality. (Garraty and Gay 1981: 608)

What sets the Ottomans apart is their equally inventive approach to overcoming the divisive particularism that ruined so many other empires built by frontier warriors. One practice included killing the brothers of each new sultan to remove rival pretenders. In other areas they retained characteristics going back to their roots as herders; Toynbee (1935, iii: 28, 42) quotes a seventeenth-century Flemish emissary who records that just as a European may enjoy a well broken-in horse, dog, or hawk, 'the Turk' appreciates a well-trained human. Their Janissaries were trained in that spirit, 'as human aux-iliaries to assist them in keeping order among their "human cattle"'. Incorporation of foreign communities, especially the 'people of the book', Jews and Christians, on the other hand was arranged according to standard imperial practice.

Their advance against Austria–Hungary took the Ottomans to the gates of Vienna in the late seventeenth century. After that, the empire was forced to concede a transformation of its frontiers into boundaries and hence rein in frontier nomads whose forays into Russia and Poland now amounted to breaches of international law (Abou-el-Haj 1969: 467, 471). It proved equally difficult to overcome the corporative state/society complex of the empire itself. European states even exploited this by so-called capitulations. These granted them the right to protect the Christians incorporated as foreigners in the Ottoman empire, thus restricting its sovereignty from the out-side. Marx describes (*MEW*, x: 172–3) how the capitulations France had obtained earlier were systematised in 1740, when Paris secured a protectorate over all convents of the 'Frankish' religion and all Frankish visitors of Holy Places – note the Crusader terminology. Russia in 1774 followed the example, albeit under a treaty; Napoleon in 1802 also placed relations with the Ottoman empire on a treaty basis. This would develop into a stepping stone of imperialist encroachment more generally, as concessions, which at some point (as in 1890s China) would come to include the customs system and territorial leases in the port cities and coastal areas.

Russia emerged from conquest by Swedish Vikings known as 'Rhos'. Arab chroniclers describe them sometimes as traders, sometimes as warriors, sometimes as both. In the tenth century, the Swedes sailed down Russia's lakes and rivers for trade until they reached Byzantium, where they hired themselves out as mercenaries. Along the way they subdued the local population, who nicknamed them Varangians, white squirrels. 'The Varangian realm in Russia', Perry Anderson writes (1996: 175–6), 'was a commercial empire built fundamentally on the sale of slaves to the Islamic world, initially via the Khazar and Bulgar Khanates, and later directly from the central emporium of Kiev itself.' Kiev was one of two centres created by the Varangian conquests, the other being Novgorod. Norse gradually melted into Russian (both Indo-European languages) as their rule extended southwards. Kiev became the core of the future empire following the adoption of Greek Orthodox Christianity (and many other aspects of Byzantine civilisation) under Vladimir 'the Great' in 982. But as Boyer notes (1992: 247), it was by then already difficult to establish whether Vladimir should be considered a Scandinavian or a Russian. A characteristic of all Viking settlement was their absorption, within a generation, into the existing culture – an aspect we will see was crucial in the synthesis between sea-nomadism and imperial universalism in Western Christianity's frontier formations.

Kiev in the twelfth century had to be given up in the face of pressure from the Pecheneg (Patzinak) nomads operating from the steppes along the rivers Don and Donetz. Having retreated to Moscow as the new capital, the empire sought the succour of another nomad people which had initially threatened them, the Kipchaks (Polovtsis in Russian), the founders of the kingdom of Georgia, to ward off the threat of the advancing Mongols. Nomad empires as we saw will tend to split in succession crises, and in the course of the fifteenth century the Mongols further subdivided into separate khanates. This allowed the Russian empire to take recourse to the key protective strategy in empire/nomad relations, the recruitment of auxiliaries. Allying himself with the Crimean Tatars (Tatar being the generalising name used for all nomads from the trans-Baikal area), Tsar Ivan III defeated the remnants of the Golden Horde, but was thrown back to Moscow by the Kazan khanate. The

Tatars/Mongols at this point were still militarily superior; as Chaliand reminds us (2006: 176), the front-loading musket of the Russians was slower and had a shorter range than the bow and arrow.

In the mid sixteenth century, Ivan 'the Terrible' reorganised the army and created a service nobility at the expense of the landed aristocracy. This enabled the empire to subdue the nomads, except for the Khanate of the Crimea (supported by the Ottoman empire, to which it was tributary; Abou-el-Haj 1969: 472). The Crimean Tatars in 1571 and 1591 even sacked Moscow, imposing a tribute which Russia continued to pay until Peter the Great assumed the throne at the beginning of the eighteenth century. The Crimea was annexed only in 1783 after Catherine II defeated the Ottomans. This expansion towards the south and into Siberia has often been compared to the North American frontier; but the relationship which Russia established over its newly acquired territories was typically imperial. As Wolf observes (1997: 183), 'in contrast to the North American trade ... the Russian fur trade relied mainly on tribute – that is, payments in fur made as tokens of political subjugation'.

For its expansion, as well as to fight off Asian nomads, the Russian empire relied on the unique phenomenon of home-grown quasi-nomads, the Cossacks. Often runaway serfs, the Cossacks (from the Turkish *kasak*, 'nomad') in the fifteenth and sixteenth centuries settled in the southern steppes along the Dnepr and the Don rivers. They adopted nomad social organisation and in wartime or periods of civil unrest were recruited as cavalry by the autocracy. Neither southern Russia nor Siberia would have been conquered without them, because only they could match nomad mobility in warfare (Lattimore 1962: 150). In Trotsky's view (1978, i: 29), those enterprising elements in the peasant population who in the West became city dwellers, craftsmen, or merchants, in Russia became Cossacks. Trade in the expanding Russian empire therefore was left to Tatars, Armenians, and Jews. The Jews, upon their expulsion from England and France at the turn of the fourteenth century, had been actively welcomed by Casimir 'the Great' of Poland to assist in the kingdom's commercial development; with the annexation of Poland they were incorporated into the Russian empire where they specialised, as Engels notes (*MEW*, viii: 50), in selling manufactured products to the countryside.

What also makes the Russian experience unique is that the strategy of incorporation was not, as in Turkey, terminated by a national revolution entailing the persecution of minorities. It was in key respects reproduced in the USSR by the policy of national self-determination, albeit a policy directed, like state socialism generally, from above. In the larger scheme of foreign relations, however, the Russian empire's role was always that of a frontier formation against the Asian nomads. 'The function Russia had in European history', Gramsci writes (1975, ii: 714), 'was the defence of Western Europe against the Tatar invasions, it was a frontier (*'antemurale'*) around European civilisation against Asiatic nomadism.' This was a catalyst of the dissolution of the empire of Western Christianity, as it allowed the survival of units of a size that would otherwise not have been feasible.

Before proceeding, let me sum up the main aspects of the empire/nomad mode of foreign relations.

In terms of the *occupation of space*, the empire is a sedentary for-mation, relying on an agricultural core; nomad pastoral tribes or tribal confederations, on the other hand, are characterised by mobile occupation of space. Both develop their concept of space from these different practices. The universal sovereignty claimed by the empire, and the actual presence of nomads and other barbar-ians, are reconciled spatially on the frontier. Socially, the frontier facilitates mutual adaptation and accelerated social innovation, for which it then serves as a conveyor belt, spreading new practices far and wide. Imperial cities also function as frontier sectors in this sense; resident foreigners here (and on the frontier) are allowed to retain their own social customs as part of a policy of incorporation.

Protection in the empire/nomad mode revolves around recruit-ment by the empire of foreign auxiliaries (often, nomad cavalry) to protect the frontier against other nomads (the policy of *divide et impera* in Rome, 'ally with the far away to fight the near by' in China, and so on). The frequent consequence will be that frontier warlords seize power in the empire themselves.

Exchange, finally, proceeds by tribute, the provision of slaves, or the marrying of princesses of the empire. A particular form of tribute is obtained by taxing commercial diasporas resident in imperial cities.

Let us now investigate the experience of China along these lines.

THE INNER ASIAN AND SEA FRONTIERS OF CHINA

Foreign relations in Asia for over two millennia revolved around a struggle between the dominant sedentary empire, China, and the nomad peoples on its frontier. Although the 'Inner Asian frontier', as

Lattimore baptised it in the 1920s, is largely made up of a single primary milieu (some 10,000 kilometres of almost continuous grassy terrain from Manchuria to Hungary), not all lands on it were occupied by nomads: Xingjian, notably, was based on cellular oasis agriculture, itself exposed to Kazakh nomads (Lattimore 1962: 171; 212). The Silk Road trade route to the west, dating from Roman times, ran across this oasis system.

The Inner Asian frontier constituted what Lamb calls (1968: 130) 'the great road of nomad movement, used from the earliest times of which there exists any record and only closed in the modern age of political evolution based on the technology of the Industrial Revolution'. China and the pastoralists to its north provide the classical pattern of empire/nomad foreign relations. The empire incorporates nomads for its defence against others and establishes tributary exchange relations across the frontier; the auxiliaries, entrusted with the keys to the empire, seize power themselves on occasion. Yet when they establish themselves as imperial dynasties over China proper, they are invariably converted to its culture, enfolded into the structures and practices developed by the literati ruling class. Certainly the mobility and open-mindedness of the nomads would pervade the empire, as when the Mongol rulers of the Yuan dynasty set out on a course of overseas expansion, or when the Muslim admiral of the famous Treasure Fleet of the early Ming dynasty sailed as far as Africa (and according to a recent account – Menzies 2003 – even around the globe). Ultimately, however, the Chinese empire absorbed all frontier development back into the imperial structure again, in the way that the gravitational attraction of a large planet does not allow smaller objects to escape its orbit. In Western Christianity on the other hand, the frontier formations did escape this gravitational field, because there was very little in terms of material administrative–military power to tie them to the centre, as we shall see in the next chapter.

China's imperial development can be shown to have passed through three long eras characterised by initial peace and prosperity, each gradually succumbing to internal disturbances and crisis (J.S. Lee, as in Sorokin 1985: 562, Fig. 8). There is no transcendent historical 'mechanism' involved here, I simply use these cycles to organise the argument and to avoid drowning in a sea of facts and dates. The periods are the following:

- The period of early empire formation, culminating in the dynasties of the Qin (Ch'in) from 221 to 207 BC and the Han, from 206 BC to AD 220. The consolidation of the Silk Road to Central Asia and beyond against the steppe nomads, and the tribute system, date from this era.

- The second period, beginning with the (part-Turkic) Tang, 618–907, followed by the Song (Sung) dynasty and ending with the demise of the (Mongol) Yuan from 1279 to 1368. This era consolidated the empire as a bureaucratic and class structure; in foreign relations, imperial fortunes fluctuated, notably when the Song (the 'northern Song' period runs from 960 to 1127), were pushed to the south ('southern Song', 1127–1234) at the hands of advancing nomad power. The Tang, and even more so the Yuan, on the other hand infused the Chinese empire with nomad dynamism, both on land and at sea, without ultimately freeing themselves from the gravitational pull of the centre.
- The third period saw the empire closing in on itself after a last spectacular series of seaborne exploits. It comprises the Ming dynasty (1368–1644) and the Manchu Qing (Ch'ing), which lasted until the proclamation of the republic in 1912.

Let us look at these epochs in turn, analysing each in terms of the occupation of space, protection, and exchange.

Early Civilisation and the Beginnings of Nomadism

The development of a Chinese ethnos begins with tribes such as the Zhun, Di, and Hu, who subordinated and partly exterminated neighbouring tribes. Some tribes, such as the Turkic-speaking Xiongnu (Hsiung-Nu) and the ancestors of the Tibetans, evaded subjection by retreating to the steppe and taking to herding. As they 'replaced the large predators that usually, in natural conditions, controlled the growth of the herbivorous animals' (Gumilev 1987: 20), these pastoralists and hunters developed into the mobile, nomadic counterpoint of the growth of a sedentary Chinese empire.

Occupation of Space. Conquest stands at the outset of Chinese development, as it did in the Fertile Crescent. The Shang kings of the second millennium BC fell victim to the Zhou (Chou), a related people who overran the Shang from the north. The Zhou rose to power in the struggle with nomads along the Inner Asian frontier, whilst consolidating an agricultural base along a north–south axis. Millet and wheat were grown in the barren north, rice in the fertile and hospitable south, along the Yangtze river. The language and writing were products of the north, close to the frontier; Chinese character script developed already in the first millennium BC, perhaps even earlier (Ostler 2006: 134–5). The southward spread of Chinese settlers and their language was made possible by cast-iron tools and weapons, which they obtained from around 500 BC. Thus the resource base was created that in turn supported holding the frontier in the north. There are also traces of very early contact with Indo-European westerners – the very idea of sovereign authority seems to have reached China in this encounter. Barber (1999: 201) interprets the fact that the ancient Chinese term for court magician and chief medical officer, '*m^yag*', comes from the Iranian *magus* (related to 'might', as power, in English) as an indication of this.

When the Zhou were defeated by nomads in 771 BC, political disunity ensued, in what is known as the 'Warring States' era (403–221 BC). But China as a civilisation had established itself sufficiently to exert a cultural influence and 'sinicise' the non-Chinese border peoples drawn into these struggles (Zhang 2001: 46, n. 15; Diamond 1998: 330–2). Confucius and other wandering sages developed their doctrines in this era, Jaspers' 'Axis Age'. Their teachings articulated the new level of socialisation, but the ethics of empire they elaborated still lacked a formation to which it could be applied. As Collins concludes (1998: 138), 'the structure of clan society was subjected to new geopolitical relations, a cosmopolitan arena that simultaneously replaced old symbolic frameworks while offering opportunities to mobilize movements beyond and across local regimes'.

The empire that finally took shape with the Qin and the Han dynasties in the third century BC was therefore based on 'institutions long known in theory [which] had at last been applied to practical working efficiency on the scale required' (Lattimore 1951: 321). It was in a final struggle between the two rivals in north and south, Qin and Chu, respectively, that the empire was unified. Qin was itself a frontier formation, to the north-west of the actual Chinese heartland. It originated in the 'western marches', in which feudal nobles had been left behind to cover the rear of the retreating Zhou state. To the civilised Chinese at the centre, Qin was considered as semi-barbarian. Yet when the Qin emperor, Shih Huang Di, famously ordered the burning of all books except those on medicine, religion, and agriculture, this fostered the unification of Chinese culture, now that all prior diversity was destroyed as far as written records were concerned. In his claim that the world was united under his sovereignty, the emperor gave expression to the imperial universalism on which China's foreign relations were henceforth premised (Giles 1915: 118–19).

Protection. The early Chinese kingdoms were characterised by perennial warfare which gradually grew in scale. In the centuries following the Zhou collapse, the war chariot was replaced by horse cavalry, which the Chinese adopted from their nomad enemies in the north. The Zhou had been neither nomads nor horse-riding warriors; they still fought from two-wheel, horsedrawn chariots (Lattimore 1951: 307–8 & 337). Judging from the the Chinese words for chariot, wheel, spoke, axle, etc., these must have been obtained from Indo-European speakers (Barber 1999: 123, 127). Horses were not indigenous, and since China is ill-endowed with grassland, getting hold of them was a major problem. Hence there was always a premium on recruiting nomad troops. The Qin cavalry that helped Shih Huang Di to power in 221 BC, already included tribal groups enlisted as auxiliaries (Lattimore 1962: 105–10). Crucially, however, there was also conscription of Chinese soldiers directly by the state; an intermediate warrior aristocracy on the frontier recruiting their own troops, as in mediaeval Western Christianity, did not take root. Warlordism would be a recurrent phenomenon over the millennia, but there would be no frontier feudalism able to break away from the empire. The centre could maintain discipline without assistance and it had powerful means to do so. Chinese archers, already equipped with the superior Turkish bow of laminated wood, in the Han era developed the trigger-operated crossbow, which gave rise to the saying that one Chinese crossbow man was a match for ten nomads (F. Wood 2002: 48–50; Hucker 1973: 568). As in other empires, arms trade with the nomads was forbidden, in order to retain the advantage.

Still in the Qin period, the Xiongnu (Chinese for 'fierce slaves', sometimes seen as ancestors of the Huns, sometimes conflated with them) posed the gravest threat to the Chinese. They conducted deep raids into China between 200 and 166 BC; at one point their army is said to have numbered 140,000 horsemen, although Mann (1986: 233) reminds us that nomad mobility was often mistaken for numbers. The pivot of empire/nomad struggles was always the vast pocket of steppe enclosed by the northernmost loop of the Huang Ho river, the Ordos. The nomads who controlled the Ordos posed a permanent threat to the empire; the Han conquered it, settling it with several hundreds of thousands of Chinese, but this would not endure. Even the Great Wall of the Ming, which connected earlier sections into the continuous structure that still stands today, did not in the end enclose the Ordos (cf. maps in Lattimore 1962: 100 and Chaliand 2006: 52).

The wall against the Xiongnu erected by Shih Huang Di was still defensive. Wu Di ('martial emperor' of the Han), who took power in 157 BC, shifted gear to a forward policy, driving the Xiongnu back into the desert. The Xiongnu had pushed the Kushan (Yuezhi in Chinese) as far as the river Oxus (Amu Darya); there they would later establish their Kushan empire, after having declined Wu Di's offer of an alliance against the Xiongnu. The Chinese policy of 'ally with the far away to fight the near by' in the end depended on the willingness of nomad peoples to reciprocate. This was an uncertain factor given that they could always move further along the frontier as the Kushan had done, away from the fault line with China, to India and Persia (Weggel 1980: 197–8; Barber 1999: 122–3).

In the two centuries straddling the beginning of the Christian calendar, the Han emperors also conquered Korea, Guangdong, and Indochina, whilst subduing the nomadic tribes in Tibet. However, this sapped their ability to withstand the nomads in the north. In the third century AD the empire found itself in a deep crisis: between 221 and 280 population declined from 50 to 7.5 million taxpayers (Gumilev 1987: 28–9). Its demise was given the final push by the great migrations, the world-historic sweep of Asia's nomads in the fourth and fifth centuries, which also contributed to the fall of the Gupta empire in India and the Roman empire.

Exchange. The steppe was suitable for herding but not, at the prevailing level of development, for agriculture. The nomads had an abundance of meat, hides, and pelt; what they needed were grain and textiles. They had overcoats but no underwear, proteins but no carbohydrates. The Chinese population would gladly trade, but the Qin and Han emperors took trade in hand themselves in order to finance protection. This was often the cause for nomad raids (Gumilev 1987: 27). The stakes were raised when the Han mission to the Kushan-Yuezhi brought back information about the great cities of Ferghana, Samarkand, and Bukhara, revealing that there were distant societies that were civilised too. This upset the idea that China was surrounded by barbarian nomads and that beyond them there was only wasteland. Following Wu Di's campaign against the Xiongnu, the Silk Road was created, along which horses from Ferghana now could be imported; Chinese luxuries ended up as far as Rome, although control over the Silk Road was never entirely secure (Stein 1984: 19, 24–5). The Indo-European rulers of the oases of the Tarim basin were uneasily incorporated and yielded to Chinese sovereignty mainly because of the nomad threat. Sogdian, an Indo-European language related to Persian, was the lingua franca of the Silk Road (Ostler 2006: 108, 140, cf. 168–9).

The tribute system emerged under the Han. It served at first to win allies against the Xiongnu, to whom the first Han emperor actually had to pay tribute himself (Zhang, 2001: 52–4). But then, the tribute system was a complex give-and-take anyway. It implied that the tributary, when in China, should receive gifts from the emperor of greater value than his tribute. As Lamb puts it (1968: 27), 'while in theory paying to the Chinese, in fact the tributary would be in receipt of some kind of Chinese subsidy'.

Thus, in periods of Chinese economic and political decline, the tributary system could prove very expensive, and any attempt on the part of the Chinese to reduce their tributary commitments, could only lead to the ... paradoxical demands of the tributaries to increase the frequency of their missions.

Once the Han empire disintegrated in the third century AD, several kingdoms, parallel dynasties, and the '16 barbarian states' (nomad principalities in the north of China) existed side by side. The barbarians, having acquired a sense of empire through frontier interaction with the Chinese, now began to govern themselves as states, but although superior in warfare, they were few and far between and failed to consolidate their rule. Only one of them, the Northern Wei dynasty (fourth to sixth centuries), held out, by combining a Chinese-style civil administration with nomad military organisation (Meskill 1973: 63–4; cf. Lattimore 1935: 56). It was created by the Tabgach (Toba), a confederation of Turkic speakers and Tibetans who defeated the Huns when the latter revolted against the Chinese in the early fourth century (the Huns would then migrate westwards and a century later, under Attila, penetrate deeply into the Roman empire). Typically, the Wei state was Chinese in the eyes of the steppe nomads, but barbarian to the Chinese. 'In essence, though, it started a particular series of frontier formations not to be related to any one culture, through they all consisted of a combination of Chinese and nomadic elements' (Gumilev 1987: 32–3). The Chinese gradually prevailed in the Wei state; in 500, Turkic language, costume, and customs were officially outlawed (Ostler 2006: 140). The ruling dynasty was deposed a generation later, amidst growing internecine struggles. The Chinese suffered defeat against the Arabs in 751 (in Kirghizia), but when the Tibetans became too powerful, the caliph of Baghdad, Harun al Rashid, reopened negotiations with China in a reversal of alliances (Chaliand 2006: 76). Throughout this period, however, and irrespective of its political fortunes, the hegemony of Chinese civilisation remained intact.

Expansionist Departures Under the Tang and the Mongols

The second long era begins in 618 with the imperial dynasty of the Tang. It restored unity to China and ushered in a period of prosperity of almost three centuries. Under the Tang and from 1279, the Mongol Yuan, the exploratory spirit traceable to nomadism animated the Chinese imperial outlook, without however transcending the limits of its auto-centric culture in the end. Having to rule the vast empire with its encrusted administrative culture seriously constrained expansionist designs, whilst the established literati class handling day-to-day government was difficult to get round for a non-Chinese dynasty such as the Tang or the Yuan (and later the Manchus).

The Tang rulers were descended from the Toba confederacy that had brought forth the Northern Wei earlier, and were part Turkic. In typical frontier fashion, they gave Chinese civilisation a mighty push by opening up the Chinese mind to the outside world. Their conquests produced a curiosity about foreign peoples and their customs, which stood in marked contrast to imperial complacency and mental closure (Levathes, 1994: 34). Confucians frowned on the religious promiscuity displayed by the Tang and disapproved of the interest shown by the court in things foreign; the introduction of Turkish dress and weapons into the imperial army caused outright offence. Tang rule accelerated the longer-term trend of Chinese migration to the south, notably to the wealthier Yangtze valley, and around 740, some 40 per cent of the Chinese lived south of the Huai river (in between the Huang Ho and the Yangtze), against only 20 per cent in the early years of the millennium (Gumilev 1987: 33–4, 62).

However, everything frontier-based dynasties undertook to consolidate their rule tended to reinforce the Chinese empire as the central node of the larger formation. In their attempt to provide the imperial bureaucracy with qualified candidates, the Tang introduced the examination system; but this only reinforced the position of the Chinese scholar-gentry, the guardians of literacy and ideological orthodoxy, who proved an insurmountable obstacle for every non-Chinese ruling class. Even in the century of insecurity between 860 and 960, when Buddhism, Islam, and certain strands of Christianity such as Nestorianism made inroads via the frontier,

Confucianism, the ethical system of the empire, remained unaffected. Its prestige was such that it could show tolerance to these religions as long as they refrained from proselytising. In the twelfth century, (neo-)Confucianism was codified into a unified doctrine, further reinforcing its unassailable hold as an imperial ideology (Giles 1915: 211–4l; Gumilev 1987: 43–4). What could frontier nomads, often illiterate, possibly hope to achieve as rulers over the Chinese?

The Khitan, the dominant group in the Liao dynasty of the Manchu confederation, succeeded in pushing the Song to the south in the early twelfth century. But then they had to find a way to govern the newly conquered Chinese. An additional problem here was the lack of any linguistic affinity. Chinese is a monosyllabic tone language with the verb coming second in a sentence, whereas Turkic, Mongol, and Tungus (Manchu) are polysyllabic languages with the verb at the end (Ostler 2006: 138). So even though the Khitan were also agriculturalists, it was not so easy for them to merge into a neighbouring sedentary society as it had been for the (Germanic) Vikings in frontier sectors of Western Christianity – just as different world-views were more pronounced in China than in Europe. The Khitan invented a script based on Chinese, but in the effort of adjusting to the requirements of rule in a wealthier society, they lost their frontier spirit and were defeated by the Manchu Jürchen, who had retained their nomad ferocity (Meskill 1973: 143; Lattimore 1935: 56).

The Mongols, who in the late thirteenth century took control of China as the Yuan dynasty, likewise made a serious attempt to develop a state apparatus of their own and avoid being absorbed into the existing Chinese imperial state. However, they were less civilised than the Turkic-speaking branches of the Asian steppe nomads and lacked a unified language and a script. Therefore the Mongol Yuan dynasty, in order to circumvent the Chinese scholar-gentry, recruited Uighurs from the oases of Chinese Turkestan to develop Mongol as a written language and create an alternative civil service. As to religion, Genghis had still been tolerant, partly in an attempt to neutralise the holy-war fervour of his Muslim enemies; his sons and successors typically adhered alternatively to Islam, Nestorian Christianity, or other creeds – all alien to the Mongols' own shamanism and reverence for the sky, Tengri. As rulers of China, the Yuan adopted the Lama-Buddhism of the Tibetans. 'They wanted to make the Mongols a permanent ruling class', Lattimore writes (1951: 81–2), 'with a code of its own sanctioned by an organized religion.' Khubilai Khan, the Yuan emperor, later asked the father and uncle of Marco Polo, Venetian traders visiting his court, to bring to China a nucleus of Catholic priests to create a national culture and state structure separate from the Chinese, but these never arrived – and neither did Marco Polo himself, according to Frances Wood (1995; cf. Chaliand 2006: 35–6, 141). This brings us to their foreign relations.

Occupation of Space. One factor in the mobile occupation of space by the nomads, besides transhumance and finding new grazing grounds, is the response to climate fluctuations. Periodic droughts often played a role in propelling nomads into adjacent sedentary societies. Ellsworth Huntington thus distinguishes a 'rhythmic alternation, possibly of world-wide incidence, between periods of relative desiccation and humidity, which causes alternate intrusions of Peasants and Nomads into one another's spheres' (as in Toynbee 1935, iii: 17; cf. 438–9; cf. F. Wood 2002: 181–4). The Arab conquests in the seventh century and the Mongol ones of the thirteenth would have been thus determined; Perry Anderson (1996: 126) refers to the same dry cycle in his discussion of European agriculture.

Gumilev too develops a climatic theory, based on the amount of rain on the steppe (1987: 21–2, 24). This is determined by the intensity of sunlight, which shifts the trans-tropic baric maximum over Sahara/Arabia northwards or southwards (the other maximum in the northern hemisphere, that over the North Pole, is stable because sunlight has little or no influence on it). Increased solar activity moves the trans-tropic maximum northwards, pushing up the region of low pressure that acts as a gully through which moist Atlantic air flows into Eurasia as cyclones causing precipitation. In Gumilev's account, the fourth and third centuries BC were periods of increased precipitation on the steppe, because of southern cyclonic tracks; yet the Caspian, fed by the Volga with its basin in the central zone of European Russia, was 8 metres below its present level. In the first to third centuries AD, on the other hand, the steppe dried out, but the level of the Caspian rose 4 metres again, and so on and so forth. Since Gumilev stresses that these changes took much longer than contemporaries would have been able to observe for themselves, the question arises how nomad action could have been a response to them.

This takes us back to the argument in Chapter 1. Human communities *exploit* the relation with nature; as Lattimore argues (1951: xlii–xlviii), nature is not 'an impersonal machine' that 'does' things with humans. 'Drought … affecting the pasturage', he notes elsewhere (1935: 54), 'may be a stimulus toward migration and conquest; but it is not in itself a *creative* power.' So whilst there is a climatic relation between large-scale movements of nomad peoples relative to empires along the steppe gradient stretching from Hungary to Manchuria or the Afro-Arab desert fringes, these movements are always part of social pressures by empires to obtain tribute, and the pressures exerted by nomads for trade. The former are centripetal (drawing nomads into the orbit of empire), the latter centrifugal (releasing them from its grip and allowing more equitable exchanges to take place).

It was the interaction of the conditions that favoured the barbarians – both those of forested Europe and those of the Eurasian steppe – with the conditions that favoured the great civilized empires; it was this interaction and not fluctuations of climate that for a whole age of history set the rhythm of the pulse of Asia and Europe. (Lattimore 1951: xlviii; on the climate theory cf. his 1962: 241–58.)

There is no doubt, however, that the mobile concept of space of the nomads, their exploratory spirit, generated a more daring, outward-looking mindset on the part of the empire whenever their power over it increased.

Protection. The Tang protected the empire's land frontier with Turkish and half-Turkish cavalry, their warhorses immortalised by the characteristic sculptures in which the horses have oversized bodies relative to their heads, symbolising strength. Through a system of alliances they held sway over the Mongols, Chinese Turkestan, Manchuria, and Tibet; although the rise of Tibetan power in the second half of the eighth century forced them to accept support from the Arabs (Chaliand 2006: 76). The Tang also perfected the canal system, work on which had begun under their predecessors. Thus surplus grain from the Yangtze valley could be shipped north to supply the imperial garrisons. The Tang dynasty, Lattimore observes (1951: 414), was 'in many ways … the most Chinese dynasty China ever had, but it was founded and maintained by using the wealth of China to subsidise "barbarian" troops'.

The Song emperors, who prevailed amidst the disunity following the Tang, faced the nomads again from a weaker position. Compared to their predecessors, who had been well-versed in dealing with barbarians, Song diplomats and military commanders, who knew only Confucius and Mencius, found themselves at a loss in confrontations with Tibetans, Mongol-speaking Khitan and Tungus-speaking Jürchen on the Inner Asian frontier, who by now had also obtained gunpowder – a Chinese invention already several centuries old. In spite of superior numbers China suffered serious reversals (Gumilev, 1987: 25). The empire had to conclude treaties with the Liao ruler of the Khitan in the eleventh century, promising to pay annual tribute; the southern Song did the same, under pressure from the Jürchen and Tatar nomads of the Jin dynasty. The Jin state was established in the twelfth century and China initially joined forces with it to defeat the Khitan (Meskill 1973: 128–9; Zhang 2001: 54). The Khitan then regrouped further west and formed the Karakhitai empire, stretching from northern China to the Aral sea (bastardised into 'Cathay' and into the Russian word for China, Kitai). They fought the Chinese but also inflicted defeats on the Seljuk Turks. Since there were Nestorian Christians among them, this gave rise to the Prester John myth of a Central Asian Christian empire ready to rush to the aid of the Crusaders, to which we return in the next chapter.

The hard-pressed southern Song empire meanwhile sought to compensate for its retreat and loss of territory by developing naval power. In 1132 the first permanent Chinese navy was established, since Guangzhou (Canton), the new capital with its one million inhabitants, was vulnerable from the sea. The development of new ships, naval gunpowder weapons, and the compass accompanied these changes. The navy became a force in its own right; a fleet commanded by defected Song commanders and merchants in the early thirteenth century was made available to Genghis Khan when his Mongols moved on Beijing (Levathes, 1994: 43, 48).

The Mongols were not indigenous to the sector of the frontier that is now Mongolia. Gumilev claims (1987: 89–90) that their roots go back to the Cheshi principality in the Turfan oasis, in the Uighur region of Xingjian. When defeated by the Chinese in AD 67, the survivors were resettled on the eastern frontier beyond Lake Baikal. The clan society from which Genghis rose only formed by the end of the tenth century under the semi-legendary tribal leader, Bodonchar. Genghis emerged when the clan structure began dissolving again and more and more men drifted off, often organising their own retinue, as had been done by Timur, or the Germanic warriors on the Roman *limes*. Genghis too was of illustrious ancestry but had lost his tribal status. The contemporary traveller William of Rubruck was perhaps not far off the mark when he

claimed that Genghis began as a cattle thief before he rose as a challenger to the Mongol ruler, Unc Khan, based in Karakorum
(Komroff 1929: 113). A 'khan' among the Mongols and other
nomad tribes was a war leader, not really elected but elevated by
acclaim by the other warriors. When peace returned, the khan was
just a herdsman like everybody else.

Now as Lattimore observes (1935: 55), 'Deeply engrained in the
Mongol consciousness is the feeling that any Mongol horde which
can master other Mongols, can master anyone else in the world.'
This was certainly the case with Genghis (Müller and Wenzel 2005).
The future conqueror began by sidelining the tribal chiefs and organising the Mongols in a decimal order (groups of 10, 100, 1000, and so
on), thus centralising command. With this unified army he took
Beijing in 1215, after having swept away the Jin Tatars. At the time,
the Mongols were content with plundering the city; they preferred
concentrating on the Shah of Khorezm, the ruler of Iran, and central
Asia. With some 100,000 men, Genghis in a few years destroyed the
Shah's larger armies, taking Samarkand and Bukhara. Genghis' troops
meanwhile were not a 'national Mongol' army by any means – we
are looking at tribal society, and the Mongol columns included
Tatars and many others. They defeated the Kipchaks (Polovtsis,
mentioned already as founders of Georgia) and the Russians in the
north, and finally, the Tanguts of the Xi-Xia (Hsi-Hsia) state in
China's north-west (Chaliand 2006: 127–8). Both the Chinese and
their nomad opponents by now had cannon to replace catapults, a
key innovation that changed the nature of warfare a century before
this happened in Europe.

Genghis died in 1227. The centrifugal forces characteristic of
nomad tribal society proved stronger than Genghis' arrangements
for his succession. True, under the nominal sovereignty of his son
Ogedei Khan, infrastructure such as the mail service remained
intact, but the territories were divided amongst Ogedei and his
brothers, each commanding their own troops. The Mongol khans
continued their campaigns, defeating (with the assistance of the
Song dynasty) the Jin state in the 1230s, conquering Korea, and
then turning west again for renewed attacks that left Kipchaks,
Russians, and an army of crusading knights beaten, and Hungary
occupied. Another turbulent succession upon the death of Ogedei
left the Mongol realm further divided.

In 1253 the Mongols held their great council. Mönkhe Khan, who
had succeeded his brother Ogedei, cleverly hoped to prevent the

eternal divisions of the nomads from breaking up their realm by dispatching his nephew (Genghis' grandson) Khubilai, widely known to have Christian sympathies, to complete the conquest of China. Hulegu, one of Genghis' sons and a worshipper of Maitreya (a mystical trend in Buddhism), would launch a 'yellow crusade' to capture Jerusalem (Gumilev 1987: 194–5). Thus the chances of fraternisation and absorption were kept to a minimum. In 1258, Hulegu's troops captured Baghdad. A year later, the Mongols were in Gaza, mingling with Crusaders and causing great confusion among them: were these men the saviours of Christianity, Prester John's troops, or bloodthirsty savages? However, the death of Mönkhe forced Hulegu to return to Mongolia, and this created the opportunity for the Mamluks of Egypt to finish off both the remaining Mongol force in Palestine and the Crusaders, effectively ending the era of the Crusades altogether. As Ilkhan of Iran, Hulegu returned to fight the Golden Horde to his north throughout the thirteenth century. In the end both the Ilkhans of Iran (the successors to Hulegu) and the Golden Horde converted to Islam, without otherwise overcoming their rivalries.

Khubilai meanwhile conquered China, as Mönkhe had instructed him to do. In 1276, Guangzhou fell, and three years later he was enthroned as the ruler over China, founding the Yuan dynasty. In true nomad spirit, further conquests were seen as the next step, but they ran into unexpected difficulty. First there was the failed attempt to conquer Java, and then Japan came into sight, but that campaign too ended in disaster.

Japan in many ways was itself a frontier formation. Its archipelago was settled by successive waves of Asians reaching its shores from nearby Korea. Via the Korean peninsula the Japanese also acquired the Chinese character script for what is otherwise an entirely different language. In the sixth century AD, sizeable populations of Koreans and Chinese from Manchuria lived among and effectively educated the earlier settlers. But then, as Storry writes (1967: 31), the Japanese have been characterised, whenever they were brought into contact with a civilisation other than their own, by 'a quite indefatigable curiosity, a passion to learn, and an aptitude for choosing, borrowing, adapting, and "japanizing" foreign ideas and techniques'. This is almost a cliché now, but it was not their only frontier trait. Under the Tang, Japanese embassies visited their capital, Ch'ang-an, to learn more and pay tribute. The archipelago's warrior clans sought to emulate the Chinese imperial order in the minutest detail; but island location also permitted, as in the case of England, the growth of imperial ambitions. Japan had all the qualities of a (maritime) frontier power – mobility and adaptability, as well as a commercial and a warrior ethos combining these qualities in the respective areas. When the Mongols landed, first in 1274 and (after Khubilai Khan had ascended to the Chinese throne) again in 1281, the Japanese were saved in both cases by typhoons (*kamikaze*) that struck the Mongol fleet. In between the two invasions, the defenders had also greatly improved their ability to conduct large-scale military operations and this led to the definitive abandoning of the operation after the second attempt (Müller and Wenzel 2005: 328–32).

In 1368, the Mongols were defeated by the Chinese in a campaign in Yunnan that ushered in the Ming dynasty. As Lamb concludes (1968: 35), conquest in the way practised by the Yuan dynasty was 'quite uncharacteristic of the general pattern of Chinese policy', and it was this general pattern which henceforth would begin to reassert itself.

Exchange. Under the Tang, writes Zhang (2001: 52), the tribute system 'witnessed its most aggressive and rapid expansion and institutionalization'. One reason why trade was always dressed up as tribute was because trade outside the control of the state was seen as a dissolvent of imperial control. This certainly applied to strategically important imports, such as the purchase of horses for the imperial cavalry (Braudel 1981: 346). When powerful merchants controlling the coastal grain trade began privately to accept tribute from foreign merchants at the turn of the fourteenth century, the empire struck back with force and reasserted its authority. Confucian disdain for trade resurfaced and the grain trade was placed under strict control, the *guang du shang dan* policy ('government supervision and merchant operation', Levathes 1994: 55).

The communities in the coastal provinces of Guangdong, Fujian, and Zhejiang had a shipbuilding and seafaring tradition that goes back to the Yi peoples, incorporated into the Han empire around 100 BC. But it was only under the Tang that seaborne trade developed a real momentum. Silk had been traded across overland routes; porcelain provided the impetus for Indian Ocean trade in the seventh century. Both the Silk Route (actually, several parallel routes) and the porcelain seaborne trade were controlled by Persian merchants (Levathes 1994: 35–6). After the loss of the north, the southern Song in the twelfth century found itself closer to the sea frontier and the maritime commercial traditions of the region; I have mentioned their naval exploits already. The dominant outlook as a whole veered towards greater openness. Hindu and Arab manuals on navigation were studied as the disdain for foreign insights waned, although the Song were Chinese purists in many respects – this was the age of the neo-Confucian synthesis.

As we have seen, a key aspect of the imperial way of organising exchange, and dealing with foreign communities generally, is incorporation coupled to taxation. Landlocked Ch'ang-an, the Tang capital, with its one million inhabitants, had markets for indigenous produce and a 'western' market for exotic goods. There were 4,000 resident Arabs. Guangzhou, too, was host to large foreign colonies – Persians, Indians, Arabs, and Malays, active as traders, artisans, and metal workers. A Bureau of Merchant Shipping established in the eighth century in the same city set import duties at around 25 per cent to make the foreign traders tributary to the empire. As foreigners, the diaspora traders were exposed to resentment from the Chinese, and massacres occurred with some regularity as Tang authority diminished. The last of these massacres, which involved the death or more than 100,000 foreigners, contributed to the dynasty's downfall (Levathes 1994: 38–9; Attali, 2003: 173).

Exchange flourished under the Yuan as well, as the land frontier was now under complete control. The vastness of the empire, all under a single, outward-looking authority, facilitated trade. This was the *Pax Mongolica* that allowed the safe passage of travellers such as Friar John and William of Rubruck to China. Chinese banknotes played an important role in the trade with Islam and along the Silk Road (Braudel 1981: 452). The Mongol rulers vigorously pursued the Song strategy of seaborne expansion and geared up to a massive shipbuilding programme. The Yuan ships were bigger than those of the Song or any European ship, and allowed the Chinese to wrest the spice trade from the Arabs. After 1350, when the Mongol empire disintegrated into a number of separate khanates, the overland routes became more dangerous and seaborne trade even more important (Curtin 1984: 120–1).

The Closure of the Sea Frontier

The Ming ('enlightenment') dynasty (1368–1644) is usually seen as the high point of classical Chinese civilisation. China's population doubled in this era, its trade in silk and porcelain soared, and by terminating the use of paper money and reverting to silver bullion it raised the stakes of long-distance trade – inadvertently providing a lever by which the Spanish, using silver obtained in the Americas, were able to break into Asian trade (Frank 1998: 109–12). It was under the Ming, and in spite of a final, spectacular upsurge of seaborne trade, that the Chinese empire definitively turned away from the sea frontier to devote all its attention to the steppe again. Let me briefly go over the different aspects of its foreign relations with this in mind.

Occupation of Space. The move back to imperial closure begins in 1402, when Zhu Di, the fourth son of the founding Ming emperor Zhu Yuanzhang, ascended to the throne. Zhu Di moved the seat of government to Beijing (renaming it thus, 'northern capital' instead of 'Beiping', northern peace) one year later. More than 100,000 households were moved to Beijing, and the infrastructure of its food supply, such as the Grand Canal, was repaired and upgraded. Between 1417 and 1420, one out of every 15 Chinese was engaged in the construction of the Forbidden City, the imperial centre (Levathes, 1994: 46). Thus the empire signalled its intention to turn inwards, concentrating on the core area.

This was not just an imperial whim. It reflected the weakening of the productive base, which diminishes the means to engage in foreign relations along a broader front. 'Already beginning in the 11th century, but particularly after the 17th century', Duchesne writes (2001/2: 451; cf. Shiba, 1994), 'the per capita acreage of farmland in China had begun to oscillate around a descending trend line'. Through struggles between different court factions and social classes, these realities were transmitted to the level of the imperial state. The nomad impulse might have fostered China's orientation towards the outside, but the empire obviously could not neglect its agricultural foundations. 'The political economic conflicts between the southern maritime and northern continental orientations and interests', Frank sums up (1998: 108), 'were increasingly resolved in favour of the latter.'

The Manchu rulers who took over the empire in 1644 no longer represented nomadism in terms of a particular conception of space. Two sedentary empires, the Muscovite and the Manchu (both of nomad ancestry certainly) were now closing in on each other across the steppes of Asia, strangling the Eurasian nomads. Western commercial expansion was a major factor here. 'In this ecumenical society, with its dynamic economy, there is no place for the arrested civilization and the static economy of the nomadic horde revolving perpetually round its closed annual cycle' (Toynbee 1935, iii: 20–1).

The Treaty of Nertchinsk of 1689 that divided the Inner Asian frontier between the two empires, Braudel comments (1981: 98), showed the nomads in their true state, as an impoverished section of humanity having reached the end of the road. The nomadic impulse would continue to operate in foreign relations, but from a different angle – that of the West.

Protection. Zhu Yuanzhang, the founding Ming emperor, in the *Zu Xun Lu* ('Ancestral Injunctions') expressed his concern that by continuing foreign trade and foreign military campaigns, 'future generations might abuse China's wealth and power and covet the military glories of the moment to send armies into the field without reason and cause loss of life' (as in Levathes 1994: 123). This was a sharp break with the expansionism of Khubilai Khan, and it was reflected in the organisation of protection. 'What was striking about the Ming army, was the extent to which it was conceived as a stationary force, and thus primarily defensive' (Meskill 1973: 160). As always, nomad auxiliaries served on the frontier as well. Zhu Di made arrangements with the Uriyangqad Mongols around Beijing, withdrawing Chinese garrisons north of the Great Wall as a sign of goodwill and effectively leaving Inner Mongolia to the Uriyangqad. Sinicised under the Yuan, they fought under Ming commanders against the northern Mongols, who were envious of the trade opportunities enjoyed by the Uriyangqad (Lattimore 1951: 85). The empire also stabilised relations with the Jürchen of Manchuria by bestowing military titles on their chieftains (thus nominally placing them under Chinese sovereignty), if only to keep them in reserve against the 'wild Jürchen' of north Manchuria.

Zhu Di's characteristic designation of himself as 'lord of the realms of the face of the earth' greatly annoyed his contemporary, Timur Lenk, the Turkic conqueror. However, as we saw, Timur perished on his campaign against the empire. His successors preferred an accommodation with Zhu Di and resumed tribute payments, i.e. trade (Levathes 1994: 124–8). From around 1420, however, the tribute system was beginning to prove more difficult to operate. China suffered from famines and the empire was provoked into military campaigns against unwilling tributaries, whilst the Uriyangqad Mongols withdrew their support. This only further persuaded Zhu Di's son, Zhu Gaozhi, surrounded by Confucian scholar-gentry still sidelined under Zhu Di, to put all emphasis on withdrawing from the frontiers and entrench in a defensive position. It was he who famously decreed the termination of seaborne trade. Upon his death in 1425, his son persisted in this strategy, whilst Manchurian Jürchens joining with western Mongols (Oirats) resumed their incursions in the 1440s (Levathes 1994: 168; Weggel 1980: 196).

As the empire weakened, the Manchus in the north-east, who had been tributary to the Ming, joined in the incursions. They began their ascent by unifying northern forest dwellers and southern nomads and then subduing the (part-)Mongol tribes of Manchuria. The Manchu chief, Nurhachi, in the early seventeenth century was able to transform a confederation of nomads into a dynasty, very much as Genghis had done, by reorganising the tribes and replacing military chieftains by centrally appointed officials. Whilst the Mongols to the west and in Central Asia were kept at arm's length, the Manchus looked on China as the 'exploitable' sedentary base in which to anchor their power (Lattimore 1935: 75). Nurhachi was never able to defeat the Ming army decisively, but when invited to Beijing to assist in internecine fighting among the Chinese, he decided to stay. Thus the Qing dynasty was established.

To enable themselves to rule the empire, the Manchus also sought to unify state and 'church' (Lama-Buddhism). They meanwhile took care to maintain the frontier zone as a world separate from the empire, and keep it in a state of poise. This was to be their privileged staging area; others, including their Chinese subjects, were to be kept from using it in this way. Since they were culturally sinicised, however, the Manchus soon lost their peculiarity as foreigners in the eyes of the Chinese. As Lattimore emphasises (1935: 95), they were simply the ruling class and increasingly assimilated the outlook of imperial China, sharing in its decay after 1850.

Exchange. Emperor Zhu Di was surrounded at his court by eunuchs linked to commercial enterprise, and trade flourished. Porcelain production in Jiangxi province was stepped up to provide an export commodity much sought after abroad. Still in the late Ming period, along with raw silk, sugar, alum, and zinc, it was a major export, sold by south Chinese merchants for silver from Japan and the New World (Souza 1986: 5).

Certainly the official status of trade was still that of tribute. As Takeshi Hamashita has argued (as in Frank 1998: 113–14), the tribute/trade system evolved as a constellation with China at the centre and south-east Asia and its Chinese settlers on its periphery, in turn linked to networks that interlocked with European trade in due course. Later, even east African representatives, after some prodding, came to kowtow at the imperial court. Shogun Yoshimitsu of Japan had been among the first to pay a visit to Zhu Di, greeting him with a humble 'your subject, the King of Japan' – a reminder of Japan's frontier position and a gesture much resented by later shoguns. But the result was that Japan was given the right to limited trade (Levathes 1994: 123). Again, much of the apparent puzzle about why foreign rulers were so eager to pay their respects becomes clear once we see that, as a recognised tributary, a foreign state was awarded market rights to sell to the Chinese public. Certain favourite tributary states, such as Korea, actually had permanent market rights. As Frank writes (1998: 115),

[the] ranking of tributaries in concentric circles with China in the centre may seem excessively ideological to us, but it rather accurately expressed an underlying reality: the entire system of multilateral trade balances and imbalances, including the subsidiary role of India and Southeast Asia ... acted as the magnet that resulted in China being the ultimate 'sink' of the world's silver

– with bullion settlements a fact of trade whilst appearing as tribute.

To reassert central control over private foreign trade activity, Zhu Di in 1403 lifted the ban on trade and ordered the construction of an imperial fleet of warships, merchantmen, and support vessels. In four years, almost 2,000 ships were built on wharfs around Nanjing. In the period 1405 to 1433, in spite of successive decrees by later emperors terminating all sea voyages, the Great Treasure Fleet set sail to explore trade opportunities. It made seven epic journeys across the China seas and the Indian ocean, eventually reaching the east coast of Africa and, according to some sources, rounding it and even visiting the West Indies. Its legendary admiral, the eunuch Zheng He (Cheng Ho), had been captured and castrated as a Muslim boy and rose after having been adopted into the imperial household. On the first voyage of the 300-ship Treasure Fleet, Zheng He encountered wealthy Chinese merchants who had settled in Sumatra and Java in spite of Zhu Yuanzhang's ban on overseas trade (Levathes 1994: 20, 73–6, 99). Sri Lanka was a key objective on Zheng's second voyage, and China proclaimed its sovereignty over the island state, forcing the Sri Lankans to pay tribute until 1459 (Ostler 2006: 160). Menzies (2003) has made spectacular claims about the distances covered by the Treasure Fleet, and it would seem as if their cartographic legacy indeed facilitated the European 'discovery' of the Americas. For his argument that DNA traces suggest actual Chinese presence in Central America, there is at least one alternative explanation: the striking similarities between Chinese and Maya art forms and the layout of cities may also signify that 'the peoples of the Americas never quite lost the deep connection with their prehistoric origins in Asia' (M. Wood 2005: 146).

When emperor Zhu Gaozhi in 1424 ordered that 'all voyages of the treasure ships are to be stopped', envoys were recalled and the building of ships discontinued. Zheng He, the admiral, was made military commander of Nanjing. Yet the commercial interest survived, and in 1431 the admiral was dispatched again with the Treasure Fleet to restore the Chinese sphere of influence, especially in Malacca (he died on the return trip). In 1436, a new emperor finally ordered shipbuilding in Nanjing to be halted completely. Private merchants, under the protection of the eunuchs, became interlopers at the expense of the official tribute missions, to which the government reacted by reducing boat size and overseas trade. Shipbuilding and navigation, however, had definitively entered a period of decline. 'By the sixteenth century', Levathes writes (1994: 177),

few shipwrights knew how to build the large treasure ships. The development of guns and cannon also slowed, allowing the European powers to surpass the Chinese in firepower. The Chinese began to lose their technological edge over the West, never to regain it.

In 1400, the Ming fleet had numbered 3,500 vessels; in 1440, the provincial fleet of Zhejiang was down from 700 ships to half that number. By 1500, it was a capital offence to build a ship with more than two masts. In 1525, an edict followed that ordered all ocean-going ships to be destroyed. In 1551, it was made a crime to go to sea in a multi-masted ship.

The inward turn of the empire meant for the Chinese that they gave up their seaborne expansion (which, as will be remembered, had not been made for territorial gain to begin with). Hence, in Hegel's phrase (1961: 66), 'there could only be a relation with further history to the degree that they themselves were being visited and investigated'. Within a century, that would indeed be the case. In Western Christianity, a radically different synthesis between sedentary agriculture and mobile nomadism, empire, and frontier, had evolved in the meantime; this in due course would result in the maritime supremacy China had decided to forgo.

4
The Conquest of the Oceans – Ethnogenesis of the West

The West emerged as a breakaway frontier formation taking the imperial claim to universal sovereignty in its stride. This synthesis goes back to the ways in which the mediaeval empire of Western Christianity incorporated Viking frontier warriors for its protection; their descendants, the Normans, conquered England and Sicily and spearheaded the first Crusade against the Seljuk Turks. As the frontier formations grew in power in the centuries that followed, a new mode of foreign relations, sovereign equality of states, then took shape in the wars of religion sparked by Protestant revolts against the Christian cosmopolis.

In this chapter, we look at the 'Western branch' of this revolution. The conquest of the Atlantic, reorienting the Crusades first to Africa and then towards circumnavigating the earth and gaining access to the wealth of Asia, was its high road. Via maritime supremacy and overseas settlement, an Anglophone heartland centring on the British Isles established itself in the eighteenth century. Sovereign equality among liberal states offered a particular hospitality to the emergent capitalist mode of production; as we shall see in the next chapter, it was to mean something quite different for those states which formed under circumstances in which maritime supremacy and control of world trade and industry had already been largely secured by the English-speaking West.

FRONTIER WARS OF WESTERN CHRISTIANITY

The synthesis that I see at the root of the West's dominating position in the modern world was argued in an idealist fashion by Hegel in the early nineteenth century. 'The Greeks and Romans were internally mature when they turned towards the outside', he says in his lectures on the philosophy of history (1961: 468).

The Germans on the other hand began by pouring out, inundating the world and subordinating the corrupt and decayed states of the civilised peoples. Only then did their development commence, ignited by a foreign culture, foreign religion, state formation and legislation. *They have formed themselves by the absorption and transcendence of the foreign into their own* (Emphasis added).

This synthesis began with the invasion of the Roman empire by its frontier peoples, mixing into the sedentary order an infusion of barbarian audacity. 'Fifty years after the death of Charlemagne, the Frankish empire lay as prostrate before the Norsemen as the Roman empire did when faced with the Franks 400 years earlier', Engels writes (*MEW*, xxi: 147). The only reason it did not succumb to the raiders on its frontiers was because the Germanic tribes invading the Roman empire had infused it with courage and fighting spirit. 'Only barbarians are capable of rejuvenating a world suffering from a declining civilisation' (ibid.: 151). This would be repeated by the Vikings.

The Viking Impulse

The migrations that toppled the Roman empire involved the resettlement of entire peoples set adrift by nomad movement on the Inner Asian frontier. The Viking expeditions were themselves instances of sea and river nomadism, on a far more modest scale of course. Yet in terms of a 'barbarian infusion' of a new vitality, they are comparable. Boyer's argument still resonates with Hegelian idealism when he writes (1992: 406) that the Vikings 'possessed a ferment of activity, of dynamism which found itself asleep in the south. They arrived in time to breathe into the (Indo-)European personality the vigour it lacked'.

The Viking raids and conquests, taking off halfway through the ninth century, were made possible by nautical prowess and daring. The oak-beamed longship, with its square sail and single bank of oars, the mere sight of which inspired dread in Carolingian towns and settlements, was capable of negotiating the high seas as well as sailing upstream along rivers. As Engels notes (*MEW*, xix: 455–6), it had been developed in the Baltic with its many shallows and islands; protected from the Atlantic storms and tides, 'the particular shipbuilding technique and shipping experience was created which made possible the later conquests of the high seas of the Saxons and the Norsemen'.

The expeditions developed along three axes. One, the exodus from the fjords of Norway into the Atlantic. This occurred when tribal chiefs (*jarlar*, 'earls') sought to evade monarchical encroachment and compensate for loss of income and status at home. Norwegian marauders raided Ireland and Scotland and settled in Iceland and Greenland – until the cooling climate made their life there impossible and they were driven out by the Inuit Eskimos again. They also reached the Atlantic shoreline of North America before turning to raiding elsewhere (Marcus 1998: 49).

Secondly, the Danes. Here we are looking at well-organised campaigns aimed at frontier sectors closer to home. In 850 they hibernated for the first time in the north-east of England; in the ensuing decades they succeeded in widening the area under their control, levying the *danegeld* tribute on the local population. They were defeated in 886 by Alfred 'the Great' of Wessex, who pushed them back to the original Danelaw in Northumbria. Henceforth their campaigns became more opportunistic, with Danish raiders often joining Norwegians scouring the European continent (Boyer 1992: 159; Stephenson 1962: 171–2, 201–2).

The third axis was that of the Swedish Varangians, whose role in the founding of Russia was discussed in the last chapter. They profited from the displacement of trade routes with Asia from the southern to the northern frontier of Western Christianity after the Arab conquest of most of the Mediterranean coastline in the eighth century. Trade via Byzantium now had to be diverted via Russia to the Baltic and on to the North Sea and the Atlantic – the thesis developed by Pirenne (1937: pt. 2, ch.1). The eclipse of the Frisians gave the Scandinavians their chance, and Gotland emerged as an entrepôt of trade between Flanders and the Russian plains.

Frontier synthesis occurred early on. In England, West Saxon influence brought Christianity and written law to the north, whilst the Vikings left their imprint on the language; when the Normans landed in 1066, the Saxon and Danish population strands had been integrating for some time (Stenton 1966: 45; Ostler 2006: 314). The history of Normandy itself goes back to 911, when one of the Norse marauders, Rollo, after a long sojourn in Ireland, turned on the Franks but ran into powerful resistance. Accepting Christian baptism in defeat, he was granted lands in the lower Seine valley in exchange for protecting it, and Danish and Norwegian settlement dates from that time. Around 940, Gibbon records (1989, vii: 174; 163), Danish was still spoken in Bayeux, but in Rouen the language had already been forgotten.

In typical nomad mode, Viking trading guilds could be transformed swiftly for war purposes; a pattern later adopted by the Hansa, by

Portuguese traders and by the Dutch and British East India companies with their armed merchantmen. Their legendary fighting skills and ferocity led the Vikings to hire themselves out as military auxiliaries early on: sometimes to hold off further incursions by other Vikings, but also to fight Arabs and Turks in the Mediterranean. Gibbon (1989, vii: 154) relates how Prince Vladimir of Russia advised Byzantium 'to disperse and employ, to recompense *and restrain* these impetuous children of the North' (emphasis added). To meet demand, the various lineages easily mingled. The Viking force guarding Constantinople was nominally Varangian, but in fact recruited from England and Denmark. As Toynbee sums up (1935, ii: 201),

Western Christendom successfully defended herself, by force of arms, against the first fury of the Scandinavian onslaught which had threatened to over-whelm her; she then passed over to the offensive by rapidly converting to her religion and culture the invaders who had made a forcible lodgement on her soil in the Danelaw and in Normandy; and she reaped the fruits of this moral victory when she sent forth the converted Normans, as her knights errant, to fight in her service not less valiantly, and at the same time far more effectively, than their pagan ancestors had fought against her.

In most empires, as we have seen, such recruitment placed into the hands of the nomadic frontier forces the power to try and take over the imperial centre themselves. What made the empire of Western Christianity unique was the absorption of the Scandinavian sea-nomads into the frontier zones of the weak and fragmented sedentary society on which they preyed. This imbued these outlying areas with a dynamic, exploratory spirit which contributed to ethno-transformative departures from the imperial centre. This can be made more concrete by showing how the empire of Western Christianity mutated through several constellations into one in which a crusading papacy dispatched its Norman warriors to fight for the faith on foreign shores.

Christian Universalism

The paramount political myth of Western Christianity was the resur-rection of the Roman empire (Rosenstock-Huessy 1993: 489). Three reincarnations of that glorious past may be distinguished: under Charlemagne, with its centre of gravity in the West; then the 'Holy Roman Empire of the German Nation' under the Ottonians (it would nominally remain in existence until 1806); and finally, the empire of the popes in Rome, who made their bid for worldly power in the eleventh century, with the Normans as their frontier warriors. It was this last constellation that put Crusaders and Atlantic seafarers on the path of conquering the world's oceans.

Frontier interaction with the Arabs along the Mediterranean coastline served as a conveyor belt along which Western Christianity was reconnected with its own Hellenistic past. It also defined the imperial claim. Empire is based on the assumption that sovereignty is exclusive and universal, and both the worldly and the sacred aspects are required for it to have any credence. Confronting a rival monotheism, Islam, provided the necessary religious aura from the Carolingians on (cf. Rich 1999).

The rise of Islam was borne on the wings of one of the classic nomad explosions in history. Arab merchants and Bedouin tribes had long been active on the frontiers of the Byzantine and Persian empires; they actually profited from a stalemate between the two when they themselves were set in motion by migratory pressures on the Arab peninsula. Under Caliph Omar, the Arab armies, inspired by their new creed, swept along the southern coast of the Mediterranean and across Spain in the eighth century. With the Mediterranean under Arab control, southern Europe locked into the frontier systems along which passed mathematics from India, Roman law from Byzantium, Greek philosophy, and Egyptian mapmaking; but also crops such as sugar cane from India, hard wheat from Ethiopia, rice from the Middle East, and citrus trees (Gibb 1962: 49–50; Ponting 1991: 111).

Arab–Islamic civilisation rose to great splendour; as true frontiersmen, the Arabs proved fast learners. Chaliand (2006: 92) notes that in the 670s, 40 years after they burst onto the world scene, these dromedary riders from the desert commanded a sea-going fleet that threatened Constantinople. Hegel (1961: 490) writes that the Abbasids achieved their magnificent culture in the process of expansion and compares them to the Germanic peoples in this respect. But he claims that Abbasid culture lacked the enduring quality of Christian civilisation because it did not merge with sedentary society; in his view, it was based on fleeting, abstract passion, on 'foundations of generality'. Ostler (2006: 111) traces this to the Arabs' nomad roots. 'There is one thing in the cultural background which does unite all the Semites ... However successful their cities, however developed their religions and philosophies, they never escaped the memory that they had all arisen from desert nomads.'

By stopping the Arab onslaught north of the Pyrenees in 732, Charles Martel obtained the aura of defender of the faith. His son's coup d'état against the Merovingian king won papal blessing, partly because by then the popes had been bailed out by Frankish arms several times. When Charlemagne was crowned Roman Emperor by Leo III in 800, the question of who held ultimate authority, the pope or the emperor, loomed large; it would continue to undermine the imperial pretensions of Western Christianity. It certainly compromised the empire's ability to protect the frontier, fostering centrifugal tendencies. 'Modern linear borders', Teschke reminds us (2003: 66), 'were preceded in Europe by zonal frontier regions contested by semi-independent lords'. To secure their allegiance, imperial lands were given out as fiefs (from the Latin *feudum*). Imperial villas, concentrating land ownership in large, self-supporting manors modelled on the Roman latifundias, were meant to economically sustain the armoured cavalry of the frontier lords (McNeill 1991: 393). This gave frontier sectors a territorial aspect absent from nomad formations in Asia, whilst enhancing their autonomy. Production and exchange were very much wrapped up in the arrangement, as vassalage merged with tribute and bonded labour into the feudal mode of production, whilst trade declined and, as we saw, Jewish 'living money' replaced coinage again.

After the partition of the Carolingian empire, the centre of imperial unification of Western Christianity passed to Germany. Early in the tenth century, the dukes of the newly formed duchy of Saxony, on the frontier with the Slavs, assumed the title of German king. Rival claimants from Bavaria, in the frontier sector facing the Avars, had to accept that Otto I of Saxony, crowned king by the pope, in 962 was promoted to Holy Roman emperor of the German nation. A strategic marriage with the queen–widow of Italian Lotharingia then brought this important region into the imperial domain. The eastern frontier against the Slavs and the Magyars was secured by military means; the Magyars were compelled to give up nomad existence, convert, and become vassals in the defence against the Bulgarians and Pechenegs (Chaliand 2006: 111; Zettel 1986).

Yet the empire remained weak and ephemeral. 'There were no taxation, no officials, no traffic, no money, to make it possible for [the emperor] to establish a central government', Rosenstock-Huessy writes (1993: 489–90). The Holy Roman empire would never have a true capital; the emperor and his court lived off the land and travelled from one residence to the next, as did many of his fief-holders. Given the general poverty and low productivity of agriculture, all on the manor feared the day the overlord and his retinue would arrive for their regular stay, expecting to be fed and entertained (Slicher van Bath 1980: 42–4).

Since imperial fortunes depended on holding the frontier, the empire had to mobilise all available sources of legitimacy, the most important of which was the Christian religion. Otto II suffered a revolt of the Slavs on the river Elbe and defeat in southern Italy at the hands of Islamic forces. The growing pressure compelled his successor, Otto III, to move closer to the Church. This then would evolve into the third and final imperial constellation – the usurpation of the imperial mantle of the Roman empire by Rome itself, what Rosenstock-Huessy (1961: 139) calls the 'Papal Revolution'.

Otto I had already begun to appoint bishops. Like the frontier lords, these were often his relatives. His grandson in 995 even appointed a German pope (his cousin, Gregory V). Complementing these changes at the top, however, there also developed a parallel popular movement, a movement that was democratic and as we would now say, 'European'. This was the drive, spreading from monasteries in Burgundy, to purify the Church and combat the excesses of wealth and power among its magnates (Bartlett 1993: 256–7). The monastic reformers campaigned for various improvements that were highly beneficial to people's daily lives, such as combating the internecine violence of the nobility by instituting 'God's peace' on particular days of the week. They were also behind the new holiday of 'All Souls', the day after All Saints. This highlighted that everyone, not just those beatified by the Church, was entitled to salvation. Thus the unification of the empire from above was enlarged by one that came from below, or, at least, from much closer to the basis of society. This set the empire on the path of internal peace, doctrinal purity, and recovery from the Dark Ages, all through the medium of a network of dedicated monks. 'For the first time in history,' Rosenstock-Huessy (1993: 506) writes of the Cluniac order that started the reform movement, 'space was conquered by the legal personality of a corporation, scattered though it was all over the empire'. This tied the loose social fabric of a vast territory into a common normative structure, solidifying it as a sedentary civilisation even whilst the issue of ultimate sovereignty remained disputed.

The empire of Western Christianity crystallised in its final form when the popes, beginning with Leo IX, placed themselves at the head of the monastic reform drive. The Church thus brought the popular movement back into the fold, wresting it from the German emperor who had tried to do the same. The formal question of supreme authority was settled in 1077 when Pope Gregory VII forced the emperor, Henry IV, to repent for the latter's attempt to have the pope deposed by a synod of German bishops (Barraclough 1968: 83). Two prior events already highlighted the usurpation of the empire into a Catholic enterprise: the formal break with the Orthodox Church of Byzantium in 1054, emphasising the resurgence of Rome as a spiritual and worldly power; and the conclusion of a feudal treaty with the Normans five years later, giving the popes a military arm of their own to protect the frontier, and themselves from the Germans (Gregory VII had to call on his Normans straight away when Emperor Henry, in defiance of a second papal bull, came down to Italy again, but now with an army). In true imperial fashion, the Church proclaimed universal sovereignty, dispatching its frontier warriors to enforce it where needed.

Frontier Campaigns of the Aristocratic Diaspora

If we compare Western Christianity to the empires discussed in the last chapter, three particularities require our attention. One, the fact that the empire was (formally) a theocracy. *All* secular rulers were henceforth relegated to a lower plane as defenders of the faith, and made fief-holders under the pope's heavenly mandate. The popes, Rosenstock-Huessy writes (1993: 517) 'ejected the emperors and kings and vice-emperor from the Church, and assigned them one state among many as their jurisdiction'. This also worked to disseminate a new concept of politics. In Strayer's words (1970: 22), 'By asserting its unique character, by separating itself so clearly from lay governments, the Church unwittingly sharpened concepts about secular authority.' Any worldly ruler (except the emperor) successfully challenging the pope's *religious* sovereignty (on which the imperial title had come to rest) would henceforth be in a position effectively to claim the mantle of sovereignty himself, even if feudal obligations remained operative for several centuries. Protestantism, however, a democratic force heralded by the monastic reform movement, would overcome this barrier. It provided both the doctrinal denial of papal–imperial sovereignty, and a framework of class consciousness for those directly engaged in processes of exchange no longer cast as imperial tribute.

The second specificity of the empire of Western Christianity was the role of the Normans and others in what Bartlett calls the 'aristocratic diaspora', in expanding the frontier. Teschke (2003: 94) speaks of the 'magnates of the old Frankish families who had survived in the ex-marcher lordships of the Carolingian periphery – Normandy, Catalonia, and Saxony', and who now became available as conquerors. The Normans' cavalry especially acquired a reputation as legendary as their forebears' naval raids. Lombard princes considered the Normans a 'savage, barbarous and horrible race of inhuman disposition' (Bartlett 1993: 83–7; cf. Douglas 2002), traits which the Normans themselves cultivated so as not to disappoint their paymasters.

The third driver in the turn to frontier expansion was out-migration by free settlers. This was not so much a matter of a shortage of land, but of social conditions on the manors, with their bonded labour and low productivity. Colonisation of the Flemish coast and the lands east of the Elbe offered opportunities for farmers to raise output and enjoy the freedom of the towns, giving them a measure of independence from their feudal lords. Broadly speaking, the free settlers and the Norman and other frontier knights tended to migrate together, reproducing feudalism in tandem if not necessarily in harmony. Engels in a letter to Marx (as in P. Anderson 1996: 151 note) points out that feudalism was 'founded in the kingdom of the West Franks, further developed in Normandy by the Norwegian conquerors, its formation continued by the French Norsemen in England and Southern Italy', only to reach its final form in 'the ephemeral kingdom of Jerusalem'. Settlers followed the same route, moving on from Flanders to the British Isles and, eventually, to Jerusalem as well (Bartlett 1993: 111, 116). Clearly this was a contradictory process and the shift in the balance of forces heralding the end of the Middle Ages may be illustrated by the defeat of the French knights at the hands of an army of Flemish commoners in 1302.

In the Crusades, the aforementioned particularities of Western Christianity would combine into a powerful outward thrust. The papal claim to supreme authority (the German emperor was not allowed to join the campaign) and the parallel design to overcome the split with Byzantium, the availability and ambitions of the Norman frontier warriors for more audacious campaigns, and town dwellers caught in a world that was changing, all blended into the process. A profound yearning for salvation animated them all, but, as pilgrims were to find out, access to the Christian holy places on the contested southern frontier, from Santiago de Compostela to Jerusalem, was being denied by Islamic occupiers. Of course, taking to the Cross appears to us as a quintessentially mediaeval response, but a new age was making its appearance at the same time. It combined the emerging subjectivity of the free citizen with the move, heralded by the streamlining of papal authority, towards a unified state no longer stitched together from a mosaic of personal dependencies.

The actual Crusades built on campaigns in southern Italy by Norman warriors in the service of the pope. They defeated the Varangians of Byzantium and other auxiliaries and then drove the Arabs from Sicily, opening the way for further offensives. These culminated in the triumphant capture of Jerusalem in 1099. The second Crusade of 1147 was already a frontier war of the expanded empire. As Bartlett writes (1993: 263), 'each province of Catholics was commanded to attack that part of the barbarian world nearest to them'. The German emperor-elect this time obtained a licence to join the campaign. His nephew, Frederick Barbarossa, who also participated (and who witnessed the disastrous retreat from Damascus), was eventually, at 70 years of age, to assume the command of the third Crusade in 1187 as emperor himself. Leading an army of an estimated 100,000 to 140,000 men along the difficult land route, harassed by Seljuk Turks and Byzantines alike, he perished whilst crossing a river in Syria.

The Crusades were crucial in shaping a personality type that would later make its appearance in the Indies and the Americas. This combined monastic piety and abstinence (Attali, 2003: 197, speaks of 'inverted nomadism') with violent ruthlessness and was embodied in the Crusading orders of the Templars, Hospitallers, Teutonic knights, and others. Again to quote Bartlett (1993: 90), the frontier campaigns in combination with outward settler migration 'produced an outlook of confident expectation. The Frankish warriors ... anticipated an expansionary future and developed what can only be called an expansionary mentality'.

The territorialisation of political space heralding a new mode of foreign relations was pioneered by Sicily in the early thirteenth century under Frederick II Hohenstaufen, the grandson of Barbarossa and the son of a Norman mother. Frederick adjusted the state form to the administrative possibilities and requirements of wealthy Sicily, with its advanced burgher society. This could only be done by granting the popes an interest in the process, because Rome's imperial pretensions were now at their peak. Frederick solved this by making Sicily a papal fief again (as Norman warriors had done before him); in reward he gained the imperial title over Germany. The pope, whose court at that point was maintained on the income from Sicily alone, ordered that the royal seal of the fiefdom be changed to depict a map of Sicily and Apulia instead of the seal of

Rome. This, Rosenstock-Huessy notes (1961: 195–6), marks a revolution of the concept of space, one that heralds the ascendancy of the
territorial state. It would take several centuries before sovereign
equality would crystallise, but the state form first tried out in
Sicily would prove a crucial component once it did.

As military campaigns, the Crusades were not able to consolidate
the initial focus and unity of purpose. As defeats and reversals
multiplied, religious zeal turned inward, into paranoia about heresy
and the hope for a miracle. The myth of Prester John, the Christian
prince believed to be operating in the rear of the Seljuk Turks, captures
the mood. As noted in the last chapter, there actually were Nestorian
Christian converts among the rulers of Inner Asian frontier formations; like many nomads aspiring to statehood, they tended to be
eclectic in their religious tastes (Gumilev 1987). The popes however
saw them only in imperial perspective, as potential vassals and
tributaries. One pope, mistaking the halting of the Mongol attacks
after the death of Ogedei Khan as a sign of weakness, sent emissaries
with letters inviting the new Mongol emperor to submit to him as
supreme ruler under God. In his reply, Ogedei's successor, Mönkhe
Khan, consistent with his own imperial world-view, graciously
accepted ... the pope's submission! (Komroff 1929: 16–7, 20–1.) The
golden chance, one would assume, came when Khubilai Khan, the
ruler of China, actually proposed an alliance against Islam, but by
then the crusading ambitions had dissipated.

Political and even commercial ambitions sidelined armed pilgrimage
in the Fourth Crusade of 1201–04. The campaign inaugurated the
age of Venetian primacy in this part of the Mediterranean and ended
with the capture of Constantinople. It established a Latin empire
under the Count of Flanders that held out until 1261, when the
Byzantines ('Greeks') regained control. In the frontier wars for the
Latin empire, nomads were played off against each other in typical
imperial fashion. Marx gives the example (as in Gumilev, 1987: 172
n. 6) of a French Crusader commander who in 1239 concluded an
alliance with a khan of the Kipchak nomads against Bulgaria and
Rus. By now, the Crusaders were fighting each other as well. The
Knights Templar massacred members of the Order of St John and a
number of Teutonic Knights in Acre in 1241, whilst Venetians and
Genoese were battling each other at sea. As Gumilev concludes
(1987: 192), the civil war racking the North Italian cities, fought
between modernising Guelphs and conservative imperial Ghibellines,
had finally reached Palestine.

To the Islamic world, the Crusades were only one war amongst many. More important battles were being fought in the east. The recapture of Jerusalem in 1187 by Saladin, a Kurdish military chief in the service of the Seljuk Turks, was soon forgotten and there was little interest in, or respect for the 'Franks' anyway (Lewis 1975: 83–4). The vast space occupied by the original Arab conquests had by then broken up again into separate caliphates, imamates, and emirates, betraying the origins of empire in nomad society. The Umayyad caliphate of Cordoba lost its capital to the Reconquista in 1236; the Abbasid caliphate, with Baghdad as its capital and drawing on the synthesis between Persian and Arab civilisation, was destroyed by the Mongols in the decades that followed. As imperial splendour waned and the nomad heritage as well as modernistic tendencies among the elite (exemplified by the Ismailist movement) threatened to undermine the unity of Islam, the tradition of tolerance gave way to the demand for greater conformity (Rodinson 1972: 118–20). The Ottoman empire, as we saw, succeeded in overcoming certain difficulties in matters of succession; incorporation allowed a measure of diversity, but also put it at a disadvantage in relations with absolutist European states. For the development of Islam, as for other aspects of social development, the imperial context worked as a conservative force.

On the north-eastern frontier of Western Christianity, German and Swedish crusading orders were covering the colonisation drive in the Slav lands east of the Elbe and the Baltic coast. With locally recruited auxiliaries, the celibate knights of the German Order, or Teutonic Knights, in the late thirteenth century pressed forward into the tribal forest zones, the old *branibor* ('Brandenburg') referred to earlier, subjugating the original inhabitants, the Prussians (*Prutheni*). After an initial defeat at the hands of a Russian force led by Alexander Nevsky in 1242, the Knights would eventually be annihilated by a Slavic–Lithuanian army in the battle of Tannenberg in 1410. It was at that juncture that the Hohenzollerns, a German warrior family from Swabia, began their rise as vassals of the Polish monarchy, and (from 1415) as holders of the electorate of Brandenburg for the Holy Roman empire (Marx and Engels 1955: 9–10). This inaugurated the rise of Prussia as a frontier formation of the German empire and the beginnings of its reverse expansion, in Rosenstock-Huessy's analysis (1961: 420), *into* that empire.

The two other major frontier wars of Western Christianity were the Norman conquest of England and the Reconquista of the Iberian peninsula. Each in its own way was a prelude to a further series of conquests – of the Atlantic and Indian Oceans, of the Americas and the Indies. I come back to them when we discuss the 'Atlantic turn' in the next section. Let us conclude here by a brief look at patterns of exchange in each of the main frontier sectors.

On the southern Mediterranean coastline, many thousands of travelling Jewish and Muslim merchants were active in the era of the Crusades in maritime trade between Tunis and Sicily, or on caravan routes along the coast. From the late twelfth century, however, Jews and Copts were driven out by Muslim Egyptian merchants, the Karimi, operating with support from the Fatimid caliphate. Before long, a considerable slice of Mediterranean trade and 80 per cent of Red Sea trade were dominated by Karimi traders (Curtin 1984: 112–15, 121). Along the northern perimeter, as we saw, the Italian cities Genoa and Venice were active in the Crusades. Genoa obtained trade freedoms in Palestine in exchange for naval assistance in the First Crusade; the Venetian merchant colony in Constantinople grew to some 10,000 in the century that followed. They were involved in the exchange of salt, iron, and slaves from the north for silks and spices from the east. Frances Wood (1995: 113–14) gives the example of the Polo family firm which had offices along the Black Sea coast. However, as Rosenberg notes (1994: 71), the position of resident Venetians became precarious as Crusader fortunes went in reverse and home-grown Greek competition threatened their continued incorporation by Byzantium.

The Fourth Crusade brought relief, and both Venetians and their Genoan competitors greatly profited from the opportunities for trade with Asia under the *Pax Mongolica*, which also made it possible for Marco Polo's father and uncle to travel to Karakorum. The downside of increased contact with Asia was the exposure to the 'Black Death', which killed between a quarter and a third of Europe's population in that same century. It struck around the time that the Mongol empire disintegrated and Islamic merchants began to encroach on Italian trade again. With their two-humped Bactrian camels these merchants had all along controlled the overland trade; Braudel (1981: 343) gives details of their carrying capacity, half a ton per camel. The caravan trade peaked in the fourteenth century, which was also the heyday of the pastoral nomads 'who patrolled it' (Wolf 1997: 32). With the fall of Constantinople to the Ottomans in 1453, however, the centre of gravity of Italian commerce shifted to the Atlantic coast.

On the Baltic frontier, finally, trade routes established at the time of the original Muslim conquest of the Mediterranean revived in the aftermath of the Crusades. Although the Vikings had in the meantime become dispersed, Scandinavian traders were active as far as the English coast in the west and Novgorod in the east; and when German cities, merchants, and their military protectors gained control of the North Sea and the Baltic, the northern commercial orbit revived in the form of the Hanseatic League.

IMPERIAL AND NOMAD ASPECTS OF THE ATLANTIC TURN

The frontier wars of Western Christianity reached their limits with the conquest of England, the colonisation of the Baltic coast, and the Reconquista, which included control of the western Mediterranean. The quest for wealth now became a force in its own right. 'The Norman venture, on the outer margins of Western Europe', constitutes an early 'world-economy' in Braudel's definition (1984: 25); it 'laid down *the lines of a short-lived and fragile world-economy which others would inherit*' (emphasis added). True, the actual Normans, as we learn from Gibbon (1989, vii: 194), 'were no longer the bold and experienced mariners who had explored the ocean from Greenland to Mount Atlas'. But frontier boldness and predatory instinct instilled into the societies where they had settled shaped the ambition to reach the wealthy 'Indies', the lands beyond the river Indus, by sea. This took Christian imperial aspirations in its stride. Portugal was still a frontier formation, but Spain projected a more universal pattern of rule on its overseas realm. In the Protestant north, roles were divided along broadly the same lines between Holland and England.

Frontier Connections of the Iberian Conquests

Portugal had a pivotal role in the Atlantic turn of Western expansion. The county of Portucalia, originally a fief of Léon, already became a monarchy in the twelfth century. Lisbon was taken in 1147. It was a general characteristic of the Reconquista that the emerging political structure resembled a military hierarchy; landed settlement lagged behind personal bonds of military vassalage. Mounted knights organised in religious–military orders tended to be concentrated in the cities, so that clientelism rather than Norman-style feudalism was the result. This was even more pronounced in Portugal. 'In this distant frontier region', Perry Anderson notes (1996: 171), 'much of the general development of the Spanish pattern was to be repeated, and exaggerated'.

The embryo of the Portuguese monarchy was the armed military brotherhood, the Knights of Aviz, whose grand master became the country's first king in 1384. In the ensuing war with Castile, the Reconquista nobility of Portugal was decimated or ended up on the other side. The monarchy emerged reinforced, its income equalling that of the Church and far outstripping the revenues of the aristocracy. As the head of a new Order of Christ, the Portuguese king also gained control of the remaining assets of the Knights Templar after their suppression in France. Henry of Aviz was a descendant of the English house of Lancaster through his mother (the daughter of the powerful John of Gaunt, the claimant to the throne of Castile); according to Rowse (1998: 21), his personality resembled that of his cousin, the English King Henry V, in his religious, withdrawn and dedicated nature. He gained his reputation as 'the Navigator' by using his fortune to pursue expeditions along the African coast, seizing Ceuta, the end point of the African gold trade, in 1425. African gold along with ivory would later provide Portugal with the means to enter the Indian spice trade (Wolf 1997: 111–12).

Portugal's ventures along the African coastline attracted Genoese traders to Lisbon once Venice had established its monopoly on the Levant trade. The Genoese had earlier joined forces with Castilian wool producers, thus eclipsing the commercial fortunes of Catalonia (Braudel 1984: 141). However, the galleys used in the Mediterranean were unfit and the ships of northern Europe too small to permit Portuguese expeditions to venture onto the tempestuous Atlantic Ocean (beginning with Madeira and the Cap Verde islands). Therefore the Portuguese in the 1430s developed the caravel. This combined the agility of the Viking longship and the carrying capacity of the Hanseatic cog with the triangular, lateen-rigged sails of the Arab dhow to facilitate sailing into the wind (Alves 1998: 72; cf. Vollmer, Keal, and Nagai-Berthrong 1983: 100). Hull planks were fitted edge to edge, giving the vessel a flat surface (northern ships had clinkered, overlapping planking) and enhanced speed, even if waterproofing remained a problem (cf. 'Shipbuilding', in Bedini 1998: 618).

The real revolution of the caravel was the new method of relying on the ship's beam structure for strength, the 'skeleton-first' technique (as against 'shell-first', which relied on the planking, Alves 1998). This allowed increasing the payload and yet gave sufficient strength to allow the firing and recoil of heavy cannon, combining the requirements for protection with commercial profitability. A crew of 20 could operate a 30 to 50 ton caravel (Spellman 2002: 19). Bartolomeu Dias, pursuing Portugal's exploration of the African coastline, sailed round the Cape of Good Hope in caravels. The heavier type of ship he requested on his return became the 'carrack' (a term used in the north, possibly from the Irish, hide-covered *curach*; in Portuguese, the carrack is called 'trade ship', *nau da trato*). The carrack had square sails on the foremasts, lateen-rigged on the aft mast (Contente Domingues 1998: 37–8; on the *curach*, see Marcus 1998: 7). It was kept in service until the early seventeenth century. By then, carracks had reached a size of 800 to 1,200 tons, too unwieldy, and the Portuguese turned to smaller ships again (Souza 1986: 174). Many Portuguese ships meanwhile were built in Goa and Brazil from local hardwoods, as timber in the mother country was scarce.

Now the key productive force, as will be remembered, is always the community itself. Tools or 'technology' are only significant in the hands of an able people. To navigate the wind and current circuits of the treacherous, stormy expanse of the Atlantic, for instance, required a particular moral fibre. 'Nothing would have been simpler if ocean navigation had seemed a natural activity to sailors', Braudel writes (1981: 409), repeating Gibbon's verdict that Viking nautical experience and daring had been lost. 'Before this could be revived, Europe had to be aroused to a more active material life, combine techniques from north and south, learn about the compass and navigational charts and above all conquer its instinctive fear.' This was the Portuguese achievement. The 'techniques from north and south' made the caravel and the carrack possible (Arab shipbuilders had experimented with skeleton-first ships from the tenth century on; Alves 1998: 77). But these, as much as the stern rudder, the compass, and astronomy for calculating latitude, would have meant little if there had not been the human qualities to exploit them.

Maps, too, were obtained via the Mediterranean frontier. The Pizzigano map, depicting what would appear to be the Caribbean islands of Puerto Rico and Guadeloupe, was based on information obtained by a Venetian trader passing through Calicut in India in 1421, when the Chinese Treasure Fleet happened to be docked there. Another map, depicting the Cape of Good Hope, as well as the Magellan Strait at the tip of Latin America, was brought back to Portugal by Henry the Navigator's brother, Dom Pedro, from a trip to Venice in 1428, and was equally of Chinese provenance. In combination with fifteenth-century charts of the Meditterranean coastline, called 'portolans', which allowed the calculation of distances along compass lines, this gave the Portuguese and other sea captains crucial leads (Menzies 2003: *passim*; cf. 'Cartography', in Bedini 1998: 105–6).

What limited Portuguese development was the country's small population, for which slaves had to compensate. Slav and Greek slaves had long been sold by Venetian traders to work in Italy and Spain, but the Portuguese bought their own slaves in Africa to work on the sugar cane and cotton plantations of Madeira and the Cape Verde islands. In the second half of the fifteenth century, some 150,000 African slaves were transferred to these newly-won overseas possessions; the capital, Lisbon, had a 15 per cent slave population around 1600 (Ponting 1991: 195–7). Manpower shortages also plagued the Portuguese merchant navy in Asia when it came under attack from the Dutch. The loss of ships of the *Estado da India* in the period 1629–38 alone is estimated at 155, disastrous if one realises that the Portuguese fleet of large merchantmen at its peak had only around 300 ocean-going vessels (Souza 1986: 172, 174–5; Wolf 1997: 111). All along, the Portuguese seafaring tradition was more a diaspora than an extension of the home economy. Portugal's role in inter-Asian trade, for instance, was far greater than the actual spice trade from Asia to Lisbon. Even there, Souza reminds us (1986: 67, table 4.4), Portuguese involvement was dwarfed by China's. A representative example, shipping arrivals in Manila between 1577 and 1612, lists 25 Portuguese ships and 45 Japanese, against 584 Chinese; settlement in Asia was limited to a few thousand. Portuguese as a commercial lingua franca on the other hand remained in use long after its commercial heyday (Ostler 2006: 387). True, 400,000 Portuguese left for Brazil in the course of the eighteenth century, out of a total population of 2 million for metropolitan Portugal, a remarkable feat (Spellman 2002: 27). Nevertheless we may agree with Braudel (1984: 141) that just as Portugal's frontier position supplied it with the elements for its pioneering Atlantic expeditions, it also prevented the country from becoming a dominant power itself.

Spain by contrast developed imperial ambitions from the discoveries, creating a world-embracing realm in due course. 'The two fronts of sixteenth-century European expansion', Rosenberg writes (1994: 107), '... were advancing according to very different dynamics, over very different terrains of operations, and were consolidating themselves by very different mechanisms of control.' Columbus was one of the many Genoese who played a part in the Iberian expeditions after the rise of Venice. He had the bad luck of arriving to lay out his plans to the Portuguese king, John II, just when Dias came back with the news that the Indian Ocean could be reached by sailing round the Cape of Good Hope. Columbus then turned to other Iberian sponsors. He sailed west in a carrack accompanied by two caravels. The carrack, Santa Maria, measured 85 feet in length, less than one-quarter of a junk of the Chinese Treasure Fleet, the pioneers of ocean-going ventures (Vollmer, Keal, and Nagai-Berthrong 1983: 100–1; Levathes 1994: 21). Columbus had a copy of the Pizzigano map; a copy of the map brought back by Dom Pedro, with Columbus' notes on it, was captured by Ottoman raiders in 1501 and is in the Topkapi museum today (Menzies 2003: 140, 397).

The empire of Western Christianity had long disappeared behind the horizon when Columbus proclaimed Castilian imperial sovereignty over the Americas – for his Iberian sponsors that is. Upon his return a Spanish pope assigned the Western Hemisphere to Spain, Africa to Portugal, by drawing a line across the Cape Verde islands. The Portuguese however negotiated to move it 270 leagues further west so that under the Treaty of Tordesillas of 1494, their claim to Brazil was secure (Ostler 2006: 336, 337 map). This was followed by a comparable treaty for Asia, signed at Zaragossa in 1529. By then, a host of private explorers had made their way into Central and South America claiming to act in the name of king and Church. But the Habsburg monarchy, although obsessed with defending the faith, held the upper hand over the Church. Absolutism could neither tolerate aristocratic feudalism, nor allow rival clerical jurisdiction. Under the *patronato real*, the Spanish king even obtained the effective right to appoint bishops in the Americas, making the Church the servant of the monarchy (Nederveen Pieterse 1990: 104).

In the European equation, Spain by now operated as an absolutist, mercantilist state, resisting (in fighting the Dutch revolt) but ultimately conceding the transition to sovereign equality. In the Americas and Asia, however, it engaged in foreign relations along the lines of the empire/nomad mode. 'No previous empire', Ostler writes (2006: 339), 'had been gained or maintained through the control of oceanic seaways', and the Spanish experience thus constitutes a bridge between how classical land empires dealt with foreign barbarians and subsequent seaborne imperialisms. As Wallerstein argues (1974: ch. 4), this imperial lens also coloured the Spanish monarchy's perception of its European possessions, so that it lost out to the modernising territorial states in the north. The Spanish monarchy after a delay took direct control of imperial expansion, and in 1565 the 'Philippines', named after the king, were added to its possessions. Soon, however, the autocentric imperial perspective worked to abandon expansion overseas altogether. Braudel (1984: 32) in this light interprets Philip's decision in 1582, two years after having conquered Portugal, to return from his residence in Lisbon to Madrid again; he compares it to the Ming court's move from Nanjing to Beijing as a signal inward turn.

How this orientation also cancelled out the naval advantage Spain might have enjoyed transpires in Philip's Armada adventure of 1588. England, seen as the arsenal of the Dutch revolt, was to be attacked by the largest fleet ever seen; but the ships assembled in Lisbon harbour were in fact a floating land army. The Reconquista warrior aristocracy looked down on commerce and shipping; its outlook had been shaped by the imperial pretensions of Western Christianity. Supplied with little or rotten food, countless seamen died from undernourishment and typhus while the fleet was still in harbour; even the admiral perished. Officers and men from the land army were conscripted to make up the shortfall, adding more unwilling sailors. Command was now entrusted to the Duke of Medina-Sidonia, but as Padfield relates (2000: 27–9), he considered the enterprise doomed before he sailed. In the end, packed with troops to board the opponents' vessels and effectively fight a land battle at sea, the Armada was destroyed by the storms that hit the fleet and by the superior English naval artillery, fired from a safe distance in the actual battles.

In the Americas, the Spanish conquistadors found two ready imperial formations waiting for them, one in Mexico and Central America (the Aztec empire), the other along the Pacific coast of Peru (the Inca). Each happened to be in crisis and was no match for the otherwise small Spanish columns which possessed firearms, iron weapons and horses, unknown in the Americas. Small wonder the Spanish saw themselves as the *gente de razón*, men endowed with reason, confronted with an ocean of some 60 to 80 million barbarian Amerindians, a population the size of Europe's. Infectious diseases against which no immunity had been built up were to reduce these numbers drastically, but as Wolf reminds us (1997: 122, cf. 131), they would not have wreaked such havoc if merciless exploitation and unspeakable cruelty had not weakened the population to begin with. Brazil's indigenous population in 1819 stood at one-third of the pre-Columbian era; in other areas, the decline varied from 30 to 90 per cent (Spellman 2002: 28, 31; Slicher van Bath 1989: 101–5). This mortgaged the conquest, because the Spanish were not so much after land as after people, to dig up gold and silver. Under the papal treaties, all new land was theirs anyway, a truly imperial sovereignty. So when the population appeared to be melting away before their eyes, Church lawyers recommended both the import of African slaves and a measure of protection for the remaining Amerindians (Jahn 2000: 46).

The Spanish realm was divided into two vice-royalties, New Spain (the former Aztec empire), and Peru, the Inca domain. Slicher van Bath (1989: 75–6) has analysed the Spanish American possessions in terms of the spatial structure of empire, each with their respective frontier zones. Incorporation of the Amerindians was limited by the decimation of the population and the zealous imposition of counter-reformation Christianity. The Church was lenient in one respect: as it proved difficult to teach the locals Spanish, it was decided to let them use codified versions of Nahuatl in the north, and Aymara and Quechua in the south, the lingua francas of the Aztec and Inca empires respectively (Ostler 2006: 364–9; in Portuguese Brazil this role was left to Tupinambá, ibid.: 393). This facilitated conversion, although the surviving Amerindians, who were sun worshippers adhering to a cosmology of harmony, could not comprehend why they should abrogate their own religion if they were to adopt the Christian faith. In the eighteenth century, homogenisation came to include the forced adoption of Spanish and Portuguese after all. As Ostler explains (2006: 374–5), contemporaries steeped in the Enlightenment spirit that would guide the movement for independence saw the existence of separate Amerindian communities as an embarrassment; just as they were afraid of uprisings if indigenous communities were allowed to retain their own medium of communication (B. Anderson 1991: 48).

If we go over the separate aspects of the empire/nomad mode, the familiar features stand out clearly. In terms of exchange, the Amerindians were qualified as *tributarios*, tribute-payers – tribute being due in money or goods. However, given low population density and decimation, Braudel writes (1984: 390), 'America could only become something if man was shackled to his task' – by indentured labour, serfdom, or slavery. An exchange pattern of even older parentage also developed by intermarriage. Settlement was not extensive, less than a million people over the entire Spanish colonial period (Spellman 2002: 27; cf. the Portuguese figure above). The Spanish colonists were mostly young single men from Castilian crown lands and from Andalusia, many of them priests and soldiers. Exogamy was as unsystematic as it was widespread, with the result that ethno-transformation did not produce a straightforward 'racial' hierarchy. Being counted as Spanish was always within reach of successful *mestizos*, creoles; many Spanish on the other hand were destitute (Slicher van Bath 1989: 123–4). Jews, Muslims, Protestants, gypsies, and foreigners were all forbidden to go to America. This was an extension of the turn to absolutism under Ferdinand and Isabella and the suspension of incorporation in the wake of the Reconquista: in 1492, the Sephardic (Spanish) Jews had been expelled from the Iberian and foreign domains of Castile and Aragon. Thus militant counter-reformation and empire blended into a backward turn. In Marx's words (*MEW*, x: 439), 'Spanish freedom disappeared under sabre-rattling, under a rain of real gold and in the terrible glow of *autodafés*'.

Of course, the overdetermining exchange relations were those connecting Latin America to Europe. Precious metals paid for the entry ticket into Asian trade and to finance ongoing commercial ventures. Of the gold and silver mined in Spanish America between 1550 and 1800, an average 45 per cent each year went to the Levant, the Baltic area, and East Asia; 22 to 38 per cent accumulated in Spanish America. In all these destinations it ended up unproductively, as treasure. The precious metals circulating in western and southern Europe (and varying between 15 and 30 per cent of the total) on the other hand served as a means of exchange and stimulated economic activity (Slicher van Bath 1989: 162–3; cf. Frank 1998). New plants and crops (maize, potatoes, beans, and tomatoes) were brought from the Americas to Europe too, whilst the return import of wheat helped in the long climb to repopulating Latin America (Ponting 1991: 112–13).

Finally, in terms of protection, we also see traces of how the frontier of empire was held against those further out. In the Spanish American frontier zones, Amerindians constituted the majority (the Spanish lived in the core areas). These *indios de paz* accepted Spanish rule and served as a shield against migratory tribes beyond. Their political formations, the *repúblicas de indios*, were frontier creations of colonialism, 'tributary lordships', with little or no relation to pre-Conquest political formations. Indeed as Wolf notes (1997: 148), the Amerindian entities 'constituted neither "tribal" remnants of the pre-Hispanic past, nor a static type of peasant community ... They grew up in the tug of war between conquerors and conquered'. The 'wild' Amerindians they were supposed to keep at bay were called *indios de guerra*, and the Spanish rulers never entirely succeeded in subduing them. The Araucanos of Chile are a case in point. The prohibition of Amerindian slavery was not applicable to these rebellious frontier zones either: the Araucanos were captured as slaves until the late seventeenth century; the Apache and other tribes in the north, until the nineteenth.

Everywhere in the Americas, Europeans had to deal with forms of warfare that belonged to a different age and which armies of the sixteenth and seventeenth centuries failed to come to grips with – warfare conducted according to tribal rules. In Brazil, Portuguese and Dutch discovered that fighting in the jungle was different from fighting a war in Flanders, Braudel writes (1984: 58). 'The Indians and Brazilians, past masters of the raid and the ambush, turned it into a guerrilla war.'

Let us now turn to the frontier–empire combination in the north Atlantic sector of Western Christianity, with Holland in the role of Portugal and England in that of Spain – and with Protestantism the crucial differentiator.

Skies over Holland

In the words of Marx and Engels (*MEW*, iii: 177), Holland was 'the only part of the Hansa that rose to significance'. It overwhelmed Flanders when the counts of Holland gained control over the Scheldt estuary, the gateway to Antwerp; its fisheries flourished once the herring of the Baltic migrated to the North Sea due to a change to a milder climate. With their growing fleet of armed merchantmen, the Dutch were involved in endless wars with the Hanseatic League in the first half of the sixteenth century to gain and retain control of the so-called 'mother trade', *moedernegotie* (trade in Baltic naval supplies such as timber, tar, rope, and also grain). Even at the height of Holland's maritime supremacy, the mother trade would always remain the mainstay of its economy (den Haan 1977).

As a frontier province of the Habsburg empire, the Dutch were counted on to supply the naval expeditions of Charles V and Philip II with ships and equipment, but the absolutist–imperial aspirations of these rulers were bound to clash with the particular ways in which freeholding and local self-government had taken shape in the

Low Countries. Land reclamation was a pillar of Dutch ethnogenesis, first by organising sea and flood defences and, from the sixteenth century, by inland drainage; but never as a centralised hydraulic system. Equally, the pomp and circumstance of the Roman Catholic hierarchy were alien to the inhabitants of the lowlands. In the words of the sixteenth-century Protestant writer and author of what became the Dutch national anthem, St Aldegonde (as in Boxer 1965: 116), the Dutch therefore 'took in hand to restore all again to the old and former state of the Apostles and Evangelists'. The revolt against Spain began in Flanders, triggered by the 'elevation of the clerical state', the Spanish Inquisition, which, by its persecution of heretics, disrupted commerce; in 1572, a new sales tax of 10 per cent, imposed amidst a severe economic crisis, sparked a second revolt in the north (Motley n.d., i: 236; 310–13).

The Dutch were forerunners of a new world of foreign relations, but they still lived (as had the Portuguese) in the interstices of the old. The towns and cities of Holland, with Amsterdam at their head, developed as a world-embracing 'web of traffic and exchange which would eventually make up their empire' (Braudel 1984: 215), 'a fragile and flexible one built, like the Portuguese empire, on the Phoenician model'. The sedentary formations between which these trading peoples operated the carrying function still treated money as tribute to the imperial or state treasuries. For the Dutch, as later for the English, it was 'exchange value'. When the Spanish monarchy in 1575 went bankrupt for the second time, this also ruined its Bavarian financiers; Genoan bankers weathered the storm. But when the Spanish crown annexed Portugal in 1580 and its 'new Christians' (converted Jews) had to seek refuge in Amsterdam, they brought with them the banking skills that would give the city its ascendancy in finance, terminating Genoa's pre-eminence (Wolf 1997: 115). In the seventeenth century, Holland, still dismissed by Erasmus as a barbarian backwater only a century earlier, could thus rise to become the world leaders in shipbuilding, civil engineering, dredging and land reclamation, high-yield agriculture and horticulture, clockmaking, diamond cutting, as well as printing and publishing. Crowning it all were the visual arts and cartography, in which the particular Dutch conception of space has obtained its enduring testimony.

This sense of space derives from the way the Dutch dealt with their geographical condition. Holland, in Schama's words (1988: 11) was a 'country where the very elements of land and water seemed indeterminately separated, and where the immense space of the sky was in a state of perpetual alteration'. Political–religious independence and territorial reclamation were entwined in collective consciousness and also informed map-making. As W. Thongchai argues (as in B. Anderson 1991: 173), maps are always projections of a prior concept of space as much as depictions of a reality. In his atlas of 1578, Gerard de Jode uses the word *speculum*, mirror, to denote how lands, oceans, and people are all cast in the light of a unifying sky. Mercator, Ortelius, and Blaeu, who gave Dutch mapmaking its world reputation, adopted the same perspective in the seventeenth century. In 1710, a *speculum* of the star constellations by J. Danckerts had rivers and a ship at sea drawn in between Capricorn, the Great Bear, Gemini and others (Allen 1999: 48, 89). This imagery, in which the sky pacifies the treacherous embrace of land and sea, was made famous by the great painters. It also characterises the Dutch attitude to territory as something of relative value at best. Even protection against continental attackers was organised by inundating large tracts of land, the *Waterlinie*, prohibiting the passage of foreign troops from the east into (the province of) Holland.

The lack of a territorial concept of space, combined with an ingrained particularism, also postponed the creation of a centralised state until the Napoleonic occupation. Foreignness was never a concern for the Dutch; Portuguese Jews and Protestants from France and the southern Netherlands all found asylum in Holland's cities. And although the Dutch revolt, and the Eighty Years' War it sparked off, were fought under the banner of Calvinism (rather than anything like nationalism), religious diversity too was accepted as a price for commercial prosperity. A state religion requires a state, and the Dutch only achieved a conglomerate of provinces. The Stadholder, a function held by Count William of Orange and made hereditary for his descendants, was in the service of the parliament of towns and provinces, the States-General, dominated by Holland; at several junctures, the monarchist aspirations of the Orange Stadholders led Holland to dispense with their service altogether.

The Dutch assault on Portuguese positions in the Indies began around the turn of the seventeenth century. In the prior decade, they had expanded their fleet to an estimated 2,000 sizeable armed merchantmen, by far the largest navy in Europe. Even disregarding overall numbers, an armed Dutch East-Indiaman was able to outmanoeuvre a Portuguese galleon by its lighter construction. It would fire its 30 or so guns from one broadside, wheel round to fire those on the other side, reload, and so on (Boxer 1965: 69; Padfield 2000: 18–9, 58). True, with less than a million inhabitants even at the height of their power, manning these ships was always dependent on Scandinavians and Germans, but to the Dutch this was no problem either, given that neither nationality nor religion mattered much to them.

The one-sidedly commercial involvement of the Dutch trading monopolies ruled out imperial overseas conquests. The East India Company, VOC, formed to maintain price levels in the face of a glut in Eastern spices by 1600, and the much less successful West Indies Company, WIC, prioritised exchange and protection over the actual occupation of space, property over sovereignty. Land, according to the Dutch, could only be claimed if it was worked, and to possess it overseas in excess of actual need made no sense. Settlement was accordingly limited. In all, from 1602 to 1795, almost 1 million Europeans embarked on VOC ships destined for Africa and Asia (Spellman 2002: 20). But around 400,000 returned, whilst a death rate of one-quarter was not unusual, so we are looking at some 200,000 to 300,000, Dutch and non-Dutch, over a 200 year period.

In the east, the VOC in 1610 obtained the permission of the local ruler of Jakarta to set up a 'factory' (trade office). The VOC governor-general, J.P. Coen, in 1618 destroyed the ruler's army and drove out the English, who had hoped to replace the Dutch with his help. Batavia (today's Jakarta) was home to a community of Dutch settlers, 'free burghers' who aspired to become a service class for the VOC settlement. Not unexpectedly for a monopoly, however, the company saw to it that private enterprise was curtailed; and given that agricultural work on land sold to them was done by slaves and Chinese tenants, the burghers were free, though they had little opportunity to get ahead. Coen, however, had been impressed by the vigorous resistance the VOC had encountered from small Portuguese settler communities in the East Indies. He appealed to the VOC that the burghers too should be allowed to be commercially active and thus give them something to fight for if need be, but this was dismissed. When his successor repeated the request, the reply in 1651 stressed that 'the stabilisation of a real colony with burghers trading privately cannot be in the interest of the Company' (as in Blussé 1986: 25; Boxer 1977: 40–1). The attempt to dispatch Dutch girls from orphanages to the Indies to build a settler community did not work either, since there were too few of them and they behaved too independently. When the VOC finally did encourage intermarriage with locals (the same happened in Ceylon), the wives and children of these mixed unions were strongly discouraged from ever coming to Holland, just as their descendants had few career chances in the VOC settlements (Blussé 1986: 81, 84).

In Cape Town, on the other hand, a Dutch settlement since 1652, married men were released from VOC duties to settle as burghers. However, since their numbers were restricted in spite of additional immigration by Germans and French Protestants, settlers resorted to slave labour to work the land, keeping productivity low (Boxer 1965: 246–7). 'Boer' groups on the margins took to pastoralism, adopting a semi-nomadic existence pushing the frontier ever further to the north. They encroached on the lands of indigenous tribesmen, whom they killed or enslaved, until they met fiercer resistance from Bantu-speaking Xhosa pastoralists. In the closing decades of the eighteenth century the Boers began to consider themselves a separate nationality, 'natives' of Africa. As militant Calvinists, their claim to space was comparable to English settlers in North America; but they lacked a state to back them up, let alone to give the imperial imprimatur to their seizure of land. In 1795, when Holland was invaded by revolutionary French troops, the English seized Cape Town, gradually encroaching on Boer positions. The latter's northward push worked to consolidate a Zulu nation opposing them and pushing other indigenous ethnoi, such as the Ndebele (or Matabele), into what is now Zimbabwe and Botswana. Eventually they were all subdued by the British (Wolf 1997: 349–50). The Boer War brought the Dutch colonists under British sovereignty, but a Dutch-speaking population remains the majority component of white settler society (Ostler 2006: 399).

Finally, after Henry Hudson had found the entry to the river named after him for his Dutch patrons, the WIC established colonies on Manhattan and in New Netherland (perched in between New England to the north and Virginia to the south). They too attracted a mixed population, drawn both from Holland itself and from other European countries. The English claim to all of North America was obviously unacceptable to these settlers. 'In their scheme, the discoverer also had to occupy and chart the land' (Shorto 2005: 109). But they were too few and of too varied an ethnic background to resist the takeover of Manhattan when it happened. This takes us to the final and decisive form of Atlantic settlement, the English conquest of North America.

The English-Speaking Synthesis and Maritime Supremacy

English-speaking society uniquely forged the synthesis between comprehensive imperial sovereignty and nomad mobility. Maritime supremacy and overseas settlement gave it a world-embracing equivalent of the Athenian empire, of which Mann writes (1986: 204–5) that one can only begin to understand its extent by filling in the (sea-)space between the islands and coastal settlements under its control. The English language and culture has provided an enduring bond between its constituent parts, outlasting the devolution of sovereignty from empire and Commonwealth to the separate states. Foreign policy was the perennial problem of the English-speaking states; Gramsci (1975, i: 203) notes how Canada and Ireland, and occasionally also Australia, forced the British to abandon the idea of having a common foreign policy early on. But as with the EU today, this difficulty does not suspend integration.

Ethnogenesis in England resulted from a process of layer upon layer of migrating peoples; there is no fountain somewhere in the British Isles from which the West, liberalism, and capitalism, all flow. Celts, Romans, Angles, Saxons, Danes, and Normans each left their genetic imprint on an ethnic mosaic of growing complexity (Cook 2001). The foundations for a unified state though were laid by the Normans. The thirteenth-century Gough map, which drew on the inventory of feudal holdings in the Domesday book compiled after the Conquest, records the territorial spatiality of the English realm, like the Sicilian seal of Frederick II. Importantly, the Normans' administration was also based on a compromise with the self-governing tradition of the earlier inhabitants, 'English birthright'; this would prove a powerful limit later reproduced as liberalism (Escolar 2003: 38; Rosenstock-Huessy 1961: 293).

The Celtic fringe populations were not initially included in this compromise. They were looked down on as pastoralists unable properly to cultivate the land. It was in the relations with the Gaelic ethnoi that the English middle and upper classes developed notions of racial superiority which, as Calder writes (1981: 36), 'would easily be adapted to justify the enslavement of Africans and the conquest of the Indian subcontinent, and which many people of Celtic descent would come to share'. Eventually, the Scots of the Lowlands, who spoke English, and in due course the Highlanders and the Welsh too, were all integrated – but the Irish never were. In Braudel's phrase (1984: 372), 'The Irish were the enemy, savages simultaneously despised and feared.' Their use of Gaelic was seen as a threat and even under Henry VIII was interpreted as a sign of doubtful loyalty (Ostler 2006: 465).

In the closing stages of the Crusades, strains caused by monarchical centralisation and agrarian resentment against commerce and money-dealing led to the expulsion of the Jews. Jews resident in England, as elsewhere, had been excluded from landownership under the feudal constitution, but as exchange specialists they were at hand when, towards the end of the thirteenth century, cash-strapped feudal lords began to sell off land under new rules meant to increase the number of direct tenants of the English crown. However, by buying up land, 'a course of shocking imprudence' in Churchill's judgment (1956–58, i: 228), the Jews overstepped the limits of incorporation precisely when 'national' consciousness was beginning to crystallise. 'Erstwhile feudal lords were conscious that they had parted permanently for fleeting lucre with a portion of the English soil.' A wave of hatred against Jews was unleashed, culminating in their expulsion by Edward I in 1290. The same happened in France a few decades later; there, as in England, this was also a shortcut to debt clearance by the monarchy and the landed classes. In the Holy Roman empire on the other hand, incorporation was not suspended, reminding us of the different modes of foreign relations of empire and incipient territorial states.

In the fourteenth century, after the Crusades had first turned their energies to the outside, Angevin and Valois kings, Burgundian and Norman dukes, and a host of lesser aristocrats began fighting each other again. In protracted struggles over sovereignty in France (the Hundred Years' War, terminated in 1453) and the British Isles (the Wars of the Roses), the warrior class wasted itself. This allowed Henry Tudor, a descendant of Welsh marcher lords married into the House of Lancaster (a branch of the Angevin-Plantagenet dynasty) to seize power in 1458. He ended the civil war by marrying a York heiress, and, as Henry VII, set about reinforcing the power of the centralising monarchy. The English population however, unlike the French, was able to resist renewed servitude to pay for the feudal adventures; the plague halfway through the fourteenth century had created a scarcity of labour and allowed commoners to advance socially (Wolf 1997: 121–2). This further demarcated English society from its counterpart across the Channel, just as it spelled the end of French as the language of the ruling class in England.

In terms of exchange, wool exports to Flanders became the mainstay of royal income. An indigenous class of merchants and agents grew up around it, gradually displacing the Hanseatic merchants and Genoese bankers, whilst landlords converted to sheep farming by privatising common lands in their domains. The monarchy's choice of Burgundy as the key ally against Valois in the Hundred Years' War was motivated to a considerable extent by securing access to Flanders, then a Burgundian domain; controlling the Channel was a key concern too. On account of the dynastic connection with the House of Lancaster, the Portuguese assisted at various junctures. In 1419, a Portuguese flotilla sent by Henry the Navigator blocked the Seine estuary on behalf of his cousin, King Henry V (Rowse 1998: 70, 74).

The maritime outlook and commercial interest meant that the English early on joined in the voyages of discovery. Henry VII personally oversaw and paid for Cabot's journey across the North Atlantic, and in the king's accounts there are entries for ships going to the 'new-found isle' (Newfoundland), payments to 'men of Bristol that found the isle', to 'merchants of Bristol that have been in the Newfoundland', etc. The active role of the monarchy in this domain, Rowse comments (1998: 256), came naturally to Henry, who 'had spent fourteen formative years of his life in France [and] was sympathetic to French ideas of government'.

The imperial aspirations fuelled by overseas exploration were explicitly embraced by Henry VIII. When news of Luther's church rebellion reached the king in 1517, an adviser assured him that this was of less concern to England. The king was no longer a prince of the German empire, given that he had earlier donned an imperial, closed crown with two metal bands crossing it. 'The Crown of England is an Empire of hitselff, mych better than now the Empire of Rome: for which you Grace werith a close crown' (as in Armitage, 2000: 34). The expropriation of church lands in 1534 combined privatisation with royal supremacy in religious matters. It gave rise to a notion that was different from absolutism, the idea of Commonwealth. Commonwealth articulates the fact that the territory is held in common by a gentry class; the beneficiaries of property creation and redistribution according to Rosenstock-Huessy (1993: 274; cf. Tawney 1966: 248) as a result developed an attitude of 'charity and liberality' inherited from the mediaeval Church and its social functions.

Thomas More, who would go to the scaffold over his refusal to countenance Henry's break with Rome, in his *Utopia* was less optimistic and certainly was not saved by charity. This suggests a specific duality in English liberalism: 'charity and liberality' for those considered within the same civilisation and accepting its orientation; a vindictive treatment of those out of step or out of bounds.

Spanish supremacy in the Atlantic shipping lanes initially kept a lid on the aspirations to found an oceanic realm with England at the centre. Henry VII still sought to secure an Iberian alliance by arranging the marriage of his sickly eldest son Arthur with Catherine of Aragon; when Arthur died, she became the first wife of Henry VIII. Other wives would follow but the break with Rome was no soap opera. The Act of Supremacy made Henry head of state *and* Church, in true imperial fashion. Under his daughter Elizabeth, the English then dared to confront their Iberian competitors directly, 'exploiting the space opened up by the Dutch maritime companies and the "naval shield" which these provided' (Escolar 2003: 36).

In 1577, the appointment of a new Treasurer of the Navy, John Hawkins, the son of a merchant adventurer and connected by family to the queen's Navy Board, marked a decisive step to maritime supremacy. Hawkins had conducted raids to break into the Spanish slave trade and found that the galleasses built by Henry VIII, with their single bank of oars and limited sailing ability, were unfit for ocean warfare. The new 'race-built' galleon was developed to allow English captains to conduct raids and surprise attacks, as they were still no match for the more powerful Spanish fleet. With a larger sail surface enhancing speed and manoeuvrability, the low, ram-like bow of the race-built galleon had so-called chase guns mounted for forward fire. Versatile on account of its rigging, a galleon could outgun the opponent and get away quickly, avoiding the traditional way of fighting involving boarding, to which the Spanish were still committed (Padfield 2000: 24–5).

Elizabeth in 1578 claimed the title to the entire North American coastline and gave out colonial charters to her courtiers Humphrey Gilbert and his half-brother, Walter Ralegh, to colonise it (Calder 1981: 81). But it was Cromwell's policy of building a new fleet of warships, with taxation policies to pay for them, that finally shaped the ideology of maritime supremacy. His 'Western Design' placed the emphasis on the conquest of the North Atlantic. Challenging Dutch ideas about the oceans as a space open to all, the English instead looked at the seas in terms of sovereignty. Selden, writing against the principle of *mare liberum* propounded by Grotius, argued that the oceans, too, should be appropriated and made subject to law. 'For the first time in history', writes Rosenstock-Huessy (1993: 294), 'the waters were put before the continents and treated as giving laws to the continents.' The Navigation Act of 1651 was the crowning achievement of this inversion. By 'nationalising' the shipping lanes to the British Isles, it achieved what Teschke (2003: 201–2) characterises as a territorialisation of the seas. In the late eighteenth century, the ability to calculate longitude made it possible to divide the oceans into exactly measured boxes (B. Anderson 1991: 173; Sobel 1998).

Thus the seas were integrated into the striated organisation of territory, which, as Deleuze and Guattari claim (1986: 58–60), gave the West an advantage over other societies not able to see them as a single geometric grid. This was then inscribed into imperial universalism. For the Dutch, land could only be claimed as property if it was developed; for the English, setting foot on foreign soil was sufficient ground to claim it in its entirety, certainly if that land was inhabited by people lacking a proper civilisation. 'That soil, and all soil stretching out from it for as far as the metaphysical aura of discovery could be made to stretch, came under the flag of the explorer's sponsoring nation', Shorto (2005: 109) writes in his study on the Anglo-Dutch struggle over the rightful ownership of Manhattan.

The English inherited the stock of experience of earlier seafaring societies on the Atlantic coast, but maritime supremacy was not for the taking. France by the late seventeenth century emerged as the key contender to English-speaking hegemony, and its fleet was in many respects superior to that of the British navy. True, the French navy suffered from being shut out from trade with the Baltic; ships' masts for instance were assembled rather than of one piece, and tended to break under strain (Braudel 1981: 363). But as Padfield points out (2000: 4),

the reason territorial monarchs failed time after time against maritime powers was not that absolutist, non-consensual governments were incapable of building great fleets in peacetime – quite the reverse – but that they were unable to fund them in the crises of war.

Not only did they lack the fiscal and financial institutions available to the Dutch and English merchant governments, but 'they were forced to divert resources from the fleet to their armies, to fight territorial rivals frequently financed by their maritime enemy from the profits of sea trade'.

In addition, the aristocrats commanding the French land army, like their Spanish counterparts, looked down on naval warfare. They resented the powers of Colbert, the modernising minister of finances and architect of mercantilism, who was also minister of the navy. Right after their navy had inflicted a serious blow on the combined Anglo-Dutch fleet at Beachy Head in 1690, the army leaders even proposed to dissolve it altogether and replace it by cavalry militias stationed along the coast. The king decided to maintain a naval force, but it was no longer meant to attack the enemy fleet, only to harass its merchant navy, the *guerre de course* (Padfield 2000: 139). This prefigured the twentieth-century German naval strategy of submarine warfare and in the Second World War even of battleship raiding.

English maritime supremacy was achieved in the contest with France, but a much more profound transformation involved the integration of an intercontinental English-speaking realm along liberal lines. Cromwell's Protestant dictatorship first established a modern state, a Leviathan as laid out by Hobbes; this turned monarchical property into abstract sovereignty. In the concluding phase of the Civil War, however, Dutch intervention on the side of commercialising landlords fine-tuned the relationship between the English state and society, in order to maximise the opportunities created by overseas exploration and Atlantic empire. The Orange Stadholder, William III, in late 1688 won the consent of the States General to intervene in the English civil war on the side of the commercial interests and the Protestants, both chafing under the restorative absolutism of James Stuart. An intervention would tilt the European balance against France, whilst establishing a constitutional monarchy and ensuring parliamentary control of policy in Britain.

The Glorious Revolution, as its supporters baptised it, enacted the programme laid down by Locke in the *Two Treatises of Government*. First, the sphere of civil society was to be expanded to the economy, by enshrining private property as beyond the state's reach, regulated by private law. Secondly, the state's guarantee for the liberal rules on which civil society operates was to be extended to foreign lands; giving its protection of private property and contract in the words of one commentator (as in Jahn 2000: 104), 'an economically aggressive' aspect. Indeed, in Locke's view, (private) property and sovereignty are continuous. As Inayatullah and Blaney paraphrase his argument (2004: 41, quoting Locke),

The progressive enclosure of land as private property eventually produced settlements and cities that "came in time to set out the bounds of their distinct Territories". Ownership and sovereignty equally establish exclusive rights of dominion, by which property owner and political community can exclude others from the benefits flowing from or attaching to objects of property and membership in community.

The Peace of Utrecht in 1713 settled the war William had launched against France; this was the first round of a contest that would span a full century. Several of its provisions, such as France's yielding of Newfoundland and Hudson's Bay, or the Spanish cession to Britain of the right to supply its colonies with slaves, in Rosenberg's view (1994: 40–1) show to what extent commercial aspirations were at the heart of the Anglo-Dutch war aims.

British maritime supremacy was now a fact – its navy was more than equal to the combined fleets of France, Spain, and the United Provinces (Padfield, 2000: 167). But the personal union with Protestant Hanover a year later again drew Britain more closely into Continental entanglements. The North American colonies, Spellman reminds us (2002: 34), were still 'among the least valuable territorial assets secured by England' and there were as yet few signs that these lands, which had no known precious metal wealth, would eventually rise over the mother country.

Settlement across the Atlantic had been an act of defiance by Puritans resentful of the restorative Anglicanism of Charles I, and hence may be understood as an assertion of English birthright. This was given a fanatical twist by the conviction that the settlers were crossing the Atlantic to establish a new Jerusalem, indeed that they were the descendants of the ten northern tribes of Israel dispersed in biblical times. In Gramsci's words (1971: 20), they were 'the pioneers, protagonists of the political and religious struggles in England, defeated but not humiliated or laid low in their country of origin'.

They import into America, together with themselves ... a certain level of civilisation, a certain stage of European historical evolution, which, when transplanted by such men into the virgin soil of America, continues to develop the forces implicit in its nature but with an incomparably more rapid rhythm than in Old Europe.

Their religious zeal and pioneering will-power would not only generate tremendous man-made wealth, but also place it in the service of a global mission. 'Out of the Puritans' exceptionalism', Shorto writes (2005: 386) '– their belief that the Old World had succumbed to wickedness and they had been charged by God to save humanity by founding a new society in a new world – grew the American belief that their society had been similarly divinely anointed'.

In the mother country, this was not yet fully appreciated. Only in the Seven Years' War with France would the maritime, global outlook, the 'Western Design', gain the upper hand again over the European entanglements created by the Protestant succession of 1714 – and retain it. William Pitt upon the outbreak of hostilities declared that the war 'has been undertaken not to defend Hanover, but for the long-injured, long-neglected, long-forgotten people of America' (as in Draper 1997: 166–7). True, the staggering costs of the conflict, and the need for Pitt's successors to retrieve some of it by taxing the supposed beneficiaries, would contribute to the breakaway of the United States. But this in itself did not terminate the underlying ethnic bond, or suspend English-speaking imperial supremacy. It rather inaugurated a *restructuring* of hegemony by industrialisation. As Adam Smith (1910, ii: 430) reminded his readers in the fateful year 1776, 'The rulers of Great Britain have, for more than a century past, amused the people with the imagination that they possessed a great empire on the west side of the Atlantic.' But protecting and administering the North American colonies, he argued, had been costly to the empire. Instead of the loss-making 'monopoly of the colony trade', Britain should switch to the more profitable course of manufacturing and free trade, which Smith identifies in his book as being the true sources of wealth.

It would take until the 1820s before the bonds of language, culture, and property rights brought the British Empire and the United States back into the common liberal line-up that I call the Lockean heartland. This was the form in which the English-speaking West has maintained its global hegemony until the present day. In the words of Toynbee (1935, ii: 94), it represents

a commonwealth in which the binding element is not community of blood but that common obedience to a freely chosen leader and common respect for a freely accepted law which has been called 'the social contract' in the figurative language of our modern Western political mythology.

Hence Gramsci (1975, ii: 923) cautions against equating 'commonwealth' with 'empire', because there is an element of membership and free adhesion absent from the imperial equation, and which in turn allows peaceful redistribution.

This particular quality of a voluntary union also underlies the Anglophone chauvinism by which the English-speaking West distinguishes itself from narrower nationalisms. It rather amounts to what Bukharin calls (1972: 112), a 'territorial–psychological' category that casts its net more widely than the single nation. It defines a broader area as 'civilised' according to certain rules which alone bestow on it the label of 'humanity', whilst relegating those outside to barbarian status, evil or otherwise. Thus, through pseudo-speciation, the heartland claims to occupy a superior plane of civilised existence; *no sovereign equality can be legitimately upheld against it*. The notion of innate rights, modelled on English birthright, serves as the antenna seeking out candidates for inclusion into this civilised humanity.

On the basis of the Lockean mutation, then, the foreign relations of England and its ethnic offshoots would develop as a complex articulating different modes. In its quasi-imperial attitude, there are already – given the universalism inherent in the imperial concept of space – the roots for a notion of international community, indeed a global 'commonwealth'. This combines sovereign equality for its members with a homogenising liberal culture from which no deviation is tolerated. Sovereign equality is *always* based on a common normative system which also entails obligations (Delcourt 2006: 198); in this sense it marks the final form of the evolving contradiction between separate political existence and common humanity. In the case of the English-speaking West, however, we are looking at a universalism in which the rest of the world is considered a backward anomaly.

The exchange aspect of the rise of a Lockean heartland resides in the growth of the capitalist mode of production. Capital here enjoys the specific hospitality offered by the unique combination of a series of states restricting their jurisdiction to their own territory, whilst leaving transnational capital the largest possible free space. In the exchanges with the rest of the world, the West seeks to extend this hospitality by trying to pry open states that control their own societies and to dispossess the state classes that resist Western hegemony and control. I have elsewhere (2006) developed this aspect extensively; let me here concentrate on the issue of protection.

Protecting the Heartland by Mobile Warfare

The origins of Western supremacy go back to the synthesis between elements of empire and nomadism in the Anglophone breakaway from Western Christianity. In terms of protection, the English-speaking West combines *mobile warfare with a doctrine of global sovereignty*.

Maritime supremacy is another characteristic of the heartland, in which the contradictory logics of state sovereignty and global society are partially transcended. In the fleet, mobility and primacy are ideally combined. Its size and presence reflect the economic power behind it, and it can emerge at any point as a concentrated force (Deleuze and Guattari 1986: 22). Yet maritime supremacy is not just about winning sea battles, and neither is naval power always the dominant feature of Western hegemony, as the 'Long Cycle' theory of IR maintains (e.g. Thompson 1988; for a critique, Houweling and Siccama 1993). Mobility is not confined to naval manoeuvrability either. It is the principle on which the original advantage of nomad frontier raiders over sedentary empires was based, on land as much as in coastal waters and rivers; it is also available to land powers. Gramsci (1975, ii: 865–6), who turned it into a metaphor of revolutionary politics, notes that Trotsky's 'war of manoeuvre' in the Civil War was inspired by Cossack cavalry. With the development of the productive forces, new forms of mobile warfare become possible; by the logic of war, these must be adopted by all belligerents, so that the advantage of mobility cancels itself out if it is not renewed.

Control of the world's sea lanes is certainly a necessary ingredient for a global foreign policy. But it is a means to an end. As Corbett (2001: 2) writes in the opening chapter of his military history of the Seven Years' War, 'It is behind the coast-line that are at work the dominant factors by which the functions of a fleet are determined.' Hence, 'the whole study of them is based on the relations of the coast-lines to the lines of land communication, to the diplomatic tensions and the political centres of the struggle'. This underlies the 'combined' or 'indirect' military doctrine of the British, associated with flexibility and mobility (Danchev 1999).

In the First World War, however, the Anglophone powers were drawn into a type of warfare in which the combined/indirect approach, which historically had given them an advantage, appeared to have eluded them. The Western Front in Flanders and northern France especially turned into a morass of destruction. Mechanically repeated sequences of artillery bombardment, mass infantry assault through barbed wire and landmines to the next trench, machine guns mowing down the assailants, it all led nowhere. Gas warfare added its yellow clouds of grisly death. This then was the much-feared 'war of position'. 'See that little stream? We could walk to it in two minutes', Scott Fitzgerald has his hero say in a fictional 1925 visit to a French field (1968: 124–5).

It took the British a month to walk to it – a whole empire walking very slowly, dying in front and pushing forward behind. And another empire walked very slowly backward a few inches a day, leaving the dead like a million bloody rugs.

Restoring the advantage of mobility, the 'war of manoeuvre' therefore became the overriding concern of the Western allies. It took two forms, the aeroplane and the tank, the former an American, the second a British invention. Both were products of advanced industrial society, with workforces able to handle mechanical instruments and coordinate separate tasks in mass production; this new set of productive forces was then harnessed for foreign relations by all the developed states.

The tank was conceived as a caterpillar-tracked armoured fighting vehicle able to cross trenches, tear apart barbed wire defences, and crush machine-gun nests. As Cawthorne relates (2003: 26–7, 30–1), Lord Kitchener, the secretary of war, would not hear of it; Churchill, then at the Admiralty, on the other hand embraced it early on. Indeed the naval view of things was reflected in its designation as the 'landship' ('tank' was only used to keep the secret). In early 1916, the British army ordered 100 of the experimental model, the Mark I. It took until November the next year before a massed attack with almost 500 tanks at Cambrai demonstrated their capacity to decide a battle; earlier attempts had not employed their mobility in a sufficiently concentrated way. Even now, mechanical failure, dispersion after the initial breakthrough, and other problems let victory slip away again. But in subsequent battles at Soissons and Amiens, French and American troops using Renault FT-17 tanks confirmed it was a war-winning weapon, or so it seemed.

At war's end, France had produced 3,870 tanks, Britain 2,636, against only a handful of prototypes for Germany. The US military were keen to make the Renault under licence and to mass-produce an Anglo-American tank with Ford T engines, but the mood among the Allies soon changed. Conservative top brass in Britain even claimed it was time to 'get back to real soldiering' (as in Cawthorne 2003: 33), a sentiment mixed with abhorrence about the terrible destruction wrought by the war. France began the building of the Maginot line of continuous fortifications on the border with Germany. In the United States, public outrage over the 'merchants of death' seemed to draw a line under foreign military involvement once and for all, a sentiment still resonating in Scott Fitzgerald's novel quoted above. The recommendations of advocates of mobile tank warfare such as Charles de Gaulle and Basil Liddell Hart were dismissed.

Liddell Hart in 1932 even repudiated his own views in *The British Way of Warfare*, in which he concluded that abandoning the indirect strategy in the First World War had cost Britain its world economic leadership and wasted a generation. The war of position was a trap the United Kingdom should not have walked into; even mobile armies, what he called 'the land navies' of the future (as in Danchev 1999: 318), were bound to fall into it again. A policy of controlling the elements unifying the continents rather than conquering the continents one by one was the way forward, and Versailles and the Washington Naval Conference of 1922 were thought to provide the necessary diplomatic structures that would consolidate the heartland advantage won in the war and prevent another one.

The air war was the second response to the First World War stalemate. A memorandum to the British war cabinet prepared by J.C. Smuts in August 1917 predicted (as in Brodie 1970: 71 n.) that

the day may not be far off when aerial operations with their devastation of enemy lands and destruction of industrial and populous centres on a vast scale may become the principal operations of war, to which the older forms of military and naval operations may become secondary and subordinate.

'Aircraft can fly anywhere that is air', Jenkins (2002: 2), cites US General Billie Mitchell from a 1925 book; hence, 'frontiers in the old sense – the coast lines or borders – are no longer applicable'.

As with the tank, naval manoeuvrability was the inspiration. Giulio Douhet, the leading air strategist, whose ideas were embraced by the US and British military, spoke of a 'battle plane' which could do without fighter escort (it inspired all US bomber designs from the B-10 onwards), in an obvious reference to the battleship (Brodie 1970: 94–5; cf. 73). True to the British maxim, 'the bomber will always get through', mass air attack on population centres to break the will of the enemy population became an axiom early on. Crucially, both the United States and Britain settled for autonomous air forces. The German air force also was keen to develop strategic bombing, and in the Spanish Civil War it would be the first to resort to the terror bombing of civilian populations. But 'like all continental air forces, it was bound to the ground forces by the tremendous prestige and insistent demands of the latter' (Brodie 1970: 75).

As we shall see in the next chapter, the enemy in the Second World War was able to gain the advantage of mobility as long as their supply lines allowed it; the USSR in turn emulated the Nazi mode of warfare, obtaining effective parity with the West at the end of the war. The nuclear arms race unleashed by the United States and Britain was the attempt to establish global sovereignty at the top end of the destructive spectrum, which the USSR tried to follow as long as it could (cf. Aupers and van den Hoogen 1980: 81, Fig. 1). After the American fission bombs in 1945 (matched by the USSR in 1949), the hydrogen (fusion) bomb followed in 1953/4. Also in 1953, the medium range ballistic missile (MRBM) was introduced by the United States, and, in 1955, tactical nuclear weapons and the intercontinental ballistic missile (ICBM). The USSR came alongside again with tactical nuclear weapons in 1956 and, a year later, with the ICBM. So the advantage tended to be lost ever more quickly. To restore the advantage of mobility, US strategists in the late 1950s advocated the use of nuclear missile-launching submarines, mobile launchers utilising the North American rail network and its inland waterways, as well as the deployment of bombers as airborne missile-launching platforms (Brodie 1970: 396).

The submarine-launched ballistic missile (SLBM) was undoubtedly the most important of these. It was introduced by the United States in 1959, three years after the first nuclear-powered submarine (necessary to achieve the required range and independence from refuelling to carry the SLBM) had come into service. The USSR launched its first nuclear-powered submarine in 1962, and the SLBM became operational in 1964. After that, a number of innovations to increase the number of warheads on ICBMs and their ability to independently re-enter the atmosphere with their own set targets were introduced, but all were followed within a few years by the Soviet Union. By 1985, with Gorbachev at the helm, it was clear that the USSR had lost the arms race, but also that a nuclear war would spell the end of life on the planet (Velikhov 1985). Certainly the advantage of mobility was still solidly on the side of the United States when the arms race drew to a close. Of its 10,000-plus strategic nuclear warheads in 1986, some 2,000 were on land-based ICBMs, 5,500 on SLBMs, and 2,500 on aircraft, against Soviet numbers of, respectively, 6,400, 2,700, and 680 (Kennedy 1987: 503, table 47).

All along, the quest for the advantage of mobility by the West also included securing it at the lower end of the destructive spectrum. Limited war, low-intensity war, rapid deployment forces, are all forms of mobile warfare in the sense that one can decide the locale of the application of force; not only the air transport capacity but the combined air and sea power is crucial here for the indirect approach to work. In the period of deepening US ground involvement in Vietnam, a military officer writing in the *Air University Review* (Bowers 1967) typically warned that the historic advantages of the 'British way of warfare' were being lost in that conflict. However, at the end of the Cold War the West's superiority in this domain was overwhelming too. NATO in the mid-1980s had 376 major surface warships against the Warsaw Pact's 187, but owing to their aircraft carriers, NATO had 2,533 naval aircraft against 800 (Kennedy 1987: 511, table 48; the USSR had a slight advantage in submarines). This allows the West to organise protection under a global governance mode of foreign relations, as police action. But here the atavistic imperial aspect of the West's military supremacy has laid bare the contradictions between its global aspirations and the need to control the world's resources for the 'American Way of Life', irrespective of its consequences (cf. Klare 2001). Let us now investigate some of the historic determinants of this way of life.

TRANSOCEANIC POPULATION MOVEMENT AND THE AMERICAN FRONTIER

The conquest of the oceans made it possible to redistribute the world's population on a scale never before seen in history. In the wake of European settlement in the Americas, slavery and indentured labour became key forms of subordinating foreign populations to the West. The concept of 'race' emerged in the process. Racial terms such as 'Negro' or 'Indian', negating further ethnic diversity, 'mirror the political process by which populations of whole continents were turned into providers of coerced surplus labour', Wolf writes (1997: 380–1). 'While the categories of race serve primarily to exclude people from all but the lower echelons of the industrial army, ethnic categories express the ways that particular populations come to relate themselves to given segments of the labour market.'

Previously, non-Europeans had been seen as 'an amorphous mass whose common characteristic was their heathendom' (Curtin 1971: xiii-xiv). But the conquest of the oceans brought Europeans into contact with civilisations that were their match or more. Even in Africa, 'Europeans were no threat to a major African state that was internally strong until after 1800'. When the English established their dominance in the trafficking of Africans in the eighteenth century, at the expense of the Dutch, they still had to reach agreement with local African rulers first. As in the Americas, the advent of the firearm worked both to upset local structures of authority and to create new opportunities for 'entrepreneurs' operating outside them. Various 'big men', some armed with cannon, were thus in a position to negotiate with the Dutch and the English from a position of strength. These operators and middlemen turned existing patterns of slavery, which involved separation from one's kin group but otherwise allowed a slave to become a functioning member of another group, into channels for providing the European traders with captives for transport across the Atlantic. Slave wars for export, Vincent writes (1990: 215), must therefore be distinguished from tribal capture of slaves.

Africa became disorganized, many of its cultures extinguished, and the life of the whole people darkened not because of indigenous slavery but because two higher cultures – Islam and Christianity – opened a worldwide market for slaves and organized fratricidal warfare among the Africans.

In all, the population loss to Africa as a result of the Atlantic slave trade has been estimated at 6.3 million people (Fage 1969: 85, table C).

The Atlantic slave trade also worked to bolster coastal frontier formations in Africa, undercutting the formation of empires in the interior. 'By such processes', Braudel notes (1984: 436–7), 'Black Africa was more thoroughly enslaved than the history books of the past might suggest.' Even those potential empires that did emerge were geared to the Atlantic slave economy early on. The Ashanti kingdom of Ghana, one of the branches of the Akan ethnos migrating from the Sudan in the thirteenth century, formed in response to the disintegration of tribal relations as a result of the trans-Sahara trade (Khazanov 1974: 142). Provided with firearms by the Dutch, it expanded by imposing tribute in humans, thus securing a steady supply of slaves from the early eighteenth century on. This allowed the Ashanti to break the alliance between the coastal Fanti, another branch of the Akan, and the British. It would take until 1901 before Britain, having provoked the Ashanti into rebellion by demanding the surrender of the Golden Stool, the symbol of ancestral sovereignty, subdued the kingdom after nine months of bitter fighting (Wolf 1997: 212; Apter 1968: 99, 113).

The abolition by Britain of the slave trade in 1809 and of slavery in 1834 triggered a restructuring of the bonded labour supply. True, even after 1810, almost 2 million Africans were abducted, of whom 1.6 million reached the Americas alive. But debates on whether black slaves could be replaced by other forms of foreign labour had been going on for some time. The alternative that emerged, first in Britain, was the indenture system for non-Europeans (Gollwitzer 1962: 24). It was introduced in 1830 and remained in force until abolished in the United Kindom in 1916. Worldwide, between 12 and 37 million workers were transferred abroad (from 1834 until the final abolition of indenture in the Dutch East Indies and Surinam in 1941, Castles and Miller 1998: 54).

In India, as Spellman (2002: 123) documents, indentured labour was a direct consequence of Britain's mercantilist policy of shutting Indian textiles out of the British market. Besides creating the room for capitalist machine production in the mother country, this threw millions of Indians out of work and made them available as labour in the global market. This as we shall see is a more general phenomenon. When a country can no longer export goods or other forms of wealth, its rulers will turn to exporting people. Further British imperial projects like the Mombasa–Lake Victoria railway attracted tens of thousands of workers from Gujarat, the homeland of the Indian minorities in East Africa.

Chinese indentured labour was secured by military means. The second Opium War waged by the British against China in 1856–60 did not just open up the Manchu empire to narcotics. It also led to the signing of a convention allowing Chinese to work in British colonies. The United States, France, and Spain obtained comparable agreements, and from 1850 to 1875, 1.25 million Chinese signed up for indentured labour abroad. Staggering mortality rates of 50 to 60 per cent on transoceanic voyages are an indication of the human misery this entailed (Spellman 2002: 133–4).

Of course the 'West' itself, the pivot of these transoceanic population movements, also emerged from overseas migration and settlement. The transatlantic crossing of English-speaking migrants is, with hindsight, the constitutive moment in establishing the ethnic hierarchy over all other immigrant populations. Some 250,000 migrated to America from Britain in the seventeenth century, and if many other Europeans joined the trek in the centuries that followed, this initial ethnic profile decided the orientation of the United States. In 1794, Ostler relates (2006: 492), a petition of German speakers asking for publication of US laws also in their tongue, was rejected by the (German) Speaker of the House of Representatives. In the late eighteenth century, there were attempts to limit transatlantic settlement from Britain, but liberalism prevailed. Of the 50 to 60 million

Europeans who emigrated in the nineteenth century and the first decades of the twentieth, 60 per cent went to the United States, the rest mainly to the other Anglophone settler colonies and Argentina. The share of Britons, Irish, and Germans in US immigration fell from 80 per cent in 1860 to 63.9 per cent in 1890 and 25 per cent in 1920, with Italians, south-eastern Europeans, and Jews from Russia accounting for most of the remainder (Spellman 2002: 21–3, 34–5). Yet this could no longer alter the drift of ethno-transformation. When Bismarck was asked to name the defining event of his age, he mentioned the fact that 'North America speaks English' (as in Ostler 2006: xxi).

As the century drew to a close, measures were also being taken to prevent the indentured labour supply from turning into Asian immigration into the United States. Restrictions were imposed on Chinese labourers in 1882; in 1907, the Root–Takahira agreement limited Japanese immigration. In 1921, a mechanism was introduced that ensured that immigration of any particular group could never exceed a limit of 3 per cent of that group's number already in the United States. This had the effect of stopping 'yellow' immigration completely (Gollwitzer 1962: 25–6, 65; Gramsci 1975, i: 170).

The English-speaking peoples always had a preference for having areas entirely to themselves. Yet many instances of white settlement attempted under exclusively British auspices were either late attempts, or ran into large foreign populations which could not, as would North American Amerindians, Australian aboriginals, and Maoris, be exterminated, either entirely or nearly so. Sometimes these settlements were abandoned – but in all cases the British left behind a legacy of ethnic conflict. As Gott writes (2006: 22), Israel/Palestine tops the list here. Zionist colonists were allowed to establish a Jewish state on the basis of the Balfour Declaration, but 'unfortunately for the settlers, arriving during the imperial sunset, they had insufficient time to achieve the scale of defeat of the local people, amounting to extermination and genocide, that characterised the British conquest and settlement of Australia'. Sierra Leone (where Christian blacks from Britain and Canada were resettled), South Africa, Zimbabwe, and Kenya with their white minorities, but also Sri Lanka and Fiji, key destinations of indentured Indian workers for British-owned plantations, each in its own way represents an unfinished settler policy, abandoned midway, and consequently a source of continuing instability.

This takes us to how 'the West was won' and to the tribal legacy of slavery in the United States.

The Frontier in American Ethnogenesis

'Up to our own day American history has been in a large degree the history of the colonization of the Great West', Turner (1962: 1) famously argued in 1893. 'The existence of an area of free land, in continuous recession, and the advance of American settlement westward, explain American development'. The Frontier Thesis, according to Gramsci, was just a way of romanticising the development of the United States, but Turner (1962: 2–3) is no doubt right when he claims that 'This perennial rebirth, this fluidity of American life, this expansion westward with its new opportunities, its continuous touch with the simplicity of primitive society, furnish the forces dominating American character.'

Of course we have to be clear what these terms stand for. The frontier developed into the highway of American ethnogenesis, but it did so by displacing and effectively exterminating the indigenous peoples. Here the West was supplied with the type of personality and community and the means to conquer the planet; on the frontier, Aglietta claims (1979: 74), 'expansion became the dominant phenomenon of American life'. Those in the way would be dealt with harshly.

Fishing for cod in the waters off Newfoundland entailed trade in beaver pelts with locals. It drew the Europeans further inland as beaver populations were hunted to extinction; the Algonquin Amerindians were the first of successive native peoples taking up the trade, triggering competition among them for new hunting grounds (Wolf 1997: 160–1, cf. 162 map). On the European side, the key competitors were the settlers of New England and the French, the strongest European contenders to English-speaking expansion. French fur traders in Canada relied exclusively on this activity and had no choice but to be friendly with the Amerindians. The British on the other hand had a more varied economy and they were 'notorious for their crude mistreatment and fraudulent practices' in dealing with the indigenous peoples (Draper 1997: 141). When the French monarchy attempted to secure the lands beyond the Alleghenies as a zone of expansion (from Montreal in the north to their settlement in New Orleans in the south), simmering conflict exploded into the Seven Years' War, terminating French sovereignty in North America. As late as 1791, Canada still had 140,000 French speakers against 20,000 Anglophones, but as immigration resumed, English overtook French in the mid nineteenth century (Ostler 2006: 415).

The French defeat paradoxically brought about the independence of the United States. I have mentioned already how the war's costs had to be retrieved by taxing the colonies, and this was responded to in ways that the changed geopolitical configuration permitted for the first time. As Arthur Schlesinger puts it (as in Draper 1997: 180–1), 'By eliminating England's ancient enemy as an ever-present danger, [the Peace of 1763] not only weakened the colonists' sense of military dependence on the homeland but also their sense of political dependence.' The French, again paradoxically, would for several decades become an ally in the severance of the colonial bond. But this was tactical only. The promulgation of the Monroe Doctrine of 1823, with Britain a silent partner, was merely the first indication that global liberalism would henceforth be upheld by the Anglophone powers for the greater good of mankind (Smaje 2000: 152; Nederveen Pieterse 1990: 312).

France made one last attempt at a North American empire when Napoleon acquired (from the Spanish) nominal sovereignty over Louisiana, the frontier zone between the Rocky Mountains and the Mississippi. Forced to sell it again for $15 million to the United States in 1804 to finance his European wars, this doubled the territory under the sovereignty of Washington, unlocking a vast surface for further colonisation. 'Not since the Treaty of Tordesillas in 1494, when the dazzlingly depraved Pope Alexander VI had divided the Americas between Spain and Portugal', Cocker writes (1998: 197), 'had so much been given by so few for so little.'

The displacement of the Amerindian tribes meanwhile continued without a change in stride. Whilst negotiations with France were going on, President Jefferson (1969: 81–3), in a letter to the governor of the territory of Indiana in February 1803, spelled out the policy of chasing the Amerindians from their land. Predicting that 'our settlement will gradually circumscribe and approach the Indians, and they will in time either incorporate with us as citizens of the United States, or remove beyond the Mississippi', he noted that, regarding Indiana,

We presume that our strength and their weakness is now so visible that they must see we have only to shut our hand and crush them ... The Cahokias extinct, *we are entitled to their country by our paramount sovereignty*. The Piorias, we understand, have all been driven off from their country, and we might claim it in the same way ... The Kaskaskias being reduced to few families, I presume we may purchase their whole country for ... a small price to us ... Thus possessed of the rights of these tribes, we should proceed to the settling of their boundaries with the Poutewatamies and Kickapoos, claiming all doubtful territories. (Emphasis added.)

He insisted, however, that 'while we are bargaining, the minds of the Poutewatamies and Kickapoos should be soothed and conciliated by liberalities and sincere assurances of friendship'. One cannot help thinking of how Reagan embraced Gorbachev in the late 1980s. A campaign against the Creek to make way for cotton planters moving into Alabama was followed by an attack on the Seminole, a branch of the Creek ethnos from Florida, later in the decade. Creek warriors who fought with the United States against the British in 1812 were dispossessed of two-thirds of their lands at war's end; with cotton prices rising, the territories they inhabited were simply too valuable. The Cherokee, who fought under General Andrew Jackson in the same war and even adopted the required sedentary way of life, were also found to be in the way of settler land requirements; tens of thousands died on the forced marches further west (Ponting 1991: 134; Cocker 1998: 196). A comparable displacement befell the Winnebago several times, with the result that their population halved between 1829 and 1866.

In North America, the frontier phenomenon of recruiting auxiliaries by the 'imperial' civilisation primarily involved scouting by Amerindians (Lattimore 1962: 136–7). The tribal pattern of dealing with foreign communities, to which the Amerindian peoples were accustomed, greatly limited their ability to fight the United States for a sustained period. So when, in the period during and following the American Civil War, a series of brutal campaigns to subject and effectively destroy the Great Plains Amerindians was unleashed, there were initial victories but terminal defeat in the end. The Cheyennes took to the war path on the margin of the Civil War, followed by the indomitable Apaches and others. As a tribal society with limited possibilities, however, 'the Indians had no means of keeping a standing army in the field indefinitely' (W. Brandon, as in Nederveen Pieterse 1990: 313). Their communities had also been weakened by the advent of horses and guns, allowing the natives to hunt bison on a large scale. They placed into the hands of young warriors the means for independent raiding, a phenomenon familiar from nomad society (Wolf 1997: 178). Traditional authority, anchored in mythical ancestry, on the other hand unravelled.

There was no possibility for white Americans to learn from this decaying way of life, and yet the frontier retained the aspect of accelerated social development. Turner (1962: 2) highlights the continuous adaptation to natural circumstances, on which more advanced forms of social life are then superimposed; 'a return to primitive conditions on a continually advancing frontier line', yet with the 'complexity of city life' never far behind. Colonial life is a microcosm of the successive stages of social development, from hunting to trading, from pastoral herding to sedentary farming, from landed to city and factory life. On this shortened time dimension, the stages of development are compressed into each other; they create a density of adaptive choices which turn the frontier into what it has always been, a laboratory for social experimentation. At the same time, as Aglietta emphasises (1979: 80), the 'spatio-temporal environment' of pre-capitalist, petty commodity relations on the frontier was the ideal incubator of Lockean liberalism, ensuring that commercial exploitation remained the bottom line of innovation. American mass production, pioneered in the slaughterhouses along the Ohio river and culminating in mid-twentieth-century Fordism, in this sense was a frontier phenomenon.

In terms of protection, the frontier for white Americans operated as 'a military training school, keeping alive the power of resistance to aggression, and developing the stalwart and rugged qualities of the frontiersman' (Turner 1962: 15; 'aggression' was when Amerindians tried to defend themselves, but then, as Lattimore 1951: 350 reminds us, the barbarians do not keep the records). The idea that there was an enemy who had to be annihilated, that no compromise was possible, thus took root in the American mindset. In combination with the Puritan heritage, this produced the attitude that the extermination of people beyond the pale is the equivalent of 'rooting out evil' (Liberman 2004b: 24). The dangers of frontier life simultaneously impregnated the American mindset with intolerance towards strangers as well as towards opinions considered 'un-American'.

An obsessive clinging to the notion of free land and access, blended with a violent attitude to anyone standing in the way, also engendered a particular attitude to nature, one radically different from the respectful one held by the natives. By refraining from expansion, it was felt, a nation 'ceases to extend its sway' over others; hence as Cocker comments (1998: 203), 'to pre-empt such a possibility, white America now seemed to declare war on the whole world of nature'. This included the near destruction of the 25 million-strong American bison herds and the extermination of one of the world's most numerous land birds, the passenger pigeon, by 'a complex blend of American farming, industrial and hunting interests'. By the mid nineteenth century, 40 per cent of the 1 million square miles of ancient American forests had already been destroyed to clear land for agriculture; in 1880, 75 per cent. The Great Plains, although unfit for cereal cultivation, were brought under the plough in response to growing world wheat demand. This would result in the mid-1930s dustbowl, when storms whipped up hundreds of thousands of tons of thin topsoil (Ponting 1991: 256). By that time, energy-intensive mobility premised on cheap oil from the South had further consolidated a collective mentality of unrestrained exploitation of nature's riches as the hallmark of the American way of life.

In the 1890s, frontier ethnogenesis obtained a political mass basis in Agrarian Populism. The countryside's response to the world economic slump in agricultural exports, it crystallised an international imagination from the sediments left in the collective psyche by the first stages of frontier development: the original trapper mentality, the agrarian myth of the family farm, and petty-bourgeois fears of big capital. Thus were created the narrow-minded nationalism and anti-capitalism typically directed against the financial element, with anti-Semitic and anti-British overtones, which still today characterise the resistance of important sections of American society to the United Nations or to any form of regulation imposed on the Land of the Free from the outside. A conspiratorial tradition also developed which brings all the enemies of the Midwest together in a single, densely integrated bloc of Jews, Anglo speculators, and Bolsheviks (Hofstadter 1955: 78; Rupert 2000: chs 5 and 6).

The Puritan legacy with which Populism has blended supports a world-political perspective of divinely ordained conquest of the world, 'Manifest Destiny'. This phrase, coined in 1845 by a journalist on the occasion of the outbreak of the war with Mexico, set the United States on the path of fulfilling the task set by Providence to bring liberty and 'federated self-government' to the world (Portis 2004: 49). Ever since, the United States has appealed to what Stanley Hoffmann (as in Liberman 2004b: 20) calls 'the principle of difference', American exceptionalism. It has three components: protecting the promised land from contamination by atheist Europe and from foreigners generally; disseminating 'freedom' (for which read, the liberal order) to the world at large; and proselytising on behalf of Christianity across the globe.

By 1900, the frontier had generated the outlook which would support such an expansion even if many internal ills remained to be addressed. As Jenkins sums up the ascendant consensus (2002: 98), expansion 'would teach [the masses] the value of the elite's leadership', just as 'Americans would be impressed by their own collective power.' 'They would come to see themselves, as they had done in Civil War, the Indian Wars, and the colonization of new land, as *a community of heroes engaged in a struggle on which the future of humanity depended*' (emphasis added).

Woodrow Wilson shaped the Manifest Destiny doctrine to the broader needs of the heartland when he proposed the League of Nations at the end of the First World War. By then, the fantasies of Theodore Roosevelt and of Wilson himself that the colonisation of America had been part of a sweep of Teutonic peoples that had begun with the defeat of the Roman empire had been recast to remove Germany from the script (cf. Jenkins 2002: 99, 111). Wilson saw America's world role (as in Shorto 2005: 386) as rooted in 'the sheer genius of this people', allowing it to see 'visions that other nations have not seen', etcetera. Even so, the United States had certain traits in common with the constitutional states of northern Europe, such as respect for authority and law and the appreciation of the common good and evolutionary change that allow self-government. The French, Spanish, and Latin American nations on the other hand had not been educated in these values, and their democracies lacked self-discipline as a result. In 1914, Germany was recognised as belonging to this other camp after all. Otherwise Wilson and his contemporaries in the outward-looking ruling class remained convinced that the structural clash was between continental European state-led politics, 'state exigency, ... state interest, [as] superior to those rules of morality which control individuals', and the Anglo-American concept that 'right begins with the individual' (as in Jenkins 2002: 136).

The Tribal Legacy of Slavery in the South

Let me conclude this chapter by looking at how a black sub-population, abducted as slaves from Africa, remains segregated from the American mainstream. I see this as a drawback or shortcoming not of the United States alone. The Anglophone West, in combination with globalising capital, to which it offers a privileged spatial constellation, unifies the dominant trends in global social development into a hegemonic way of life; no structural feature of US society can therefore be considered a 'local' peculiarity. In American slavery and its legacy, the West's unique experience of redistributing populations on a world scale, and their continuing subordination, merely obtain their most concentrated expression.

Why Africans were preferable to Amerindians as slaves was not so much a matter of their supposed bodily qualifications as a matter of politics. The Amerindians were kept in reserve to help fight the French or the Spanish; in addition, they could be used to hunt down runaway slaves. If provoked into rebellion, on the other hand, the native Americans might draw their brethren into the fight. Africans could not appeal to nearby free tribes and upon arrival in American ports were deliberately mixed to obliterate any ethnic bond among them (Wolf 1997: 203). Yet the black slaves, made defenceless by being robbed of their indigenous tribal structures, were made part of the social structure of the United States in a quasi-tribal fashion again, in ways reminiscent of caste in India. Indeed, as Cash (1954: 36) writes in his classic study of the American South, the white inhabitants thought of their world not in the perspective of class, but of caste, 'with interests and purposes in conflict with the interests and purposes of other castes'. The treatment of Afro-Americans, Ogburn confirms (1964a: 187), can be compared to that of the lowest caste in the Indian village. As we saw, caste in turn has an aspect of tribal foreign relations.

The outcome of the American Civil War coincided in time with the liberation of the serfs in Russia. In a way the two had similar consequence: a new class had been created by law, but society was not able to accommodate it. In the United States it added a third ethnos to the white settlers and the Amerindians. As Tocqueville (1990, i: 332) wrote of his experiences in the 1830s (when most blacks were still enslaved), 'The three races, although mixed, ... do not amalgamate and each race fulfils its destiny apart.' The Amerindians in his view were doomed to disappear. The fate of the black slaves, however, was in 'some measure interwoven with that of the Europeans'. The two were 'fastened to each other without intermingling; and ... unable to separate entirely or to combine'. Proximity of one ethnos always affects another. In the words of Cash (1954: 51), in the American South, 'Negro entered into white man as profoundly as white man into Negro'.

Inequality therefore assumes the form of foreign relations imbricated with the more obvious economic aspect of class exploitation. In combination with cultural degradation, such exploitation in Polanyi's words (as in Inayatullah and Blaney, 2004: 179) causes 'lethal injury to the institutions in which [its] social existence is embodied. The result is a loss of self-respect and standards, whether the unit is a people or a class.' The black slave in the United States was and remained a foreigner, 'torn from his culture, family life, and system of values, and ... in a society that offered no adequate substitutes' (Genovese 1989: 80). After emancipation, this did not change, as Tocqueville foresaw (1990, i: 356–8). 'You may set the Negro free, but you cannot make him otherwise than an alien to the European.' Indeed, 'The European is to the other races of mankind what man himself is to the lower animals: he makes them subservient to his use and when he cannot subdue them he destroys them.'

The fate of the 'other races' is that of enduring foreignness, in a relation to the white majority best characterised as tribal. Again in Tocqueville's words (ibid.: 368–9), 'The Negroes constitute a scanty remnant, a poor tribe of vagrants, lost in the midst of an immense people who own the land.' Let me briefly go over the separate aspects of the tribal mode to elaborate this.

Slaves in the United States were fewer in number and lived in smaller concentrations than elsewhere in the Americas, so the spatial aspect of their presence would always be in the nature of sharing. To use Nederveen Pieterse's phrase (1990: 337), they were 'encircled by a white vigilante society'. The first thing that happened in the slave South after its defeat in the Civil War, was the re-establishment of white supremacy along tribal lines. Oklahoma in the 1920s was virtually ruled by the Ku Klux Klan. The Klan sowed terror in the hearts of the non-white population, whilst helping wealthy Southerners to good agricultural land and oil leases. As Tocqueville (1990, i: 368) had already observed, well before the Civil War, 'The states in which slavery is abolished usually do what they can to render their territory disagreeable to the Negroes as a place of residence.' When the needs of industrialisation mobilised millions of Afro-Americans in the course of the twentieth century, 'they remained locked in a precarious position of structural economic marginality and consigned to a secluded and dependent microcosm' (Wacquant 2002: 48). The black ghetto is a device in which foreignness is territorialised, creating the equivalent of untouchability by physical separation.

Even the tribal trajectories between eternity and life on earth are segregated in the United States. The myth of white supremacy and the white gowns and hoods and burning crosses of the KKK should be properly understood as mythical here. The concept of the white race was constructed around mythical origins such as the Anglo-Saxon, or Teutonic/Germanic, 'freedom-loving' tribes of ancient

Europe, and around the Puritan notion of a chosen people (Gossett 1963: 86–8; 185–92). 'God of course became more distinctly a tribal god than ever' (Cash 1954: 135). The former slaves on their part gave the Christian religion an indigenous inflection by weaving into it various African religious themes. The Shango cult of the Yoruba god of thunder and war, one of the elements thus inserted, is a reminder of the protective dimension involved here; as is the voodoo cult which had a special place in slave resistance to the white masters (Nederveen Pieterse 1990: 340).

Just as feud predates public justice in the tribal mode, lynching originated on the frontier as a form of mob justice when state power had not yet been established effectively. Only later was it turned against blacks in the South. The Ku Klux Klan was instrumental here, and we must recognise that it did not adopt the archaic term of 'clan' by chance. Cash (1954: 344–5) characterises it as a 'significant projection from the past into the present'; it was not only anti-black, but also anti-Jewish, anti-catholic, anti-modern, and so on. For tribal relations to obtain, there must be a reduction of the limits of the possible for the other side as well. The Klan recruits its mass base among deprived whites, and that is what qualifies it for engaging with the black sub-population in a tribal fashion. Naipaul (1989: 54) records the opinion of the black mayor of Atlanta that still today the 'tribal' struggle expresses the desperation 'of people who find that history is leaving them behind … The black underclass gets caught up in drugs and crime. The white underclass gets caught up in drugs, crime and Klan.' The poor whites of the South are equally mired in a regressive mode of social relations. In the words of Cash (1954: 138), 'Here were the ideas and loyalties of the apotheosised past fused into tightest coherence and endowed with all the binding emotional and intellectual power of any tribal complex of the Belgian Congo.' The Democratic Party in the South, its political vehicle of choice, he adds, was 'as potent an instrument of regimentation as any totemic society that ever existed'.

Emancipation in a sense enhanced foreignness. Tocqueville again spoke prophetically when he wrote (1990, i: 375) that 'if I were called upon to predict the future, I should say that the abolition of slavery in the South will … increase the repugnance of the white population for the blacks'. Indeed as Nederveen Pieterse writes (1990: 337–8), 'attitudes hardened and conflicts intensified because of emancipation as evidence that black people were beginning to count'. At the end of the Civil War, 'Jim Crow' laws introducing racial segregation were adopted in several Southern states, and informally applied in others, along with lynching, as 'the conveniences of ethnic hierarchies and the urge towards domination were still at large [and] the process of dehumanisation which had succeeded in sanctifying slavery, was active still'.

There remains the final aspect of a tribal mode – exchange. The blacks worked for the whites of course, on the lowest steps of the occupational ladder and on the margins of respectability. Today, as Wacquant argues (2002), their existence is typically strung out between the two poles of criminal activity and incarceration on the one hand, and low-paid jobs in the service industry, the military, etc., on the other. The exogamy aspect of exchange occupies a special place here though. Exogamy in tribal relations is part of the overall system of reciprocity – but not in this case: that would amount, for the whites, to marrying 'untouchables'. Sexual relations between whites and blacks in the American South have therefore assumed a particularly skewed form in that white men could avail themselves of black women, but not the black man the other way around. The Negro woman, Cash notes (1954: 87), 'torn from her tribal restraints and taught an easy complaisance for commercial reasons, ... was to be had for the taking'. The possibility of this particular type of sexual relationship, 'the relationship of the white man and the black servant woman, man and undemanding mistress', to use Naipaul's phrase, 'had left the white woman and the black man neutered' (1989: 30). Already by the eve of the Civil War, only around 20 per cent of American blacks were unmixed African. So whilst there was no recognised exogamy, there was substantial genetic intermixture (Bromley 1974a: 66 n.).

Several disturbing phenomena have resulted from this particular modality of the pattern of sexual exchange across the boundaries of difference, such as the figure, familiar from films and novels, of the Southern 'belle' addicted to alcohol. More seriously, what has been called the 'rape complex', provoked by the mere presence of blacks, turned the white woman into a sort of saint. Being absolutely inaccessible to males of the inferior tribe, she became, although tragically neglected, 'the perpetuator of white superiority in legitimate line' (Cash 1954: 87). After emancipation, the Jim Crow lynching laws centred on 'the unspeakable crime' of interracial marriage or sexual relations, meant to 'uphold the "supreme law of self-preservation" of the races and the myth of innate white superiority' (Wacquant 2002: 46). The rape complex, the pervasive fear of black men assaulting white women, meant that 'any assertion of any kind on the part of the Negro constituted in perfectly real manner an attack on the Southern woman' (Cash 1954: 119). When Naipaul in the 1980s visited Forsyth county north of Atlanta (1989: 27), a case dating from 1912 (a rape, followed by the lynching of a black man, the hanging of two others, and the removal of all blacks from the county) had only recently been judicially reviewed. Even today, many Southern state schools in the United States have racially segregated prom nights and school dances to avoid problems arising from interracial dating; private schools are tellingly called 'seg academies'.

In the next chapter we shall see that this is not the only way that tribal foreign relations have become enfolded into the social fabric of the richest and most powerful country of the world. In its inner cities, too, these patterns are reviving; but that truly is a phenomenon of global proportions.

5
Worlds of Difference

Sovereign equality as a mode of foreign relations emerged in the dissolution of the empire of Western Christianity. It constitutes the final form of political compartmentalisation of the global community; the English-speaking heartland, as we saw, is already in the process of transcending this contradiction, albeit one-sidedly and violently, on the basis of an unsustainable way of life. In this chapter, we turn to the second route out of Western Christianity, the one taken on the European continent. This too was based on the sovereign equality mode, but without the prior synchronisation of class and culture as in the north Atlantic West. As a result, contemporary global political economy and international relations converge on the heartland/ contender state pattern I have analysed at length elsewhere (see my 1998 and 2006).

The Continental nation-state model was based on the break-up of the Christian empire right across the middle, along religious, linguistic, and cultural lines. Over time, the state had to take the lead in carving out an enclosed territorial space to withstand the disruptive forces of Western hegemony. The nation-state model which the European states have adopted assumes that the foreign can be *exteriorised* from society. In fact the sedimented layers of difference enclosed by the state are pressed together rather than overcome by 'nationality'; although through patronage, language policy, and economic redistribution, state sovereignty does have important ethno-transformative effects. But as Western pressure to liberalise, in conjunction with commodification by transnational capital, erodes states' operational efficacy, the strongest, the contender states, are forced into compliance and compromise, whilst the weaker states have tended to fracture, again along the lines of internal and trans-border foreignness.

I shall first briefly discuss the evolution of sovereign equality as it emerged in the seventeenth century on the European continent, before turning to investigate the attempts of successive contenders at 'nation-statehood' amidst ethnic diversity. In many cases this has entailed war, mass migration, and mass murder; constitutionally *multi*-national contenders have sought to mitigate this in their own domain but have succumbed to centrifugal forces in the end. Secondly, we shall look at how the weaker states in the international system have actually collapsed, their societies fractured along ethnic and quasi-tribal lines. Along refugee and other migration trails, the fragments of these defunct societies feed into the cities of both the South and the North. Whether world society will be able to transcend foreignness and achieve a sustainable global governance will concern us in the final section.

THE OTHER WORLD OF INTERNATIONAL RELATIONS

Sovereign equality in Western Christianity was first established by the claims of kings and princes vis-à-vis the Church of Rome, as Protestantism. The circumstance that the rulers of the frontier lands faced a centre which in the final analysis had only religious authority, an emperor without clothes, gave a religious form to their declarations of independence. But this took two radically different routes.

On the British Isles, as we saw, the Tudor breakaway laid the foundations of a universalistic sovereignty of a new type, with equality confined to those states sharing the liberal principles on which, at a later stage, capitalist development could thrive. Calvinism, imported from Switzerland and developing through intercourse with Holland, became a driver of settlement in North America on the waves of a maritime empire. It also propelled a rapid transformation of the state from modernising dictatorship to liberal compromise on both sides of the Atlantic.

The Holy Roman empire and its appendages across Europe, on the other hand, imploded. Here Protestantism inspired peasant revolts and bloody internecine wars weakening all parties. The Lutheran reformation, like the prior, unsuccessful revolt of John Hus in Bohemia, fractured the Holy Roman empire by attacking its social structures and bringing the written word to the population directly (B. Anderson 1991: 39). Lutheranism, and Protestantism generally, were frontier phenomena, as Braudel emphasises (1984: 66), but the crowned heads of the German principalities seeking to mobilise the energies of revolt for their own purposes were not aspiring seafarers looking out on a vast ocean. Presiding over societies caught half-way between the Middle Ages and the new world, 'decomposed feudal and embryo-bourgeois,' as Engels characterises them (*MEW*, xxi: 402), they were unable to provide social development with a political focus other than the right route to heaven.

The fury with which the wars of religion were fought brought out the profound insecurity created by the social changes that were underway. Their settlement (along the lines of sovereign equality), first by the German princes and the empire at Augsburg and then by the rulers of all of Continental Christianity in the Westphalian treaties, laid down the grid on which further state formation would be based. Difference and (proto-)national collective identities were enhanced in the process; the very idea of conversion sharply demarcated faith communities from each other, forcing them to adopt a 'fundamentalist' posture as they sought to redefine themselves from the ground up in religious terms. As Rosenstock-Huessy puts it (as in Deutsch 1966: 290 n.), in every revolution, those 'who have not been revolutionised, and those who have, live in opposite universes of values, and, therefore, do not seem human to each other'. As we saw earlier, this process of pseudo-speciation is at the root of the condition of foreignness; in the modern age, it lends a vicious edge to revolution and civil war. Indeed it is played out before our eyes today, as fragments of the former Third World, defeated in the attempt at sovereign equality and caught adrift in various processes of globalisation, are finding a voice in a radicalised version of Islam, the nomad creed par excellence.

Back in 1555, the right of the German princes to decide their own religion (*cuius regio, eius religio*) divided the empire into a Protestant north, a Catholic south-east and a mixed south-west. Which denomination would be chosen was a personal choice of the ruler and his advisers (key among them the theological faculties of universities). The Augsburg agreement therefore did not mean that the empire had given up its sovereignty; there was a feeling on all sides that it was a provisional settlement (Inayatullah and Blaney 2004: 27–8; Engels in *MEW*, xviii: 590–1). Social development was highly uneven, and the imperial core areas in particular lacked the equivalent of the 'robber barons' who had been the beneficiaries of the redistribution of church lands by Henry VIII. 'Germany, like Italy, was the seat of an universalistic and supranational institution and ideology', Gramsci writes (1971: 18–19). It 'provided a certain number of personnel for the mediaeval cosmopolis, impoverishing its own internal energies and arousing struggles which distracted from problems of national organisation and perpetuated the territorial disintegration of the Middle Ages'. As a result, in the absence of a vigorous new class guiding the process, the resurrection of a national identity would only be resumed after a delay of several centuries.

The year of the treaties signed at Osnabrück and Münster (concluding the Thirty Year's War fought out on German soil and Holland's Eighty Years' revolt against the Spanish Habsburg monarchy, respectively), 1648, is usually cited as the moment at which the principle of sovereign equality was formalised and multilaterally sanctioned across Europe. Bobbitt (2002: 503) describes the treaties as a constitution for the states of Europe. However, as Teschke points out (2003: 238), they were actually concluded between rulers in their personal, dynastic capacity, along with estates and other late-mediaeval bodies, as if still within a feudal order. Under the feudal constitution, allegiance was based on fiefs granted by the feudal superior, and could only be changed on that title; pillaging or even occupying a fief-holder's lands left the feudal title intact. The signatories to the Westphalian treaties acted in this spirit (Osiander 2001: 119, 124). The Holy Roman emperor, the empire's nine electors, the other princes of the realm and the 51 free cities signed for 'Germany'; one treaty with the king of France's representative, another with the king of Sweden's. The latter's acquisitions along the German coastline, Teschke notes (2003: 239), were even ceded as imperial fiefs, making the Swedish monarch a vassal of the emperor, with voting rights in the imperial diet. The peace with Spain that crowned the revolt of the Dutch provinces perhaps came closest to an instance of sovereign equality, because it combined a religious rupture with a complete separation of territorial sovereignties. Certainly the pope declared the Westphalian treaties null and void (Bobbitt 2002: 116), but as we saw, even for the pious Iberian conquistadors he had already become merely an accessory a century earlier. England, finally, was not a signatory.

Hence the structure of modern international relations, juxtaposing an expansive Lockean heartland to successive contender states, could only emerge later, in the aftermath of the Westphalian settlement. It articulated the two fundamentally different ways in which sovereign equality was taking shape in Europe (in the English-speaking world and on the Continent) into a single constellation. But how?

Marx's rambling polemic on eighteenth-century diplomacy may not exactly be a specimen of fine historical scholarship on this matter. Yet it contains one key argument, which is that the treaties settling the successive phases of the break-up of the structures of

Western Christianity, beginning with 1648, and more particularly the treaties shelving imperial claims on the part of the Spanish Habsburgs, must be seen in conjunction with *the advent of tactical alliance making*, with liberal England, and after 1707 Britain, in the driver's seat. From a system of dynastic alliances and successions, we move to one of secret diplomacy and calculated shifts of allegiance, of which Sweden, a key signatory to the treaty of Osnabrück, became the first victim. Thus in Marx's words (1983: 68),

The treaties concerning Spain have aroused the interest of posterity, because these partition treaties anticipated the War of Succession, whilst the partition of Poland attracted even greater attention, since the final act of it took place in the contemporary period. But it cannot be denied that the partition of the Swedish realm inaugurated the era of modern politics.

Certainly, he notes elsewhere (1976: 497), absolutist centralisation along Hobbesian lines was one of the tangible fruits of the wars that ended with the Westphalian treaties. But the partition of Sweden's Baltic realm was the 'first great act of modern diplomacy'. It finally put together the European balance, which England, exploiting the rules and the guarantees laid down in 1648, would henceforth manipulate through active balancing. As indicated, England was not a signatory to the Westphalian treaties and thus had to act through other states, initially the Dutch Republic. After the Glorious Revolution and the union with Scotland, London instigated Holland's demands on Sweden in 1714 (concerning shipping access to the Baltic), according to Marx on behalf of Dutch and English private commercial interests – never mind the defence treaty with Sweden concluded in 1700. The eventual settlement (which Marx dates as of 1715, actually the treaties of Stockholm and Nystadt of 1719–21) terminated Sweden's regional supremacy. It ushered in the Russian empire as a European power, thus recruiting for British diplomacy a much more powerful ally for future emergencies (Marx 1983: 102–3).

In line with its wider commercial interests and in the name of peace, liberal–constitutional Britain threw its weight behind the reactionary continental powers against France, the ascendant contender. This was not out of love for despotism, as one observer has taken it to mean (Drischler 2006). Britain rather became the smiling witness to the dynastic game of territorial acquisition and succession arrangements, siding with Austria against Louis XIV and again in the Austrian War of Succession. Britain did ensure there would be no Austrian interlopers in overseas trade, but otherwise was happy to let the contestants fight it out (Teschke 2003: 228). In the Seven Years' War, Britain fought with Prussia against Austria and France; as early as 1762 it abandoned its North German ally again and alternately conferred with Austria and Russia over a partition of Prussian territory. In the Napoleonic wars, Austria and England were once more on the same side. Ideological antipathies against Austria (or Russia) were entirely subordinated to playing the balance of power. As Marx and Engels emphasise (*MEW*, xiv: 492–3), the novelty of British foreign policy was cool-headed calculation. Protestant England might dislike Catholic Austria; liberal England, conservative Austria; free-trade England, protectionist Austria; liquid England, bankrupt Austria – and yet Austria was the card to play.

Germany ascended to the status of the main contender of the Anglophone heartland's hegemony after 1871, with France uneasily integrated on the side of the English-speaking states. Russia remained the ally through two world wars in the twentieth century, again notwithstanding any Western 'dislike' of tsarist autocracy or Stalinist state socialism. Only when the USSR after 1945 took the place of the Axis contenders did political antagonism fully develop, unaffected by the relaxation of the despotic aspects of Soviet communism after 1953.

Contender State Nationalisms and Ethno-Transformation

One of the fissures in the Marxist theoretical legacy runs between the classical writings on capitalist development on the one hand and on national self-determination on the other. The former will usually be firmly anchored in the historical materialist approach, highlighting processes of class formation in connection with structural forces; the second easily drift off into political calculation, tactics even, in the debates on the chances and modalities of socialist revolution. From the analysis of capitalism, the Marxist classics tended to draw the conclusion that the world was on the path to what we now call globalisation, laying the foundations for socialism. On the practical issue of working-class strategy in Europe, however, what confronted them was a world of difference incompatible with existing state boundaries.

Since capital crystallised in the context of the Anglophone heartland, the cosmopolitan, globalising drive may be traced to the combined forces of capital and Western hegemony. For all other states, capital emerged on the perimeter, as a force operating from and in tandem with the liberal West enjoying a crucial set of first-mover advantages. As Teschke writes (2003: 250), 'international relations from 1688 to the First World War and beyond were about the geopol-itically mediated and contested negotiation of the modernisation pressures that emanated from capitalist Britain'. These pressures had an uneven impact, exposing pre-industrial societies to shock-like accelerations and transformations as they tried to adjust. This then triggered the particular form of national self-assertion against the West; in Nairn's words (1981: 341), 'The socio-historical cost of this rapid implantation of capitalism into world society was national-ism.' Let us review how this worked out for the main contenders, for whom a single ethnos can be assumed to have constituted the social basis of the claim to sovereign equality, including protection by a popular standing army and mercantilism.

France emerged as the arbiter between English overseas supremacy and Continental fragmentation, unable to impose itself on either. How could it overcome the centrifugal effects of the collapse of Western Christianity?

To begin with, the religious civil war with the Calvinists was settled by the Edict of Nantes of 1598 under King Henry IV, who famously gained the throne for the House of Bourbon by converting to Catholicism himself. This was the French counterpart of Augsburg, but without the territorial aspect; on the contrary, it gave the monarchy the opportunity to accelerate political–administrative unification. Detailed maps were produced 'with a view to planning the infrastructure of the kingdom and to help plan the distribution of the defensive forts and military garrisons throughout the terri-tory' (Escolar 2003: 34). A single French language was codified in the same period by Malherbe, on the basis of the Francien dialect of the Île-de-France and the *langues d'oïl* (cf. maps in Deutsch 1966: 42 and Ostler 2006: 405). The rival south-east (the region of the *langues d'oc*) lost out. Paris became the undisputed commercial and administra-tive centre, certainly, as Braudel points out (1984: 326–7), once Italian merchants had repatriated from Lyon to Genoa.

All along, the attempt to emulate English development was mortgaged by the need to preserve the existing class rule of the landowning aristocracy and the absolutist political system. As in all contender states, this produced what Gramsci (1971: 114) calls *pas-sive revolution*: the inescapable but half-hearted introduction of the new by the forces of the old. The means for modernisation had to be obtained centrally, 'through a continuous pressure, economic and extra-economic, on the countryside' (Lefebvre 1976: 36); whereas in England they ended up in private hands through commerce and enclosure. To break the peasants' resistance and neutralise regional centres of authority, Richelieu ordered the walls of provincial towns to be torn down; his successor Mazarin defeated the revolt against centralisation, the Fronde. Louis XIV then completed political unification; he also sought to homogenise the social base by expelling the Huguenots. In contrast to neighbouring Spain, which, as Perry Anderson notes (1979: 101), remained characterised by 'its semi-territorial lay-out and interminable collective ruminations', France thus obtained a centralised state power, even though socially it was still 'a mosaic of small *pays*' (Braudel 1984: 354).

The French Revolution can be understood as the shock-like adjustment to the successive impositions of unified state power; as a way of mobilising society to assert France's position in the global political economy, *passive* revolution had run its course. The accumulated contradictions between the feudal exploitation of the peasantry and the attempt to modernise, fighting off British naval and commercial supremacy *and* conducting land wars to defend the territory, all exploded in the process (Schama 1990: 62). For the first time, the unifying force of democracy pervaded the country from below. Border communities were swept along in its surge: in no part of France, Engels notes (*MEW*, xxi: 445), was the revolution more enthusiastically supported than in German-speaking Alsace and Lorraine, among the Flemish of Dunkirk, the Celts of Brittany, or the Italians of Corsica. All of them adopted the French language, disseminated through mass education, elite schools, and the literary Olympians assembled in the Académie Française. As Rosenstock-Huessy concludes in this connection (1993: 178), from the French perspective a nation is not just a territory or ethnic entity; it is a spiritual creation, communicating its inspiration to the world through language. Thus 'it becomes civilised, it counts, it belongs to humanity in the sense of the humanism of the French Revolution'. Yet given the relations of force with the liberal English-speaking world, the state soon regained the initiative in social development. Under Napoleon, its role as the brain of society, absorbing all social energy, talents, and aspirations into itself, became the model for subsequent contender states (Lefebvre 1976: 29).

This takes us to Germany. In terms of ethno-transformation, Germany's contender role can be summed up as *the failed attempt to achieve a national state under conditions of sovereign equality* (Alff

1976: 10). There are international determinants in the process which are comparable to the case of France; the ethno-transformative aspect also includes a crucial complication absent there, but ubiquitous as we move eastwards across central Europe – the ethnic differential between city and countryside. German was spoken as far north as Livonia and eastwards to the Volga. Beyond the river Oder and the upper Danube, however, German speakers (ethnic Germans and Jews) were concentrated in the cities; Slavs, Hungarians, and Rumanians populated the surrounding countryside. Even in mid-nineteenth-century St Petersburg, Budapest, or Constantinople, Engels writes (*MEW*, viii: 50), the artisan, small shopkeeper, and factory owner would be a German; the money-lender, publican, and peddler, a Jew. In Prague, Vienna, and in all the cities of the German-speaking core, too, large Jewish constituencies had grown up around the earlier nodes of 'living money'. The tortuous process of forging a German national unity against the hegemonic, liberal West would here have its most terrible impact. It was terminated only by Germany's integration into the rival blocs of West and East and, since 1991, into an expanding European structure in which forms of global governance have already replaced sovereign equality in key areas.

From its frontier position on the Baltic and the ancient *branibor* separating it from the Slavs, Prussia's rise within Germany left the imprint of militarism on the process. The revolution from above was triggered by defeat against Napoleon. The Stein–Hardenberg reforms of the state and the Gneisenau–Scharnhorst reforms of the army created institutions of renown abroad and unquestionable authority at home (Rosenstock-Huessy 1961: 418–24). Unification was then achieved by Bismarck's military victories over Austria in 1866 and over France in 1870–71. With the annexation of iron and steel producing Alsace-Lorraine, it unleashed the forces of rapid industrialisation that earlier customs union schemes had failed to achieve. 'Organised capitalism' was concentrated in highly advanced industrial centres, set in a socially backward and in the east, ethnically heterogeneous, countryside (Spohn and Bodemann 1989: 78–9). Militarism pervaded society to a degree unknown elsewhere except for Japan. As Engels notes (*MEW*, xviii: 583), upon its victory over France, the German empire had 4 million men under arms, 10 per cent of the population. Militarist nationalism articulated and sublimated the profound imbalances within the German social formation; in this case, as in Japan's, Nairn's claim about the connection with the implantation of capitalism applies without qualifications.

The decision to launch what became the First World War aimed at sustaining the challenge to the liberal West, whilst blocking the way to the labour movement and democracy, all in passive revolution mode. Modern weapons and antiquated values alike entered the fray. The German mentality at the outbreak of the war, Alff writes (1976: 163), was built around 'diffuse expressions of an expansive force, and ideologies derived from it quickly regressed to mere natural categories'. Fischer's work (1984) documents this in detail. Racist thinking, bloodbaths among Belgian civilians, and gas warfare all heralded a future few could yet imagine. The myth that defeat in the First World War had been the work of socialists and Jews stabbing the valiant army in the back then identified the domestic targets for the second stage of the German quest for world power. France, central Europe, and the Slav east were again designated as zones of expansion (Opitz 1977).

Anglo-American and Dutch investments in the 1920s made the economy a paying concern for capital again, but the Weimar republic failed to contain the Left by parliamentary means (Abraham 1981). When the crisis of the early 1930s struck, racist nationalism, which had been brewing ever since the humiliating peace of Versailles and the revolutionary upheavals of 1918–19, was geared to violent internal repression, as a prelude to a resumption of the war. Three weeks after Hindenburg appointed him chancellor in January 1933, Hitler told an audience of industrialists (Kühnl 1980: 201–2 doc. 109) that

a private economy cannot be maintained in the age of democracy; it only becomes thinkable when the people obtain a guiding idea of authority and personality ... It is impossible that one part of the people embraces private property, whilst another part rejects it ... We must now seize all means of power if we want to bring down the other side completely.

Still, his wealthy supporters were wary of the promises the Nazis had made to their working-class following on the way to power. In August 1934, however, two months after the massacre of the plebeian SA leadership by the SS, Hitler was able to declare at the Nuremberg conference of the NSDAP (ibid.: 242–3 doc. 134) that 'the national-socialist revolution as a revolutionary seizure of power has been completed ... The nervous epoch of the nineteenth century has found its final conclusion with us. In the next thousand years, there will be no more revolution in Germany.'

The German armed forces had by then developed the principles of mobile warfare applied by the West into their own concept of *Blitzkrieg*. Formally denied tanks, an air force, or a general staff, the skeleton German army wanted to trump the Allies at their own game in the next round, and it is of importance that command in 1920 was entrusted to General Hans von Seeckt, a horse cavalry man, who had served on the Eastern front. Here the Germans had been able to use movement, surprise, and encirclement, all the characteristics of mobile warfare. In the Battle of Tannenberg in the East Prussian plains, they actually employed armoured cars as 'super-cavalry'. Seeckt allowed Heinz Guderian, a captain on his staff, to prepare and conduct exercises at the tank school of the German army in Kazan, deep inside the USSR, under the secret clauses of the 1922 Treaty of Rapallo (there was also a clandestine German flying school at Lipetsk). Applying shock-troop tactics tried out on the Western front to autonomous armoured divisions with air support, Guderian created a force that would prove unstoppable until 1942 (Adair 2004: 18–20; on Seeckt, see Gossweiler 1982). When Hitler came to power, secretly developed tank prototypes began to be mass-produced by Krupp and Daimler-Benz, using the latest assembly-line technologies. They would be unleashed first against Poland in 1939, to devastating effect.

Here we see how war works as an equaliser, not only in technical terms, but also in transmitting tactical principles among belligerents. Britain and France were helpless when the German armies overran Western Europe in 1940. After a delay, mobile warfare was adopted by the USSR as well. Initially, the Soviet Union only survived the onslaught of June 1941 by dismantling large parts of its arms–industrial infrastructure and reassembling them in safe locations in the Urals. The command economy, tight party control, but also a surge of popular resistance to the Nazi invasion, all combined to accomplish this amazing feat (Werth 1964: 208–18). Certainly the Red Army after the Civil War had been transformed into a regular Soviet army on the basis of the most advanced insights of armoured warfare under M.V. Frunze and M.N. Tukhachevsky. The revolution in this respect removed any conservatism of the type that undermined British and French preparedness. However, Tukhachevsky and many of his colleagues perished in the purges of the military leadership in 1937–38, and static defence under often inexperienced commanders contributed to the incredible losses of 1941–42. Also, the gap between the evacuation of industry and the actual resumption of mass production proved almost fatal, as it took time to coordinate product lines and mobilise and sustain a sufficient workforce in new surroundings. But once the T-34 tank, with its broad tracks, high speed, and heavy gun, began to roll out of the new factories in 1942 and the Soviet command had taken steps to improve the Red Army's capacity for mobile warfare, the struggle entered a new phase (Adair 2004: 41, 44–5).

In the end, wars are won or lost by the quality of the community entering the fight, its capacity to organise itself, and its spirit – much more than by the quality of the arms it carries. Thus amidst a return to military professionalism and a tightening of discipline after the dramatic fall of Rostov in July 1942, there occurred a surge of patriotism, with all the Soviet Union's major writers involved in raising the battle cry to defend the fatherland. Women's committees urged the men to hold their ground. The party-state leadership then waded into this campaign, cautioning that the will to fight was not to be enforced by harsh disciplinary measures in the field, but by persuasion and example. This subtle shift, surprising in light of the desperate military situation, contributed to a growing mood of defiance, 'a frantic feeling in the country that if the Germans were not to be stopped [at Stalingrad and in the Caucasus foothills], the war would be as good as lost' (Werth 1964: 377, and ch. 5 on the post-Rostov reforms).

For Germany, the war in the east brought the European *Grossraum*, the enlarged living space on which its challenge to the West was premised, within reach. It now had to be reordered also in ethnic terms, in line with the Nazi ideology. Poles, Ukrainians, Russians, and other Slavs for the Nazis were indeed slaves, meant to serve as an agrarian sub-population and exposed to extreme brutality throughout the war. In addition, Germany began a programme of demographic reordering of the cities across Europe, aimed at removing the Jewish urban middle classes to make room for Germans. What began in 1933 as a boycott of shops and restaurants shifted gear when Jews could no longer pay to emigrate and were concentrated in ghettos, without income. As Germany braced itself for the struggle with the USSR, Nazi population engineers became concerned about the 30 to 50 million 'useless eaters', Jews and others, under their rule. As Aly and Heim write (1993: 15), with all resources mobilised, a labour shortage of between 1 million and

2 million, and the infrastructure strained to breaking point, the demographics of occupied Europe remained 'the only economic "factor" [Nazi planners] could still effectively change'.

In the summer of 1941 it was therefore decided that those from whom no productive contribution was to be expected should be exterminated. Even a starving ghetto needed a daily arrival of hundreds of wagonloads of provisions; the transport of people to their death on the other hand was a matter of one trip. Every day during which a ghetto like that of Warsaw remained in existence had to be balanced against the requirements of supplying the front, given that the existing rail network was already utilised to maximum capacity (Aly and Heim 1993: 296–7). This led to Auschwitz, a combination of forced labour camp and extermination site. Here and in other camps, around 6 million Jews and other undesirables were murdered by industrial methods. Soviet prisoners of war and forced labourers, Poles, and others died of malnutrition or exhaustion, or were killed upon capture in their millions, too, in an inferno of annihilation such as the world had never seen.

The murderous rationalisation of the demography along racist principles did not reverse the fortunes of war. German industry attempted to emulate Soviet tank technology with the Panther, which had the sloping front armour but not the aluminium diesel engine of the T-34, nor the particular alloy armour plating for which the Germans lacked the raw materials. The Panther was thrown into the decisive tank battle of Kursk in July/August 1943 before all mechanical problems had been solved. The other new German tank, the 58-tonne Tiger, designed by Porsche and produced by Krupp, was an even more formidable machine. It had frontal armour plating of 100 mm, impervious to penetration; at Stalingrad however, its role was reduced to that of a gun emplacement on tracks (Cawthorne 2003: 177). Indeed in the fighting retreat of the Nazi armies, the advantage of mobile warfare now passed to the Soviet side. Hitler, meanwhile holding all key positions of responsibility as minister of war and commander of the army, resorted to his own wartime experiences in the First World War to develop the concept of *fester Platz*, a fortified town not to be surrendered. The idea of not yielding an inch, derived from the struggle in the trenches, thus undercut the German army's greatest advantage, its capacity for mobile warfare. Ordered to hold their ground at all costs, entire armies were encircled and destroyed in the retreat from Belarus (Adair 2004: 66–7).

Just as the Soviet defenders finally stood their ground at Stalingrad by mobilising the profoundest survival instincts, the Germans kept fighting against all odds, in the knowledge that from the Soviet side, the retribution for the crimes they had committed would be merciless. Divided among the occupying powers in 1945, the country's western parts were aligned in the Atlantic line-up against the USSR, the east incorporated as a separate socialist state until the collapse of 1989. Germany only regained its sovereignty in the context of an expanding European Union; NATO membership keeps the English-speaking West in a position of control.

Let me conclude this section by briefly summing up how nationalist ethno-transformation affected the other main Axis powers and contenders to Western hegemony, Italy and Japan.

Italy's unification has been analysed by Gramsci as the work of Piedmont, a quasi-Prussia leading a revolution from above – but without the militaristic aspect and with a conservatism that even served to retard the process (Gramsci 1975, i: 101–2). Italy's rise to contender status had very much a residual quality in that it filled a space created by the decline of Austria and the failure of France to dominate European affairs. Hence Gramsci's conclusion (1978: 129) that 'the Italian bourgeoisie succeeded in organizing its state not so much through its own intrinsic strength, as through being favoured in its victory over the feudal and semi-feudal classes by a whole series of circumstances of an international character'. One aspect of Italy's ethnogenesis deflated its expansive force though – mass emigration. The crisis of Italian agriculture that resulted from the concentration of land ownership and the marginalisation of small producers propelled the emigration of Italians to neighbouring countries in the 1860s. As the stream of dispossessed small peasants grew, the destination moved across the Atlantic, to Argentina and Brazil; and, after the turn of the century, to the United States (Wolf 1997: 371). As we saw, English emigration involved the transfer to North America of an independent-minded, self-conscious population. For Germans, too, that was the sociological profile even though they became submerged again into English and Spanish-language societies on arrival. From Italy, however (and here Gramsci again may be taken as our guide, 1975, i: 132), it was the reserve army of labour from the south of the country that was pushed to emigrate, leaving an overpopulation of intellectuals and middle classes behind. Hence, he adds, Italian emigration to the United States, Argentina, and other destinations did not stop because the home country had restored a demographic balance, but because an equilibrium had been reached with the rest of the world.

Japan, too, can be seen as a frontier formation (of imperial China). It likewise 'turned inward' to take over the sedentary formation facing it; but there the comparison ends. As the ethnic foundations for an imperial unity under Japanese hegemony were lacking, a war of aggression ensued instead. The imperative for Japan to modernise had been brought home by the West: in the wake of the Anglo-French Opium Wars against China, it was enough that a flotilla of American warships under Commodore Perry appeared on Japan's shores in 1853 to enforce the opening of Japan's ports to foreign trade. The Japanese revolution from above, the Meiji restoration of 1868, expressly sought inspiration in the Stein–Hardenberg model of 'bureaucratic constitutionalism', which by now had become the gold standard of the passive revolution. Even more than in Prussia–Germany, however, industry was immersed in a decomposing feudal society; Norman (1940: 58) speaks of 'the introduction of capitalism into the clans'.

Japanese militarism, a by-product of the rapid transformation of a landed society by a directive state, had many traits in common with Prussia's. In both cases, they go back to their respective frontier roles combined with internal uneven development. Japan's military displayed a keen sense of naval mobility, first in the war with Russia in 1904/5, and again when they employed aircraft carriers for the surprise attack on Pearl Harbour. Unlike the Germans (and helped of course by the fact it took place at sea), they persisted in mobile warfare in the retreat, as when they used their (by then useless) carriers as a decoy force in the Leyte Gulf battle (Brodie 1970: 52).

Emigration, too, played a part in Japanese development at this stage. In 1923, the government, concerned about population size in proportion to food supply, reorganised the institutions associated with overseas settlement, introducing generous subsidies for relocation. Japanese indentured labour emigration was briefly mentioned in the last chapter. Military expansion in the 1930s also aimed at the resettlement of Japanese to mainland Asia; Manchuria's wide-open spaces as much as its resources had been at the heart of imperialist strategy from the turn of the century (Storry 1967: 189). However, as Spellman writes (2002: 143), 'the goal of demographic redistribution was never achieved and the Japanese remained a tiny and ... physically isolated minority in each of their colonies'.

Multinational Contender States

Let us now turn to two contender states which were constitutionally multinational, Austria–Hungary and the USSR. Here the very notion of ethnic homogeneity was an impossibility.

Austria–Hungary was the last remnant of the 'mediaeval cosmopolis' of Western Christianity, with a frontier sector facing the Ottomans. Comprising 14 separate nationalities, the Habsburg empire was in 1741 compelled to strike a deal with the most powerful non-German nationality, the Hungarians, to obtain their support for Maria Theresia's succession to the throne in the face of foreign opposition. In 1867, a year after the humiliating defeat at the hands of Prussia, the Ausgleich ('compromise') formally created the Dual Monarchy. However, as Rosenstock-Huessy argues (1961: 415), given the scale of concessions granted to the Hungarian nobility, the empire would not survive another deal on these lines. So when in 1918, amidst the ravages of defeat in war, the Czechs had to be accommodated as a sovereign equal, this contributed to the empire's final collapse. Let me briefly outline how Czech nationalism evolved as a separate ethnogenetic trajectory in the broader contender context.

Emperor Joseph II, who cherished the ambition to become German Emperor after the death of Frederick 'the Great' of Prussia a few years later, in 1780 initiated his policy of centralisation and imperial reform, inaugurating the revolution from above. The imposition throughout the empire of German as the official language sparked off national conflict, but in Bohemia, measures terminating serfdom and the abolition of the guilds also offered chances to reverse an economic decline that had hit the prosperous German-speaking border areas earlier in the century. The question of who would take up the task of industrialisation would have important consequences though.

Now as Halperin has argued (1997: ch. 4), the aristocracy, as a landed class liable to expropriation in a money economy, has tended to be the driving force of nationalism, not the bourgeoisie. In the case of Bohemia this was certainly how it started. Count Palacký, the key figure in early nineteenth-century Czech nationalism, even refused to attend the (German) Frankfurt pre-parliament in 1848, claiming he was a Czech and thus dissociating himself from the democratic bourgeoisie. Instead he proposed that the Slavs of the empire would form a political bloc, what became known as

'Austro-Slavism'. The 1905 revolt in Russia however raised the profile of the eastern brothers and a Slav congress convening in Prague in 1908 declared itself in favour of drawing closer to Russia, the doctrine of Neo-Slavism (Seton-Watson 1943: 186–7; Macartney 1969: 353). All non-German nationalities by now were looking beyond Austria for sovereign statehood and protection.

In the meantime, industrialisation and urbanisation were generating important demographic shifts. In 1890, half of the population of Bohemia had moved away from their place of birth, raising the identity issue to the centre of attention. In Prague in 1900, new arrivals accounted for 60 per cent, most from Czech-speaking areas (Mommsen 1963: 33; Havránek 1967: 226). The development of a Czech agro-industrial complex with its own financial sector (*Živnostenska Banka* was founded in 1865), rivalling the ethnic German textile sector linked to the banks in Vienna, furthermore entailed a process of class formation of a Czech-speaking bourgeoisie (Šolle 1969: 24, 34). Jews too now began to consider themselves as Czechs and speak the language. This in turn produced venomous eruptions of anti-Semitism on the part of German-speakers amidst a general exacerbation of antagonism between German and Czech Bohemians. After the collapse of Austria–Hungary in 1918, this would engender Nazi support among Sudeten-Germans, and, after 1945, the revenge expulsion of Germans of which the Czech communist party made itself the champion (Kosta 1978: 21).

Clearly by 1900 there was an element of international bourgeois competition driving Czech ethnogenesis, so that we cannot simply see it as an aristocratic atavism any longer. More importantly, progressive democrats and socialists were by then looking beyond nationalism and indeed, to multinational Austria–Hungary as a model for the future. This was the drift of the Austro-Marxist contributions to the national self-determination debates raging at the time. Since a large state was necessary to create the material conditions for socialism, the Austrian socialists held that an internal passport system entitling members of each ethnos to their own language and education would uncouple nationality from the territorial state as an administrative structure (Shaheen 1956: 56–7).

Lenin and Stalin attacked the Austro-Marxist theses on the grounds that these assumed that ethnic difference was a fixed instead of a historical, and hence passing phenomenon (cf. my 1996: 113–17). The Bolsheviks maintained that nationalities should strive for their own territorial sovereign state, since this would allow the workers to claim the nationality issue for socialism and outflank bourgeois particularism – whilst retaining the option of integration later. Lenin (*Coll. Works*, 21: 102–6) more particularly warned against the ingrained Great Russian chauvinism, which he feared would alienate other nationalities such as the Ukrainians for good. After the revolution, Finns, Poles, and the Baltic nations indeed broke away from the 'prison of the peoples'. But separatism could not be allowed to become a tool of Western-supported counter-revolution either. Hence Georgia and other areas hesitant to be integrated into the emergent Soviet Union were forcibly brought into it. The Baltic states were annexed to the USSR again as part of the division of Poland agreed with Hitler's Germany in 1939; parts of Poland, East Prussia and Rumania were recouped in 1945.

Ethnic diversity in tsarist Russia, however, was not just a matter of horizontally bounded territorial communities. Like central and eastern Europe, it was imbricated with class and urban/landed divisions in endlessly complex ways. In Ukraine and Belarus, large landowners, capitalists, lawyers, and journalists were Russians, Poles, Jews, and foreigners; Ukrainians and Belarussians lived on the land. In the Baltic provinces, cities were centres of the German, Russian, and Jewish bourgeoisie; the land was Latvian or Estonian. Russians and Armenians dominated the cities of Georgia and Azerbaijan, and so on (Trotsky 1978, iii: 1023).

Even in the heart of old Russia, complex ethnic legacies of a distant past persisted. Thus the Mordvins, divided into two peoples (possibly ancient tribes), the Erzya and the Moksha, had been subject to raids by Khazar and Bulgarian nomads throughout the Middle Ages. They survived the Mongol conquests and the tsarist policy of Russian settlement. All through, the two branches of the Mordvin remained separately identifiable and two languages evolved. An eighteenth-century ethnographer describes them as being of Finnish origin, and notes that the languages of the two tribes have become increasingly mixed. 'Since they have been under the Russian government, they employ themselves in the cultivation of the land; and they have a great dislike of living in large towns.' At the time of this visitor's travel (1793/4), they still held on to the tribal habit of purchasing wives, at the then current price of 10 roubles or £2 (Pallas, Johnston, and Miller 1990: 28). Fringe groups of the Mordvin were absorbed into adjacent ethnoi, such as the Karatais, who settled among the Tatars and adopted Tatar language but continued to call themselves Mordvins; or the Tyuryukhans in

Nizhni Novgorod province, who were Russified and spoke Russian in tsarist times (*Authors' collective* 1982: 51).

It is no surprise, then, that the tsarist empire had difficulty defining a criterion for all these differences. Eventually it chose language as the most reliable for the first census held in 1897, arriving at a total of 146, including dialects (Masanov 2002: 8). Only the army was entirely Russian-speaking, as it was mostly recruited from Russia, Belarus and the Ukraine; Muslims were exempt from service. Tsarist officers at the time liked to compare their army with 'the Austrians' ragbag of races and languages' (Ostler 2006: 439).

Sovereign equality between language groups had never been contemplated, neither by the tsar's government nor by the Bolsheviks. The national groupings varied too much in the degree of ethnogenesis, measured by such criteria as literacy and way of life. Lenin considered the idea of equality of nations as petty bourgeois anyway, at odds with socialist internationalism and the radical self-determination meant to support it (*Coll. Works*, 31: 148). However, as a contender to the West, the USSR had to mobilise all the advantages of a large social base including a common language (Russian), and yet preserve its commitment to national self-determination – including, very much along the lines of the Austro-Marxist theses, the right to one's own language and culture. In the Soviet census of 1926, not language, but 'ethnicity' was therefore taken as the criterion of difference. Each of the 194 ethnoi thus found was assigned either a union republic, an autonomous republic, a *krai*, an *oblast* or a *raion*. Those who did not qualify for an administrative–territorial unit of their own were termed *narodnost'* (national grouping). Hence as Masanov emphasises (2002: 8), the official ethnic diversity of the USSR was not the result of actual ethnogenesis, but imposed from above; an aspect of the confiscation of the social sphere by the contender state. The Soviet state went beyond even the Austro-Marxist project by bringing in, through the back door, the criterion of territoriality, again from above. Sometimes territory was enlarged as a reward for good behaviour, as when Khrushchev 'gave' the Crimea to Ukraine; in harsher times, it was taken away entirely, as in Stalin's deportation of the Crimean Tatars.

Ethnicity thus became an artificial construction not unlike the colonial boundaries drawn across Africa. Once the policy of the Soviet leadership to keep the USSR together began to unravel, real diversity clashed with the often fanciful dividing lines. Carrère d'Encausse (1979: 58–9) in the 1970s identified a crucial rift when she observed a 'clear-cut line of cleavage in Soviet demography' between the western republics, with their lower than (Soviet) average population growth, and the Central Asian and Caucasus republics, characterised by rapid population growth well above the average. In a prophetic recommendation concerning these fast-growing and modernising ethnic communities in the southern USSR, she argued (1979: 88) that 'Soviet policy must bank on the continuing dynamism and particularism of these peoples, and not on the standardization of the Soviet population's behaviour patterns.'

However, a challenger to the West tends to congeal into the contender posture precisely in this respect. The dramas of Yugoslavia, Armenia and Azerbaijan, Georgia and its breakaway regions, but also the petty chauvinisms in the Ukraine, Moldova, and the Baltic states, all testify to the anomalies created by the revolution from above and the tectonic forces that are unleashed once the structures created by state ethnic ordering begin to move and collide with active ethnogenesis (imbricated with class formation) from below. The role of the West has of course been momentous too, as I have argued elsewhere (2006: chs 7, 8 and 10). Playing on ethnic chauvinism provided a lever for carving up the contender state; it has certainly influenced the new nationalism in post-Soviet Russia, shaped also in the response to the ethnic rebellion of Chechnya.

TRIBAL TRAILS AND URBAN JUNGLES

If contender states such as Austria–Hungary or the Soviet Union, each containing highly civilised populations and commanding tremendous wealth and resources, in the end failed to maintain their integrity in the face of the triumphant West and succumbed to internal centrifugal forces – what about the more fragile formations further out on the periphery? The sovereign equality mode, the grid on which a contender state's claim to independence is made, does not by itself bestow the power to vindicate this claim. For most of the world's states, their only chance to survive intact is by using the geopolitical manoeuvring space created by the heartland–contender struggle for those on its margins, drawing premiums and licences from the main contest in order to bolster their own development (Berger 2001: 213; on Africa, see Lavelle 2005).

The nation-state model, by its implication of ethnic homogeneity or at least stability, and the need to mobilise society behind some sort of contender posture, creates strains on the less powerful states which their state classes managed only, and in hindsight superficially, as long as the Soviet Union challenged the West. The USSR was able to provide clients with the resources to bolster state power, forcing the West to do the same. Now that it has collapsed, the linchpin of that order has been removed. Although China's ascent is no doubt invigorating certain weak states, notably in Africa and Latin America, the bandwidth of its contender posture is confined to its immediate raw material needs. It compares in no way to the challenge posed by the Soviet Union in terms of the political ramifications of its socialist birthmark, planned economy, and military parity with the West.

The historical role of the modern state consists in abolishing the 'autonomies' (Gramsci's term, 1971: 54) associated with ways of life other than the dominant one, and relegating them to a private sphere distinct from citizenship. In most post-colonial states, this process remained incomplete, and when great-power patronage fell away, it was in many cases reversed. The capacity of what Marx calls the 'natural powers', viz., the original communities or castes, to 'reach agreement with the state' (*MEW Ergänzungsband*, i: 419) is in fact enhanced again; but the 'natural powers' themselves have left their original condition behind, too. Their identity and life-world, indicative of ethnogenetic trajectories often different from the ethnos from which the state class emanates, is also a product of ongoing socialisation. The intervention of the West in the lives of peoples on other continents was and remains a key threshold in this process.

As a result of the discoveries and the colonial encounter, the way of life that previously appeared as natural or God-given is cast in a new light and opened up to questioning. There was always a difference, however, between how this worked out for those for whom discovery broadened the limits of the possible, and for those who were the 'discovered'. What was new about the critical utopias of Thomas More, Francis Bacon, and Swift, Benedict Anderson argues (1991: 69), was that they could be presented as distant but otherwise as contemporary; 'the discoveries had ended the necessity of seeking models in a vanished antiquity'. The distant fantasy islands were metaphors for how *their own world* should be remade.

On the other side of the equation, the effect was of a different nature, although also 'critical' with respect to existing authority. In the case of the Tupi–Guarani Amerindian community in Brazil, Clastres (1987: 214–15) describes how the advent of Europeans led to 'an awakening of society itself to its own nature as primitive society, an awakening, an uprising, that … had destructive effects on the power of the chiefs'. Very soon after the initial encounter, indigenous preachers were going from one group to the next, inciting them to go and search for the Land Without Evil, the earthly paradise; thus articulating that their original community had expired. The fantasy world of spirits and dreams thus assumed an earthly form, too, but not as an exercise in political philosophy. The Land Without Evil *existed*, and it had to be *reached*; assimilating the foreign way of life imposed from the outside became the high road for getting there.

Various indigenous elites in the colonial context sought to interpose themselves as mediators between the superior foreign world and their own discredited way of life. Not unlike shamans and priests in the authentic tribal context, they offered to lead their community to the promised land; in this case, to national statehood. But unlike the religious officers of old, the authority they claimed was being negated at the same time by colonial rule; the more so to the degree that they embraced a Western lifestyle, dress, and idiom. It made the Westernisers 'internal strangers' in their own milieu, with aspirations incomprehensible to others, or just out of reach. Membership of their community was 'placed in question in everyday forms of social interaction' (Lubkemann 2003: 76).

The Westernised elite in early twentieth-century Bengal, the Bhadralok, offer an example of what happens if national aspirations are developed with disregard for the uneven impact of foreign rule on indigenous society. As Broomfield recounts (1968: 60), 'There existed in Bengal at this time a number of distinct levels of politics, and, for a politician to be successful, he had to be capable of speaking in different idioms.' The Bhadralok were *un*successful, and to keep them off balance, the British created separate Muslim electorates, to which they gave favourable treatment. This led the frustrated Bhadralok to take recourse, paradoxically, to 'communalism and terrorism' (ibid.: 281). Ghandi's donning of indigenous dress and his all-India *satyagraha* campaign can be understood as a counter-strategy, trumping the British at their own game; and one only has to think of how the Islamist Hamas movement has long been supported by Israel to tackle the Arab nationalist Fatah from within the Palestinian ranks, to emerge as the more radical opposition recently (Enderlin 2006), to see that this game continues to be played along these lines.

Indigeneity thus becomes a contested political terrain itself, but never in its pristine form. *No* community bond can survive the

colonial encounter intact. Foreign rule undermines the entire cosmology built around its relationship to nature and to others. In the
case of the tribe, its identity by totemic lineage is distorted by what
Hilda Kuper calls (as in Vincent 1990: 219) 'new types of death and
the attitude to the dead'. Thus for Swazi tribal people,

Death by disease, death under the baton of the police, the whip of the
farmer ... is neither a noble sacrifice, nor is it regarded as a politico-economic
venture which will benefit the people and maintain the culture of the dead
worker.

In the colonial context, therefore, tribal bonds were recast as
structures of survival premised on a perceived 'cheapness of individuals'. On the surface, they are reinforced, but no longer with the
same complex of meaning attached to them. With sovereignty gone,
what remains are only lines of fracture and fission in the face of
foreign authority, to which tribal labels become attached. 'Instead of
organizing the sheiks and the chiefs against the [Westernised] "revo-
lutionaries" in the towns, native committees organize the tribes and
confraternities into parties', Fanon writes (1968: 118–19). 'Confronted
with the urban party which was beginning to "embody the national
will", ... splinter groups are born, and tendencies and parties which
have their origin in ethnic or regional differences.'

Decolonisation cannot overcome this as long as it is merely a
compromise with the former rulers to allow continued access in
exchange for a flag and a national anthem. Only modern state formation can hope to create a common citizenship, but this process
precisely is stagnating or even reversed. Migdal (1988: 29) quotes a
Senegalese minister as saying that clans, 'a Senegalese evil', are growing in strength. They have largely lost their connection with kinship
or ancestry and are instead channels of political, sometimes violent,
competition. Yet they engage in this competition in ways 'not sanctioned by the state and ... under rules different from those propounded by the state'. After independence, such cleavages pose a
direct threat to the unitary post-colonial state, because 'tribalism in
the colonial phase gives way to regionalism in the national phase'
(Fanon 1968: 114).

As a result, 'hill peoples against peoples of the plain', or other
interethnic distinctions, only indirectly refer to the original foreign
encounter once colonisation intervenes. In the genocide of Rwandan
Tutsis by Hutu militias in 1994, for instance, there was a legacy
juxtaposing Hutu cultivators to the originally pastoral, Tutsi warrior

class; but this had been interfered with by the Belgian colonial authorities by bolstering the Hutus. The Tutsi on the other hand more recently aligned themselves with the sweep of English-speaking influence across the formerly Franco-Belgian sphere of interest in Africa. When Tutsi exiles in the early 1990s began military operations from Uganda, the death of a Hutu president served as a signal for Hutu Interhamwe militias set up by the government to unleash well-prepared mass killings of the indigenous Tutsi population. So ultimately we are speaking of a modern event, premised on planning and media indoctrination, even though the incompatible life-worlds of farmers and pastoralists are a sediment of mutual perception (Nederveen Pieterse 1990: 238–9; Braeckman 1995).

In neighbouring DR Congo, formerly Zaire, tribalism is being recast as regionalism along the lines suggested by Fanon, aggravated by the influx of Rwandan refugees and by transnational struggles for control of the country's vast mineral wealth. Three to four million Congolese were killed in a protracted massacre, partly as a result of civil war, partly by the military intervention of the Western proxies, Uganda and the new Rwanda. They were also instrumental in imposing a new constitution on Congo, dividing the country into 26 provinces. With a guaranteed 40 per cent stake for each region in the proceeds of its own mineral exports, elections held in 2006 worked to foster centrifugal forces on top of privatisations that were already creating insecurity for hundreds of thousands of workers (Braeckman 2006: 12–13).

In the Niger delta of Nigeria, Western oil companies, using strategies from the same hymnbook, have cherry-picked certain tribal groups, whose modern identity dates from their role as partners for the British colonial authorities, to protect or otherwise participate in the extraction and transport infrastructure. Thus Chevron–Texaco preferentially employs Itsekiri, a coastal people who as slave traders had contact with Europeans early on, but not Ijaw or others. Indeed, as Zalik writes (2004: 113), 'the crystallisation of tribal identity through traditional authority structures central to colonial indirect rule [also] shape[s] the oil industry's divisive and clientelistic relations with local communities' (on the Ijaw, cf. Wolf 1997: 217).

In the Darfur region of Sudan, oil concessions to China and desertification have activated complex dividing lines between black African cultivators and Arab pastoral nomads, although it is the state class concern to maintain control over its oil-rich areas which lends the crisis its violent, genocidal edge (Prunier 2007). In the descent of

Somalia into warlordism, energy issues were likewise involved in what otherwise appears as the most straightforward case of state collapse; and many more examples might be added.

The idea then that authentic ethnic divisions are kept under a lid of some sort, whether by colonialism or by state socialism, only to come back with a vengeance once that lid is removed, is a misconception. Africa here is not different from Yugoslavia. Ethnogenesis and ethno-transformation are continuous processes in which new forms of exploiting nature and new ways of life, a changing interethnic milieu, and shifting perceptions of identity, take the place of prior ones. If prior forms of dealing with communities occupying separate spaces and considered outsiders make an apparent comeback, such a return is never complete either. If it occurs, it is by definition anchored in a regressive development of the productive forces, including the level of civilisation of the community and the quality of the state role. This also transpires in the neo-tribalisms crystallising around migration trails and refugee flows.

Migration and the Spatial Matrix of Globalisation

At some point during the 1970s, it might have seemed as if the world had finally conformed to the idea that foreign relations be made entirely coeval with inter-state relations of the Westphalian type. Yet it was then that the back door of the state system swung open again. The already feeble results of the weakest states' development efforts evaporated in the debt crisis, and states lost their capacity to maintain themselves as protective structures. Their populations as a result became directly exposed to the capitalist world market and to the violence of world politics (Vieille 1988: 247). As African and Latin American shares in world exports of goods declined to record lows, their societies shifted gear to exporting people, very much as China had done after the Opium Wars and India after British tariffs shut out its textiles. State collapse and warlordism have only accelerated these emigration flows (Overbeek 1995: 28, export figures in table 1.1). After the collapse of the Soviet bloc, a descent into mass poverty on an unprecedented scale has turned many former Soviet and allied People's Republics into exporters of people, too. The same goes for the Philippines, Bangladesh, and so on.

The bottom line in the process, inevitably, is the exhaustion of society and nature by over-exploitation. Senegalese fishermen complained for years that giant floating factories from EU countries were methodically depleting their coastal waters, leaving little or no fish for them to catch. In 2006, EU action was finally taken – not against over-fishing by its fleets, but against attempts by Senegalese using their flimsy fishing boats for a final try to reach the Canaries, in many cases paying for it with their lives. The UN High Commissioner for Refugees identifies some 20 million people as falling within his remit; half of those are internally displaced or stateless, some 8 million have crossed international borders (Stevens 2006: 53). Displacement for ecological reasons, such as desertification and rising sea levels, involves some 25 million, a figure expected to rise to 200 million in the coming half-century if no major change of policy is achieved (McCarthy 2006).

For most migrants, Davis' conclusion applies (1999: 27), that 'the sheer survival needs of households and communities dictate the increasingly difficult and dangerous trek northward'. It is there that they will find the other world, the world in which they hope to escape the agony of their current existence, the Land Without Evil. In the process of migration, however, the people on the move become foreigners once again, and their ethnicity is redefined. This is a process of ethno-transformation in its own right, whether in the collapse, in the flight, or on arrival. 'The dynamic nature of culture', Castles and Miller write (1998: 37), 'lies in its capacity to link a group's history and traditions with the actual situation in the migratory process. Migrant and minority cultures are constantly recreated on the basis of the needs and experience of the group and its interaction with the actual social development.'

In terms of foreign relations, the migratory experience induces a specific return to tribal patterns, as the state is by definition left by the wayside. In the words of Klein-Beekman (1996: 441), 'International migration is fundamentally concerned with spatiality and with the exercise of power through spatial practice.' Certainly, he adds, 'the state intervenes to (re)negotiate the boundary separating the foreigner and the citizen – the excluded from the included'. But since the migrants have left the state and are trying to reach another one (and there is an important legal distinction but little practical difference here whether they are refugees or seeking work), no sovereign authority is specifically concerned with their claim to space or their protection. Refugee camps and transit zones are officially outside the legal sphere of the host state and usually under the exclusive jurisdiction of humanitarian organisations (Stevens 2006: 66).

In tribal foreign relations, ancestry as we saw informs the claim to space. For migrants caught between a country of origin and an uncertain destiny, this becomes a matter of intense emotional attachment, the more so as their way of life is being reduced to the survival minimum in most cases. Identity, Willems argues (2003: 36),

can be viewed as a map comprising differently shaded regions. In general, at least two regions are shaded here, those of the country of birth, and, as people grow older, the realm of childhood, the landscape people take for granted at the time and yearn for later.

This constitutes the core component of a new collective identity that is constructed once 'immigrants add a different country to that map when they move away to a new society where they try to settle'.

Along the way, they are exposed to all kinds of threats. There is no protective structure in place to keep these at bay except for the idealised bonds of ancestry, often in sharp contrast to the wealthy and highly developed new environment they find on arrival. Hence, as Castles and Miller emphasise (1998: 37), a sharp regression towards tribal or religious 'fundamentalist' defence mechanisms may occur 'precisely [as] the result of modernisation [which is] experienced as discriminatory, exploitative and destructive of identity.' In terms of exchange, low-paid service jobs or dangerous manual work (if not the actual selling of their bodies) connect the newcomers with the foreign worlds they move into; remittances provide the link with the community of origin.

Reaching a safe haven, or getting stuck or worse on the way, fits into a zonal structure of population movement analysed by Rufin (1991). State collapse and inter-communal strife or ecological exhaustion in the country of origin; regional refugee camps; onward migration to the North under the auspices of state selection; and finally, residence with a passport – these are the main way-stations in the process, with large masses of people left behind at each stage. Let us go over each of these stages briefly.

The refugee camps on the imaginary frontier are the first port of call. Today, at least 3.5 million people live in sprawling camps in Africa and Asia (Stevens 2006: 53). Many of these camps emerged in those areas where, in the second half of the 1970s, 'Contras' were being recruited by the US to fight progressive and/or Soviet-supported state classes and liberation movements (Rufin 1991: 69–74). Turning entire societies into ghost states as arsenals of the Contra effort, this created transition points between the increasingly lawless South and the beckoning North. We may think of Afghanistan, with the adjacent tribal areas of Waziristan in Pakistan, home to many Afghan refugees; Ethiopia in combination with Somalia; several states of central America, the one a reservoir of Contra forces and refugee populations for another; Cambodia and Burma, and so on. In the 1991 Gulf War, 1.3 million refugees from Iraq's Shia population, encouraged by the United States to revolt against Saddam Hussein and ferociously repressed without succour, fled into Iran, whilst half a million Kurds got stuck in the mountain passes to Turkey, eventually being sent back into northern Iraq (Stevens 2006: 56–7). The area around Goma in DR Congo near the Rwandan border, the Darfur region of Sudan, and adjacent areas in Chad, provide further examples. The occupied territories around Israel, too, are reservoirs of desperate humanity held captive by borders. Human dramas of genocidal proportions are being played out in these zones, where migration trails have become blocked and exhaustive exploitation and the fixed territorial structures of state sovereignty become fatally conflated.

The next station for refugees on the way out of a collapsed state, war zone, or ecologically devastated region is reached when contact is established with the state offering a potential final destination. This contact can be in the recipient country after informal/illegal entry, at the actual border, through an embassy abroad, or even by visits to camps by representatives of the prospective host states seeking out those with qualifications. Salter (2004: 177) speaks of a 'diffuse regulatory mobility system' with three pillars: 'documentation, border policing, and international regulation'. This is the step that leads us into a 'world of difference' in which states enjoy the full possession of their sovereign powers; they use these as gatekeepers splitting up the displaced communities into those who can cross into the sovereign territorial jurisdiction of the recipient state and those who cannot. Thus, as Gabriel writes (2004: 164), 'migration policy emphasising the "high-skilled" becomes a means by which the nation-state creates a world-class labour force and secures comparative advantage'. 'Nation' might well be dropped here, because we have left the national–ethnic foundations of the state behind and are now in the realm of 'commercialised sovereignty' (Palan 2003: 157) or what Bobbitt calls (2002: part 3) the 'market-state'.

This gets us to the final stage, legitimate residence. At some point, this includes an option of return (i.e. without giving up the right to re-enter the host country again). This moment can come with the restoration of order, if the reason for flight was state collapse and warlordism, of legality after dictatorship, or otherwise. Even when ecological exhaustion lay behind the migration, those 'having made it', may return as tourists on an income secured elsewhere. In all cases, the assumption is that migration improves the material situation of refugees. Obtaining the right to return (and come back in again), or actually being *forced* to return, is a matter of selection, too. This blends into a more general distinction between those with credit and often multiple passports who can go where they like (and whom Attali calls 'hypernomads', 2003: 30) and the permanently displaced ('infranomads' in Attali's terminology). In modern-day Canada, for instance, those with sought-after transferable skills may obtain full citizenship, but Philippine women seeking work as domestics are only admitted under highly regulated conditions crucially involving the obligation to go back to the Philippines (Gabriel 2004: 166–7, 174–5).

Along the circuits linking area of origin and newly-occupied spaces, ethnogenesis and ethno-transformation continue, with many aspects of pre-modern modes of foreign relations in evidence. More and more communities 'have become effectively transnationalised' (Davis, 1999: 27), which is not the same as, say, 'globalised', because mutual foreignness persists among them. Migrants through the ages have clung to 'the myth of the short-term sojourn', as Castles and Miller call it (1998: 216; cf. Kolko, 1976: 69). This fantasy of eventual return works to maintain foreignness relative to the host ethnos as well as other immigrant communities, resulting in 'isolation, separatism and emphasis on difference'. This has usually been reciprocated by host communities feeling threatened by foreign presence; equally, different ethnic groups are often assigned their own job categories to raise the rate of exploitation and undermine any solidarity along class lines. Even today, when Latino immigrants in the US already represent, according to Davis (1999: 9), 'the fifth largest "nation" of Latin America', they in fact remain separate among themselves by the criterion of endogamy (with, for example, Mexican immigrants marrying within their own community in the United States; ibid.: 13).

As with commercial diasporas, trust found in family and ethnic connections allow community bonds to be operative over large distances. Where state protection is deficient or lacking, quasi-tribal 'transnationalities' at the lower end of the social spectrum offer their members a measure of social insurance in the informal economy (Castles and Miller 1998: 171). Sweatshop production sites and the supply of smuggled workers, but also the import and distribution of narcotics, are often controlled by ethnic communities for confidentiality. Friman (2004: 106–10), gives the example of Japan, where the indigenous *yakuza* syndicates monopolise the amphetamine market, whilst Iranians, Thais, and Koreans control niche markets for opium and cannabis.

Codes of honour bind migrants and communities of origin into quasi-tribal obligations and ritual, in the criminal underworld as much as above ground. Portuguese nationals working abroad as migrant labour, for instance, are typically welcomed back on their annual return trips; they help with building houses and are greeted with festivals organised to distribute the gifts they bring. However, when emigrants are seen 'as having pursued prosperity that was unshared and unresponsive to family and community obligations', as in the case of those who went to the colonies, they are less welcome on return (Lubkemann 2003: 81–2).

These quasi-tribal bonds may even reflect the effects of capitalist exploitation back into the ethnic domain entirely. Thus immigrant Turks and Turkish Kurds working in Holland's steel and shipbuilding industries found themselves subject to ridicule and loss of honour on their annual holidays in the south-east of the mother country when these industries were closed down as part of neoliberal restructuring in the 1980s. As Bovenkerk and Yeşilgöz (1998) document, as a way of saving face at the Turkish end of their tribal trail, some of them then took to transporting drugs back to Europe to compensate. This made them more 'foreign' again after having been briefly part of one of the most militant sections of the Dutch working class. This process can be seen to occur, on a much wider scale, in the world's inner cities.

Urban Tribalisms

The net effect of all migration is urbanisation. In many ways, today's big cities have become refugee camps in their own right, or contain such camps in the form of shanty towns, the 'mega-slums' of the South (Davis 2004: 5). As Castells observes (as in Catterall 2003: 192), these polarised conurbations 'oppose the cosmopolitanism of the elites, living on a daily connection to the whole world ..., to the tribalism of local communities, retrenched in the spaces that they try to control as their last stand against the macro-forces that shape their lives out of their reach.'

Foreign relations here are condensed in the same time-space. In a city, the familiar and the foreign are immediately present; they offer the opportunity to experience the psycho-geography of being at home and wandering far from it (Maffesoli 1997: 81–2). Lefebvre (1970: 56–7) calls the city 'the concrete contradiction' – it is the place where the possible meets the impossible, and where the greatest density of opportunities exists. For those largely excluded from these opportunities, there are endless barriers to entry into the spaces of the privileged, but distance is no longer among them. Neither is the attractiveness of the dominant way of life any less compelling. As Fanon puts it (1968: 130), 'The shantytown sanctions the native's biological decision to invade, at whatever cost and if necessary by the most cryptic methods, the enemy fortress.' Whether in the London borough of Peckham, the Parisian *banlieue*, or the mega-slums in the South, the utopia of the different world, the world of comfort and security, is ever present, just as the world of the spirits was in the tribal past. Time on earth is submerged into 'eternal time', as with the Australian aboriginals, but in today's 'culture of urgency', the two are immediately connected in the here and now. All activity is centred, to quote Castells again (1998: 160–1), on

the idea that there is no future, and no roots, only the present. And the present is made up of instants, of each instant. So, life has to be lived as if each instant were the last one, with no other reference than the explosive fulfilment of individualised hyperconsumption.

The mode of production is obviously a key determinant in this process. Fragmented labour markets have demolished traditional structures of socialisation, both in the family and at work, so that many young men 'grow up outside these codes, lacking important symbolic affirmation' (Williams 2001: 48). When the key productive force, the community, lacks or loses certain cultural and psychological qualities (such as education level and participation in associational civil society, and the civic sense of honour that comes with it), its dealings with others suffering from the same regressions and transformations, but considered as outsiders, revert to the tribal mould. Thus the mode of foreign relations we associate with highland New Guinea or Amazonia may reassert itself again, even if the original limit of walking distance as the spatial measure is suspended by, say, the availability of a 4 × 4, and the handgun replaces the bone-tipped spear.

As we have by now examined many examples of tribal foreign relations, some authentic and some recontextualised in modernity, let me present a few illustrative instances of how, at the lower end of the axis of exploitation, their re-enactment takes shape in the modern urban experience.

Space is occupied in the tribal mode on the basis of ancestry first. It is only territorial to the extent that kinship relations demarcate particular places, investing them with the imprint of the sacred. The football stadium in a modern city is certainly such a place, and emotions may run high when a visiting side enters it. Here quasi-ancestry ('belonging' to a club by birth, residence, or choice) inspires and entitles groups of youth to 'being there alive', to use Marx's phrase. It infuses them with the energy to proclaim their presence authoritatively. Campbell and Dawson (2001: 63) speak of '[a] joyful spatial domination, an appropriation of social space. Away fans, with their colours, songs, chants and styles, are always making a statement and staking a territorial claim: "This is us! This is ours!" '.

The lack of education and training which leaves only simple, pre-adolescent tests of will, 'fooling around', open to those for whom other routes to self-esteem and 'respect' are closed takes on a less innocent form in the case of urban youth gangs. In his study of Los Angeles, Davis (1990: 316) describes how hundreds of black, Latino, and Asian gangs – Cambodian boat children, Filipinos, Vietnamese, and Chinese – develop quasi-tribal relations on the margins of mainstream society. The gangs, or 'sets', owe allegiance to more comprehensive 'peoples'; in the LA case, the Crips and the Bloods. The actual ethnic composition of gangs is less important here than the 'adopted' difference through quasi-ethnogenesis. In Los Angeles, black youth gangs are open to Latino members, or license crack dealerships to them; whilst Latinos also fight each other, such as Salvadoreans against established Chicano gangs. Territories have a core area, with graffiti trails strung around them, but also may overlap (cf. the police map of core areas in Davis 1990: 301).

In Spain's big cities, gangs with a background from across the Atlantic (Puerto Rico, Ecuador, and other places) are also called 'Latinos'. They have taken root in a context of widespread unemployment and alienation among young immigrants. The Spanish Latino gangs, like their North American counterparts, function as 'hybrids of teen-cult and proto-Mafia', to use Davis' phrase (1990: 300), cut off from education, clubs, work. In the words of one observer of the Madrid and Barcelona gangs cited by Burke (2006: 38–9), 'there are no channels of communication into the migrant communities … They live in a world that is separate from the mainstream of Spanish society'.

This is even more pronounced in Brazil, where the 'First Commando of the Capital' (PCC in Portuguese) of São Paulo state acts like a sovereign power ruling an underworld comprising both the state prisons and the streets of its cities (de Barros 2006: 16). Combining aspects of revolutionary organisation and mafia, the PCC, nicknamed 'the party', has created its own spatial infrastructure in São Paulo state, disbursing aid to the poor, bicycles for children, and administering justice on its own accord as if no state authority existed; all paid for by revenues from the drugs trade which it largely controls. The PCC represents a world of its own, expanding thanks to the zero tolerance penal policy of the Brazilian state, which keeps pumping adolescent delinquents into the sphere of its alternative jurisdiction.

Encountering others under these conditions is as much a cause for nervous excitement and as potentially dangerous as the meeting of two Amerindian parties in the Brazilian jungle cited in Chapter 2. Enzensberger (1994: 21–2) speaks of 'molecular civil war' among groups of young men bereft of the patriarchal and family structures 'whose function was to harness their testosterone-fuelled energies, their impulsive actions and their blood-lust through rites of initiation'. Gang members are still subjected to tests of courage and fighting skills, but these have been largely stripped of the codes of honour with which they were invested in the past. Juvenile delinquency may indeed be the response of adolescents to ambiguous adult roles in communities lacking initiation rites (Tiger 1970: 192).

Yet tribal protection, as will be remembered, is not 'war' in the sense of planned, strategic violence with the aim of destroying others. Not unlike their authentic forebears, urban jungle warriors are there for the 'social drama', and for 'a sense of belonging, for competition, achieving "hour" and inflicting shame on opponents' (Williams 2001: 48). This is played out in streets shared with non-tribals; gangs trying to impress others may even commit seemingly irrational violence against random passers-by, such as physical attacks filmed and shared on mobile phones. Enzensberger (1994: 106) evokes the image of passengers entering the subway compartment as 'intruders', confronting a 'sedentary clan of compartment-occupants' and ready to fight over 'ancestral' territory. What is tribal about this is that it is often the 'lack of respect', in past and present, that triggers violence. The most innocuous gesture may become an insult and an elicitor of hostility for somebody who already feels humiliated by society in general. 'Implicit in threats to self-esteem',

S. Feshbach writes, 'are the impotence and diminished status of the injured party' (as in van Dijk 1977: 121).

Tribal patterns of exchange crucially centre on the exchange of women. There are also material forms of exchange with the outside world, but these as we saw rather resemble the incorporation of commercial diasporas by empire. In the quasi-tribal exchange of women, on the other hand, the uncertainties that young men across the ages have had about sexuality play out in the urban context very much along the lines of clan ritual. Manliness is still a key asset, and if education has not provided more civil alternatives, violence becomes the way of upholding 'a code of personal honour that stresses the inviolability of one's manhood' (R. Horowitz and G. Schwartz as in van Dijk 1977: 130). 'Lurking uncertainties and anxieties ... about sexualities and the body', Williams notes (2001: 53), 'routinely helps to produce exaggerated and macho bodily displays ... and aggressive public performances including verbal and non-verbal abuse, usually centred around accusations against their rivals of homosexuality and other forms of sexual "deviance".'

Male dominance, grafted onto men's role in claiming sovereignty over space and protecting it, originally operated to link the (re)productive capacity of the community with others through the exchange of women. In the regressive mutation to urban jungle, male dominance tends towards more brutal forms. The Spanish Latino gangs referred to earlier, obsessed about sexual identity and manhood, use serial rape to punish girls for disloyalty (Burke 2006: 39). Here the primitive sexualisation of women in rap music videos, pumped out round the clock by dedicated television channels and websites, works to socialise contemporary youth susceptible to it.

Now whilst in one corner of the urban jungle the black rapper rules supreme over his 'bitches', in another, forced marriages, capital punishment for adultery or for otherwise bringing shame to the family, and comparable practices serve to uphold masculine dominance too. Among immigrant communities, fathers may find themselves entirely dependent on the respect of their peer groups; demonstrating that one's wife and daughters are under control, becomes crucial to retaining that respect. As prestige becomes more fragile, 'sexual prohibitions become absolute and punishment for transgression increases' (Meillassoux 1981: 45; Eldering 2002: 158, 259). It is at this point that 'honour' turns into the obsessive concern of elders and men generally, to be avenged with mutilation or death if violated (Johnson 2001). As Lind writes (1969: 48),

Where the old community ties and sanctions have broken down to a considerable degree, there is a tendency for the male to over-react in his effort to reassert his traditional role and ... [to] resort to brute force in order to maintain his authority when the older sanctions fail.

Let me now, by way of conclusion, turn to a more optimistic perspective – albeit an 'optimism of the will' in the face of massive challenges. This is presented here as a programmatic outline only; it obviously requires a separate study if all its implications are to be properly dealt with.

NOMAD ROUTES TO GLOBAL GOVERNANCE

The analysis of cities as tribal spaces is not just a metaphor. It is my claim in this study that the real complexity of foreign relations as we are experiencing them today can be dissected by distinguishing successive modes of dealing with foreign communities, of which the tribal is simply the first to have crystallised in time. There are real regressive tendencies operative in the current period that make tribal forms more ubiquitous, as the way of life of many hundreds of millions is collapsing back into primitive existence. Indeed the processes in which the past seems to catch up with the present, apparently eclipsing the future, may be revealing that we have entered a revolutionary epoch of a particular kind.

What we are experiencing today is an exhaustion of the social and natural substratum on which economic reproduction, under the market discipline imposed by globalised capital accumulation, rests. Hence the contradictions between the productive forces and productive and foreign relations produce crises from which a key feature of past transitions is missing. The classical Marxist understanding of revolution was that new productive forces spawn new social forces, which then struggle to gain power and reorder society to make it conform to the requirements of their further development. Instead, the transformative momentum now appears to be generated by a *falling away* of productive forces, including cultural stasis or regression. This strains the existing patterns of social relations without offering obvious alternatives to replace them. There will be no end to innovation; but as nanotechnology or stem cell therapies illustrate, the tendency will be towards more subtle and delicate forms of managing the relationship to nature. Even genetic modification of plants must in this light be distinguished from, say, razing Borneo or Amazonia by slash-and-burn agriculture. This does not mean that there is no future; we must rather think about it in terms appropriate to a 'crisis of regression'. Revolutions are always an adjustment of social relations to the limits of the possible. If these in important respects are becoming narrower, the adjustment must be of a particular qualitative type, too, for instance by allowing democracy, culture, and education to compensate for reduced wealth and material consumption.

Foreign relations are as much a key to the solution to the crisis of regression as the need to transcend capitalist discipline. Global governance has been projected by the West to serve the needs of the capitalist mode of production, through which the rich exploit the planet and its population. This is now being resisted to such a degree that there is a growing resort to force in order to *compel* others to 'develop' along the lines of Western preferences (Duffield 2001). This generates strains and tensions, just as it works to proliferate actual violence across the globe. Indeed as Hardt and Negri write (2004: xi), 'The possibility of democracy on a global scale is emerging today for the very first time ... but the primary obstacle to democracy is the global state of war.' So how can we conceive of a way out of this contradictory state of affairs?

Marx left us a tentative scenario for a transformation in terms of modes of production, not of foreign relations. As I have argued throughout this book, however, the two are imbricated closely because they are anchored in, and serve to develop, a common fund of productive forces. In *Capital*, iii (*MEW*, xxv: 485–6), the conditions are outlined under which an 'associated' mode of production, building on certain inherent tendencies in capitalist development, might come within reach. This would involve:

1. The re-appropriation of the social labour process by the self-conscious 'collective worker', reunifying the various fractions into which the workforce has become disaggregated over the last century – as technicians, designers, manual labourers of all types, managers, transport and infrastructure regulators, and so on.
2. In the domain of property and distribution, political action to restore control over the world of finance, which in mature capitalism degenerates into speculative operations and outright swindle. To safeguard actual production, Marx argued, private financial transactions would at some point have to be curtailed if not altogether suppressed. Keynes of course made his name in

the 1930s attempting to do just that; I will come back to him below.

To this twofold structure of a revolutionary transition, cast in terms of the mode of production (a transition to the associated mode in the domains of the labour process, property relations, and distribution), I would add three moments of potential transformation in terms of foreign relations. These by definition would have to cover the issues of sovereign occupation of space, protection, and exchange. Here we are looking at a transformation towards democratic global governance, with sovereignty vested in the different communities of which the world's population is made up, and administered by the United Nations and its functional organisations and regional institutions. The three moments of the transition would then be:

3. In terms of occupying space, a multiplication of sovereign spheres, from cultural autonomy of communities claiming a separate existence and granted the minority rights of ethnic law, via subregional, state, and supranational democratic institutions to the UN.
4. In terms of protection, a multilateral framework for security, based on the established collective security regime of the UN and police action for protection against violence.
5. In terms of exchange, the equitable organisation of the world's productive capacity. Obviously this can only be meaningful if it coincides with the transformation towards a sustainable, associated mode of production (1 and 2) and within the limits of the possible set by the need to preserve the biosphere.

I will confine myself here to arguing that the subject for this transition is being shaped by the events of the last few decades; but let me indicate first which structural transformations and tasks are apparent in the foreign relations domain.

Overcoming the Heartland–Contender State Divide

As we saw in Chapter 1, Marx considered the sovereign occupation of space 'the great communal labour which is required … to occupy the objective conditions of being there alive'. This meanwhile has become a global issue facing humankind as a whole, because the threats to the biosphere today pose an immediate challenge to 'being there alive'. However, the need to preserve the environment cannot be posed in the abstract. The threat to it emanates from the way of life developed in the English-speaking West and from the exhaustive effects of the discipline of capital on society and nature.

As I have argued elsewhere (2006), it was the 1970s project of a New International Economic Order (NIEO) that triggered the neoliberal drive and this in turn has brought the planet to where we are today. There were many contradictions and drawbacks in the NIEO project(s), but the idea of a truly comprehensive and universal framework for managing world order is today coming back with a vengeance. As the bill is being prepared for a quarter of a century's enrichment of one section of the world's population, the United Nations is again gravitating into the forefront as the obvious framework for coordinating the tasks facing humanity today. The debates in the Security Council on the eve of the Anglo-American invasion of Iraq in 2003, in which the French made themselves the mouthpiece of the worldwide majority against the war, demonstrate that the political categories of government and opposition have a purchase at this level. The protection of the biosphere would inevitably become the preoccupying agenda item of such a global pluralist politics.

UN pluralism may then in turn activate the process of democratisation in the member states. Equality among states can gain ground once the UN reclaims a role in managing the response to climate change and the economic processes involved in it. Democracy and self-rule must begin locally, in the spheres of production and daily life. However, the parliamentary form of debate by political representatives of collective interests, accompanied by the transparency created by old and new media, would be revitalised if this level of global governance were included. The diversity of the world is not an obstacle to its being represented at successive levels of artificially delineated entities. Indeed transcending primary community allegiances is what we saw that a 'true state' is about. It was Marx's claim (in *MEW Ergänzungsband*, i: 419) that social forces should not be present here in a corporatist sense; it is only as 'spiritual powers, resurrected at the level of the state, in their political reincarnation, [that] the natural powers are entitled to vote in the state'. Therefore Monbiot is right when he argues (2003: 110) that 'parliamentary democracy does not depend on a strong sense of community'.

The abrogation of the West's superior sovereign claim, required for democratic global governance through the UN, is proceeding already in the area of protection. After a brief and uneven attempt at conversion in the wake of the collapse of the Soviet bloc, Wall Street investment banks and the Pentagon by the mid-1990s were again overseeing a massive consolidation and merger drive of the US arms industry. This has resulted in a debt-laden defence sector dependent on arms export growth and increased US military outlays (Oden, Wolf-Powers, and Markusen 2003: 20). The war without end declared in response to the attacks on the Twin Towers, and clamoured for by the spokespersons for the Anglo-American military–industrial complex since the 1970s, is related to this economic transformation; neither world public opinion nor the Security Council have so far been able to rein in these forces. Yet the need to neutralise and peacefully disarm the most aggressive, nuclear-armed states of the West – the United States, Britain, and Israel – is a precondition for a truly global governance of protection. This would have to be the result of a democratic resurgence in the aforementioned countries, for which the potential exists; there is no way it can be imposed from the outside. But there can be no question either that the English-speaking West and its Zionist outpost maintain their superior sovereignty in matters of life and death on account of ideas about chosen peoples, Manifest Destiny, or the imperial universalism that England took in its stride as it turned away from Rome and towards maritime supremacy.

In fact, the West may already have lost the historical advantage of mobile warfare. The 'War on Terror' has turned the heartland into a sedentary force unable to keep the mobility of its opponents in check. The United States and Britain in Iraq, and Israel in its campaign in Lebanon in 2006, have demonstrated a new vulnerability in spite of their massive military superiority. As Shaw argues (2005: 140), the War on Terror has created a situation in which

The future of Western warfare does not depend only on the decisions of the West itself ... The West may not be able to choose, simply, to avoid wars; it may have wars thrust upon it. The worst danger is probably a sort of extensive (but less intensive) 'Israelization' of the West, or at least of the USA: immersion in many unending, unwinnable, if low-level wars and the corresponding brutalization of state and society.

This can only undermine the liberal principles on which the West has emerged and flourished, just as it destabilises the international order in which capitalist globalisation reached its present form. The 'general global state of war' sparked off by 9/11, Hardt and Negri claim (2004: 5), among other things implies that 'war has ... become virtually indistinguishable from police activity'. Here we see how the imperialist West prepares the ground for global governance.

In terms of exchange, finally, overcoming the heartland–contender state divide and the North–South gap behind it requires first of all a solution to the debt crisis. This obviously dovetails with the aspect of a clampdown on speculative finance, item 2 above. Associated with the name of Keynes, measures in this spirit were enacted in the United States and a number of other countries in the 1930s, but in the 1970s they were rescinded (see my 1984: 262–9). Meanwhile the intricacies of global financial flows have become far more complex; the imbalances created by them are incomparably more unstable and potentially wide-ranging. This time the survival of the human species itself is at stake.

There is however a second aspect of Keynes' legacy which is equally topical today. This concerns his proposals, tabled for Britain in the negotiations with the United States in 1944, for a post-war monetary order. True, they were rejected; the framework for financial and monetary order established under the alternative proposals by Harry Dexter White for the United States has turned the world economy, by several further twists (most recently, in the response to the credit economy generated by the NIEO drive), into a pump-priming mechanism by which the world's poor are subsidising the rich. Yet Keynes' alternative plan for global clearing has lost little of its original validity. It would have made exports less attractive for states with a trade surplus and imports more so. In combination with methods of preventing capital flight, structurally unequal exchange among economies would be turned into its opposite as prosperity spread across the world economy instead of being concentrated. 'Sixty years on, the case for an International Clearing Union, or a body built on similar principles, appears to be stronger than ever', Monbiot (2003: 169) concludes in his review of the Keynes proposals in the light of current practice. Combined with such demands as a 'Tobin tax' on speculative finance, fair trade, and encouraging the consumption of locally produced food (and goods generally), this would indeed be a suitable centrepiece for a reform programme.

Unlike the changes in military affairs, however, these economic reforms are not already in the process of being realised. Here we must turn to the issue of defining the social subject of any turnabout.

In the Tracks of Transnational Capital

Every revolution in world history has had a collective subject, a particular class that became the bearer of the process, the executor of the transformation towards a different order – amidst the mass insurrection necessary to speak of a revolution from below. As I have argued at greater length elsewhere (1998: ch. 5), the transition from the capitalist to the associated mode of production, and from Western hegemony to democratic global governance, would have its executive arm in the social stratum that forms in the process of widening and deepening socialisation of labour, the managerial *cadre*. It is this 'new middle class' of experts and professionals that in the current historical epoch has emerged as the social force associated most directly with the potential reordering of the social relations governing world society.

The element of mass resistance is therefore not to be dismissed. But as little as the peasants who fought feudal lords or oriental despots were able to change society without outside help, the nameless billions exploited by capital today can be assumed to constitute a force capable of introducing a different social order. The circumstance that this will have to include a fine-tuning of humanity's relationship with nature in the context of a narrowing of the limits of the possible only makes it less desirable to forgo careful consideration of the options and merely bank on a popular insurrection. This is not a plea for a new vanguardism. Only by meeting the needs and aspirations of the mass of the world's population on their own terms will the viability of an alternative order as an advanced democracy be ensured.

There is no doubt that the broader cadre stratum today is still overwhelmingly enlisted in the effort to ensure the hegemony of the West and the global discipline of capital. The comprehensive attempt to weld every aspect of social relations worldwide into a functional whole subordinated to capital accumulation is also operative in this domain. Indeed as Jenkins puts it (2002: 261–2), the mainstream cadre 'increasingly see themselves as part of an international system which is enabling mankind to realize its sovereignty through the global extension of liberal capitalism'. Their role is inscribed in a neoliberal strategy of hegemony presented as 'good governance' with a global sweep, but on the lines laid down by the West. This is captured by Drainville (2005: 889) when he writes that

Central to 'global governance' as a hegemonial strategy is a broad attempt to assemble a global civil society in which to embed neoliberal concepts of control. Key here are twinned processes of severance and recomposition. At once, the making of global civil society involves (i) cutting off social forces and organizations willing to work within a global market framework from other social contexts and (ii) re-assembling the lot into a functional and efficient whole that will work to solve global problems and, in the process, fix the terms of social and political interaction in the world economy.

Let us see how this can work out if we assume that contradictions in capitalism as well as the contradiction proper to foreign relations, between communalism and the human community, continue to be operative. The global market framework that Drainville speaks of must be upheld in the context of regional, sometimes world-embracing product chains; 'fixing the terms of social and political interaction in the world economy' in that setting requires the constant attention of managerial auxiliaries, our cadre. Now the cadre in capitalism are not capitalists. Their commitment to the capitalist property regime is ideological, not anchored in productive assets owned by them. In fact they are permanently enrolled in a training school for how to run a global political economy; today by following the rules of the Western way of life, free access, if need be by force, and private profit; tomorrow, possibly, other rules. Key among their tasks, directly and by training new generations, is the organisation of the collective worker already referred to. As capital seeks out ever cheaper and more amenable sources of labour power, incorporating them into the most profitable combinations across ever longer product chains, it generates this social force by connecting workers of different nationalities into a single, potentially world-embracing proletariat.

The cadre's role in the process consists, according to Hardt and Negri (2004: 113, who speak of 'immaterial labour'), in producing social relations that serve to connect the different links into a chain, and the chains into webs.

Information, communication, and cooperation become the norms of production, and the network becomes its dominant form of organisation. The technical systems of production therefore correspond closely to its social composition: on one side the technological networks and on the other the cooperation of social subjects put to work.

In the process, foreignness must be neutralised and ideally overcome, even if the aim of restructuring is usually to utilise such differences in order to raise the rate of exploitation.

The collective worker, then, is distributed over different stages of the production process, in different functions and at different levels of direction and execution, remuneration, and training; but also in a particular location and belonging to a community often foreign to others. Now as recent research in the area of the organisation of transnational product chains has documented (Merk 2004, 2007), managing a product chain implies the standardisation of the conditions under which the successive nodes of such a chain operate and are interlocked. This includes 'information, communication, and cooperation', as well as ensuring minimum working conditions, if only to avoid risk to the reputation of the final seller of the branded product. It is in these conditions that specific categories of cadre have gravitated into a role where their concerns are beginning to converge with those of the actual workers. Once we realise that the cadre originate as a specialised layer of the workforce – like engineers, for example – it will be obvious that claiming that they are in the process of reconstituting themselves as part of the 'collective worker' is not just wishful thinking. Where anti-labour laws prevent actual trade unions from forming in their own right, corporate social responsibility departments of large Western firms even intervene on occasion with subcontractor operations, taking on the role one would expect the local unions to play.

In the process of overseeing and actually travelling along the product chains, the cadre assume definite 'nomadic' roles, in the sense that there is a regular displacement to clearly defined spaces, not random migration. We are looking at a circular pattern of movement aimed at integrating the extremes of spatial distance and foreignness. As quasi-nomadic auxiliaries of transnational capital, the cadre play a role in directing long-distance product chains into more or less internally compatible processes of handling semi-finished products at various stages. Not only do these cadre, like all frontier nomads before them, therefore have a better than average insight into life across the foreign divide; they also operate in a conjuncture in which the hegemonic power of the English-speaking heartland is being eroded as its energy-intensive, consumption- and profit-driven way of life is becoming evidently unsustainable.

Socialisation under capitalist conditions remains an alienated form, reified and renaturalised in the consciousness of the producers. As was pointed out in Chapter 1, foreignness is a key aspect of this alienation. The integration of global product chains, however, requires standardisation and a movement towards common norms which cannot leave foreignness intact. If the managers of a semi-finished input produced in Thailand cannot communicate with those using it in an assembly plant in Austria, there will be delays and cost overruns. So, to quote Hardt and Negri again (2004: 125), 'the traditional structure of otherness' must be abandoned altogether, and a 'concept of cultural difference based on a notion of singularity' must be discovered instead, In other words, foreignness cannot survive the organisation and operation of global product chains.

The current period is one in which pressures to overcome this contradiction are in evidence. Obviously, this is primarily attempted from the vantage point of the hegemonic West, by making everybody speak English, think in market terms, and adopt the Manhattan way of life. Yet that is precisely what will not work locally, and the more people become aware of and take pride in their own cultures, the more they will develop reservations about seeing their primary identities alienated from them. They may speak some business English but they will resist assimilating the entire package. The question that remains is why our managerial 'nomads' would ever give up the privileges associated with their role for capital, privileges which allow them to enjoy the Western way of life. A class after all is not just a functional category, but a social force whose outlook converges on a common perspective when the going gets tough.

Global Governance in the Plural

Let me briefly go over the different moments of cadre class formation in the recent period. This may give substance to the claim that a new class is once again advancing socially and politically, as it did in different circumstances in the 1930s and the 1970s (cf. my 1998: ch. 5). The cadre are now global, and in a position to push and enforce the transformations identified earlier. My argument is that anti-globalisation activists, non-governmental organisations (NGOs), and the cadre in mainstream international organisations, consultancies and actual corporations, each in their own way as distinct class 'fractions', are the protagonists of this process.

The anti-capitalist, alternative globalisation movement deserves a place of honour in this respect. During its heyday in the late 1990s, it drew a wide, colourful spectrum of activists from across the globe into the campaign against the Multilateral Agreement on Investment (MAI). The MAI would have been, if enacted, the exact opposite of the NIEO movement of the 1970s. Whereas in the projected NIEO, corporations were to be placed under scrutiny by states and the United Nations, the MAI boldly projected a global sovereignty of capital, from which no state was to be exempt. In the wake of the 1992 Rio Earth Summit, concern over such a framework for investor access and control was articulated, notably in France, where a power-ful popular protest movement against neoliberal 'market reform' erupted in the winter of 1995/6. This movement brought down the right-wing Juppé government, but also spawned new forms of trade union organisation and the ATTAC network, inspired by the idea of a Tobin tax, which soon radiated beyond France.

In 1996, we learn from Mabey's account (1999: 60–1), the alterna-tive globalisers began to interlock with groups from other countries concerned over the MAI plans. In October 1997, a first consultation between NGOs and the OECD took place over the global neoliberal investment regime, because this was seen to preclude the turn to a sustainable global economy that had been judged necessary in Rio. One year on, a veritable mass movement had erupted over the issue, echoed in resolutions by the European Parliament and many local government bodies. One aspect of this strand of resistance was the use of the Internet as a means of rapid, global communication – also to provide NGOs and social forces in the South with the necessary information to take action. This highlights the extent to which the Internet represents a productive force which in the hands of those opposing capitalist sovereignty and Western hegemony can be turned against them, widening the limits of the possible for those in favour of a different world order.

In the United States, meanwhile, legislation that aimed to acceler-ate neoliberal trade reforms ran into serious opposition. To prevent this opposition from hardening, the Clinton administration in late 1997 withdrew its 'Fast Track' trade negotiation proposals for later consideration. In 1999, the US movement against Fast Track merged with the worldwide anti-MAI campaign to protest against the Millennium Round trade liberalisation negotiations of a World Trade Organization ministerial-level conference to be held in Seattle. Mobilised through the Internet, more than 40,000 demonstrators sent a shock wave through the world, which led the journalist William Pfaff (as in Rupert 2000: 151) to conclude that the idea that economic issues could be negotiated in isolation from political and social issues 'had been dealt a blow from which it will not recover'.

'Seattle' became the undisputed high point of the movement, and from there a summit-hopping phenomenon developed that for a brief period seemed to establish itself as a disturbing force at every meeting of the multilateral and supranational organisations that form the regulatory infrastructure of global capitalism. Importantly, these events were festivals of difference, united but not homogenised in the resistance to market discipline. They greatly contributed to spreading the idea that cultural specificity is not the same as foreignness, but can add up to a powerful movement which yet retains its human diversity, indeed celebrates it as a source of collective self-confidence. In the World Social Forum initially convened in Porto Alegre, Brazil, the movement obtained a key organisational node. It achieved great publicity successes such as the widely publicised telephone debate with the neoliberal World Economic Forum in Davos.

However, 9/11 and the anti-Islamic backlash that ensued, dealt a massive blow to the playful counter-culture of the summit-hopping anti-capitalist nomads. It is hard to avoid the conclusion that Anglo-America's War on Terror is again today enormously widening the foreign divide. The logic of the 'clash of civilisations' has eclipsed the debate over whether capitalist discipline imposed on the planet has been beneficial or a disaster. The alternative, anti-globalisation movement has subsided, its protest activism contained by improved policing and moving the summits to places difficult to reach.

The initial impact of a militant colourful vanguard placing itself at the head of a globally constituted 'collective worker' has thus largely been dissipated again. But this does not mean that the effort was therefore wasted. Not only did the activist wave publicise the issues of survival of life on the planet and the murderous effects of World Bank and IMF recipes imposed on states the world over; it qualitatively raised the level of awareness of how the world economy combines people in incomparable circumstances, from leisurely consumption to modern slavery, into a community of fate. Its collective wisdom is still in the process of being recorded and disseminated (e.g. Scholte 2003). This was also the first time that a new generation of activists broke away from the drugs and dance monoculture propagated by neoliberal media. More importantly, it was the first time a Left movement constituted itself not as national first, to grapple with internationalism later, but directly as a movement on the global level, at the same time rejecting any limitation on the full expression of its diversity. Finally, not unlike the activists of May 1968, who were absorbed into traditional left-wing parties and expanding welfare state apparatuses in the 1970s, many from the 1990s anti-globalising generation were and continue to be recruited into the expanding NGO sector.

The NGOs constitute the second framework of cadre mobilisation. They are one vector in what Duffield (2001: 2) describes as 'a shift

from hierarchical and territorial relations of government to polyarchi-
cal, non-territorial and networked relations of governance'. They
operate in a process that is moving towards global governance, albeit
one driven by the West and pursued under the imperatives of
globalising capitalist discipline. The United Nations has awarded
consultative status to 1,500 NGOs and in 2000 hosted a 'Millennium
Forum' for them, but as Monbiot has argued (2003: 80), this should
not be confused with democracy. Largely financed from state coffers,
the NGOs rather are part of the restructuring of the state role
towards global governance which at best allows new channels of
interest group representation to be woven into existing ones. As
Braithwaite and Drahos put it (2000: 31), the state in the drift to
neoliberal global governance mutates into a force 'constituted by
and helping to constitute webs of regulatory influences comprised
of many actors wielding many mechanisms', and the NGOs are key
among them.

NGOs in this context operate very much as soft, compensatory
consultancies; often not even that soft, but as real business operations. As Siméant observes (2005: 875–6), they are not global either.
Contemporary NGOs are truly frontier operations because they are
overwhelmingly founded, recruited, and funded by the West and
then dispatched into the periphery. The French medical NGO,
Médecins sans Frontières (MSF), is only one example of a host of such
networks grafted on the earlier activisim. It was set up to overcome
the limits of a bureaucratised, conservative Red Cross, but its own
requirements for professionalisation and the need to attract experienced health specialists with language skills willing to sign up for
longer tours of duty have aligned it closely with the exploitative
Western attitude as it more and more needs to 'hunt' for staff in the
areas where it is supposed to assist development. The need to have a
presence in rich countries with a tradition of support for charity, like
the United States or Japan, has further worked to deflect NGOs' rules
of engagement in the direction of the mindset prevailing in those
countries which are also pivots of global wealth and capital accumulation. 'Thus, perversely, representatives of "civil society", held
to be antithetical to economic actors, regulate some of their relationships through the use of the same instruments multinational
corporations use' (Siméant, 2005: 874).

Clearly the NGO sector represents a step back from the recognition
of difference in this respect, certainly if compared to the anti-capitalist
activism. Yet their subordination to globalising capital and its

homogenising culture should not blind us to the fact that within both the NGO sector and the formal international organisations, as well as within and between corporations, important shifts in practices and outlook are noticeable.

This takes us to the third level of cadre involvement I look at here, the institutions associated with the regulatory infrastructure of global capital. They have been operating as straightforward relays of neoliberalism for two decades now. A specialised cadre in the Bretton Woods complex and the WTO, in the OECD, and in those functional bodies of the UN and EU most closely involved in the world economy have been active all along in ensuring that market solutions are being prioritised as the high road of problem solving, whilst the state is stripped of its responsibilities in the area of social protection. These recommendations were ultimately derived from principles of 'best practice' – defined by reference to the extremes of exploitation. This 'best practice', benchmarking management concept has spread like wildfire across the global political economy, and into politics as well, entailing a depoliticisation of administrative practices. The concept of 'governance' has actually come up in this very context, as a set of administrative practices conforming to neoliberal mantras (Tidow 1999: 308–9).

However, those travelling across the globe to ensure that best practices are actually being adopted have had to integrate into their appreciation what happens on the ground. This applies to the field officers of the aforementioned institutions as well as to the cadre of what Cutler, Haufler, and Porter (1999: 10) call the 'coordination services firms – multinational law, insurance, and management consultancy firms, debt-rating agencies, stock exchanges, and financial clearinghouses'. They too belong to a common culture which appears to transcend foreign relations, albeit principally in the sense of capitalist cosmopolitanism. Yes, they are 'a globalized new professional middle class, who regardless of their country of origin, tend to speak a common language and share common assumptions' (Deacon 1997: 180). Yet as they travel along the frontiers between North and South, they find that the practical implications of their prescriptions often contradict each other. Indeed they may begin to take into account the dislocations caused by privatisation, inequality, state withdrawal, and other practices contributing to the exhaustion of society and nature, which are hard to avoid once one leaves the confines of the international airport. Dispatched to find ways around national and other cultural sovereignties in order to impose market discipline, this cadre may return with experiences rather closer to those of the NGOs, and conclusions comparable to those of the anti-globalising activists. As indicated, corporate responsibility officers of large companies travelling along the production trails to the darker side of the global economy may come to share some of these shifts of perspective too. Many of them may question whether neoliberal globalisation is a sustainable process in the longer run. In this sense grassroots protests and activist ferment can begin to resonate among them.

The concerns of this frontier cadre can be in the nature of doubts, second thoughts, or articulate criticism. Whatever their form, they will feed back into the main institutions, and here the labour, health and environmental departments are typically the first port of call. To quote Deacon again (1997: 61),

Human resource specialists [of international organisations] have a degree of autonomy ... which has increasingly been used to fashion an implicit global political dialogue with international NGOs about the social policies of the future that go beyond the political thinking or political capacity of the under-pinning states.

A senior World Bank official has even made the case for instituting ratings agencies which will monitor state and corporate behaviour as to the observance of those rules that are vital to humanity's survival on the planet (Rischard, 2002).

In all international organisations, there are variations, cross-currents, and departures from the neoliberal mainstream. The World Bank Environment Department is home to 'heretics'; so is the ILO and, to some extent, the EU. The OECD directorate that deals with human resources and labour, UNICEF and the UNDP, and the Council of Europe too, in one way or another deflect the outright application of neoliberal policies away from 'best practice'. The cadre active in all of them in that sense must be considered as relays and possibly allies of forces seeking to resist such policies. Even within such arcane structures as the standards agencies in which many of the technical aspects of the transnational socialisation of labour are being encoded, there are conflicting perspectives. Those for whom property rights are the vantage point of standard setting and monitoring regularly find themselves in conflict with those who seek to expand the domain of rule-based product and process standardisation from the point of view of managing the conditions under which actual production takes place. In Graz's words (2006: 119):

rather than a public/private, or state/market divide, we are looking at a rift confronting the advocates of further socialization of international standards (that is, bringing standard-setting bodies into a universal legal domain), and advocates of a commodification of technical standards (minimal sector and market-based standards, universally recognized).

The idea therefore that nothing can be gained from engaging with the Bretton Woods institutions and other international organisations, Deacon maintains (1997: 218), is mistaken.

The empirical evidence suggests ... that a war of positions ... *is* being fought within and between international organizations; that through the support given to labour movements and their representatives in ministries of labour ... a connection to local social forces can be developed; and that international [NGOs] and their complex connections to local civil society are part of this war of positions.

Will all this converge on a will to change course, away from the suicidal trajectory which the West has imposed on world society? The only reply to this question here can be that the globalisation of capitalist discipline has unified the 'workers of the world', people of all colours and continents, to a degree that no socialist programme has ever been able to achieve. True, this common grid of experiences tends to be overwhelmingly one of humiliating exploitation and the demoralisation that accompanies it. Yet it has also worked, paradoxically, to awaken people the world over to the values of authenticity and diversity, the treasure trove from which alternative social forms and ways of life will have to emerge. The frontier as the limit of imperial penetration, as the most unstable and sensitive zone of the empire, the sphere of maximum friction, once again allows alternative forms of existence to confront each other directly – in world cities, on the tribal trails from the periphery to the North, on the trips that managers make to the remote outposts where the inputs of the global product chains are fed into the system. The constitution of a collective worker, in which crucially, the cadre are reunified with other workers from all across the globe, takes place on this frontier.

As I have argued in this book, the frontier was always the zone of adaptation, learning, and innovation. Its subterranean attraction, as the place where the 'barbarian' lurks, lends an ambivalence to imperialism which works to absorb the barbarian counterpoint into the dominant culture, producing hybrid identities and split loyalties. Civilisation, in the sense given to it by Elias (1987) of a domestication of the instincts, indeed presupposes and creates the barbarian opposite. The Wild Man, unrestrained, instinctive, lustful, and immediate, not only represents danger and instability; he also embodies a subconscious temptation to the civilised. The building of walls to keep the barbarians out cannot in the end suspend the actual interaction. This holds for the wall on the southern border of the United States meant to contain Mexican and other Central American immigration, as much as it applies to the wall erected by Israel to keep out the Palestinians. Apartheid has always been the weak link in imperialism: the barbarian, Nederveen Pieterse writes (1990: 360–1), is already among us and even inside ourselves.

The imperial frontiers are not only geographical frontiers, where the 'civilized' and the 'barbarians' confront and contact one another; they are also frontiers of status and ethnicity which run through imperialized societies, as in the form of the colonial 'colour bar' ... This frontier is also the locus of a genetic dialectic, a dialectic which in the midst of the most strenuous contradictions gives rise to that strangest of cultural and genetic syntheses – the mulatto, mestizo, half-caste ... the living testimony [and] proof that East and West did meet and that there is humanity on either side.

Once 'difference is appreciated as a resource for internal self-reflection and social criticism', Inayatullah and Blaney conclude (2004: 49), it will contribute to overcoming the foreign as an exploitative set of relations. There is no doubt that the option of conciliating difference equitably in the course of history has tended to lose out to the compulsion to dominate and exploit, exacerbating foreignness in the process. However, respect for the natural milieu, hospitality through the ages, commercial brotherhood, religious ecumenical movements, socialist internationalism, and, more recently, the militant diversity championed by the alternative, anti-globalisation movement, have all along offered a counterpoint of common humanity. As the limits of the possible are being narrowed, this legacy may become our lifeline to survival.

References

Transcriptions of foreign proper names have been standardised to the current English versions with the alternative in parentheses after the title; names with prefixes such as 'al-', 'van', or 'von', are listed under the main name.

Abou-el-Haj, Rifaat A. 1969. 'The Formal Closure of the Ottoman Frontier in Europe: 1699–1703'. *Journal of the American Oriental Society*. 89 (3). 467–75.

Abraham, David. 1981. *The Collapse of the Weimar Republic: Political Economy and Crisis*. Princeton, N.J.: Princeton University Press.

Adair, Paul. 2004 [1994]. *Hitler's Greatest Defeat: Disaster on the Eastern Front*. London: Rigel.

Aglietta, Michel. 1979 [1976] *A Theory of Capitalist Regulation: The US Experience* (trans. D. Fernbach). London: Verso.

Aleksejev, V. 1974 [1969]. 'About Racial Differentiation of the Human Species: Primary Centres of Race Formation', in Bromley 1974b.

Alff, Wilhelm. 1976. *Materialien zum Kontinuitätsproblem der deutschen Geschichte*. Frankfurt: Suhrkamp.

Allen, Phillip. 1999 [1992]. *Atlas der Atlassen: De kaartenmakers en hun wereld-beeld* (trans. S. Brinkman). Alphen: ICOB.

Alves, Francisco. 1998. 'Genealogy and archaeology of Portuguese ships at the dawning of the modern world', in Raffaella D'Into and António Alves Martins (eds) *Nossa Senhora dos Mártiros: The Last Voyage* (trans. J.C. Abdo). Lisbon: Editorial Verbo.

Aly, Götz, and Heim, Susanne. 1993 [1991]. *Vordenker der Vernichtung: Auschwitz und die deutschen Pläne für eine neue europäische Ordnung*. Rev. edn. Frankfurt: Fischer.

Amin, Samir. 1973. *Le développement inégal*. Paris: Minuit.

Anderson, Benedict. 1991 [1983]. *Imagined Communities: Reflections on the Origin and Spread of Nationalism*. Rev. edn. London: Verso.

Anderson, Perry. 1996 [1974]. *Passages from Antiquity to Feudalism*. London: Verso.

—— 1979 [1974]. *Lineages of the Absolutist State*. London: Verso.

Apter, David E. 1968. *Ghana in Transition*. New York: Atheneum (rev. edn. of *The Gold Coast in Transition*, 1955).

Armitage, David. 2000. *The Ideological Origins of the British Empire*. Cambridge: Cambridge University Press.

Aron, Raymond. 1968 [1961]. *Peace and War: A Theory of International Relations* (trans. R. Howard and A. Baker Fox). New York: Praeger.

Attali, Jacques. 2003. *L'Homme nomade*. Paris: Fayard.

Aupers, G.J., and van den Hoogen, Th.J.G. 1980. 'Theorieën over de bewapeningswedloop', in Ph. P. Evers and H.W. Tromp (eds) *Tussen oorlog en vrede*. Amsterdam: Intermediair.

Authors' Collective. 1982 [1977]. *Present-day ethnic processes in the USSR* (trans. C. Creighton et al.). Moscow: Progress.

Balibar, Étienne. 1975 [1968]. 'Sur les concepts fondamentaux du matérialisme historique', in L. Althusser et al., *Lire le Capital*. 2 vols. Paris: Maspero.

Barber, Elizabeth W. 1999. *The Mummies of Ürümchi*. London: Macmillan.

Barraclough, Geoffrey. 1968. *The Medieval Papacy*. London: Thames and Hudson.

Barros, João de. 2006. 'Prisons brésiliennes, du désastre social aux mafias: Quand l'organisation du crime surpasse celle de l'Etat', *Le Monde Diplomatique* (December). 16–17.

Bartlett, Robert. 1993. *The Making of Europe: Conquest, Colonization and Cultural Change 950–1350*. London: Allen Lane/The Penguin Press.

Beal, S. 1884. *Buddhism in China*. London: Society for Promoting Christian Knowledge.

Bedini, Silvio A. (ed.) 1998 [1992]. *Christopher Columbus and the Age of Exploration: An Encyclopedia*. New York: Da Capo Press.

Berger, Mark T. 2001. 'The Rise and Demise of National Development and the Origins of Post-Cold War Capitalism'. *Millennium: Journal of International Studies*. 30 (2). 211–234.

Bliss, W.L. 1965 [1952]. 'In the Wake of the Wheel: Introduction of the Wagon to the Papago Indians of Southern Arizona', in E.H. Spicer (ed.) *Human Problems in Technological Change*. New York: Wiley.

Blussé, Leonard. 1986. *Strange Company: Chinese settlers, mestizo women and the Dutch in VOC Batavia*. Dordrecht: Foris.

Bobbitt, Philip. 2002. *The Shield of Achilles: War, Peace and the Course of History*. Harmondsworth: Penguin.

Boehm, Christopher. 1984. *Blood Revenge: The Anthropology of Feuding in Montenegro and Other Tribal Societies*. Lawrence, Kans.: University Press of Kansas.

Borochov, Ber. 1972 [1937]. *Nationalism and the Class Struggle: A Marxian Approach to the Jewish Problem*. Westport, Conn.: Greenwood Press (written 1905–16).

Bovenkerk, F. and Yeşilgöz, Y. 1998. *De mafia van Turkije*. Amsterdam: Meulenhoff-Kritak.

Bowers, Ray L. 1967. 'The British Approach to Strategy: Perspectives for the U.S.'. *Air University Review*, November–December. http://www.airpower.maxwell.af.mil/irchronicles/aureview/1967/nov-dec/bowers.html (accessed 22 February 2007).

Boxer, C.R. 1965. *The Dutch Seaborne Empire, 1600–1800*. London: Hutchinson.

—— 1977. *Jan Compagnie in oorlog en vrede: Beknopte geschiedenis van de VOC*. (trans. A. Alberts). Bussum: Unieboek/De Boer Maritiem.

Boyer, Régis. 1992. *Les Vikings: Histoire et civilisation*. Paris: Plon.

Braeckman, Colette. 1995. 'Condamner les victims, absoudre les bourreaux: Autopsie d'un génocide planifié au Rwanda'. *Le Monde Diplomatique* (March). 8–9.

—— 2006. 'Elections sous pression à Kinshasa: Le Congo transformé en libre-service minier'. *Le Monde Diplomatique* (July). 12–13.

Braithwaite, John, and Drahos, Peter. 2000. *Global Business Regulation*. Cambridge: Cambridge University Press.

Braudel, Fernand. 1981 [1979]. *The Structures of Everyday Life: The Limits of the Possible*. Vol. I of *Civilization and Capitalism 15th–18th Century* (trans. S. Reynolds). London: Collins.

—— 1983 [1979]. *The Wheels of Commerce*. Vol. II of *Civilization and Capitalism 15th–18th Century* (trans. S. Reynolds). London: Collins.

—— 1984 [1979]. *The Perspective of the World*. Vol. III of *Civilization and Capitalism 15th–18th Century* (trans. S. Reynolds). London: Collins.

Brennan, Teresa. 2000. *Exhausting Modernity: Grounds For a New Economy*. London: Routledge.

Bridge, G. and Watson, S. (eds). 2003. *A Companion to the City*. Malden, Mass.: Blackwell.

Brodie, Bernard. 1970 [1959]. *Strategy in the Missile Age*. Princeton, N.J.: Princeton University Press.

Bromley, Yulian V. 1974a. [1971]. 'The Term *Ethnos* and its Definition', in Bromley 1974b.

—— 1974b. (ed.) *Soviet Ethnology and Anthropology Today*. The Hague: Mouton.

—— 1977 [1973]. *Ethnos und Ethnographie* (in German transcription, J. Bromlej; trans. W. König). Berlin: Akademieverlag.

—— 1978. *Ethnography and Ethnic Processes*. Moscow: USSR Academy of Sciences.

Broomfield, J.H. 1968. *Elite Conflict in a Plural Society: Twentieth-Century Bengal*. Berkeley: University of California Press.

Bukharin, Nikolai. 1972 [1915]. *Imperialism and World Economy* (foreword by Lenin). London: Merlin.

—— 1976. *Économique de la période de transition: Théorie générale des processus de transformation* (in French transcription, Boukharine; trans. E. Zarzycka-Berard and J.-M. Brohm). Paris: Études et Documentation Internationales (written 1919–20).

Burke, Jason. 2006. 'Gang wars shake Spain's Latin quarter'. *Observer*. 15 October. 38–9.

Buzan, Barry and Little, Richard. 2000. *International Systems in World History: Remaking the Study of International Relations*. Oxford: Oxford University Press.

Calder, Angus. 1981. *Revolutionary Empire: The Rise of the English-Speaking Empires from the Fifteenth Century to the 1780s*. London: Jonathan Cape.

Campbell, Beatrix and Dawson, Adam L. 2001. 'Indecent Exposures: Men, Masculinity, and Violence', in Perryman 2001.

Carrère d'Encausse, Hélène. 1979. *Decline of an Empire: The Soviet Socialist Republics in Revolt* (trans. M. Sokolinski and H.A. La Farge). New York: Harper & Row.

Carstairs, G.M. 1957. *The Twice-Born: A Study of a Community of High-Caste Hindus*. London: Hogarth Press.

Cash, W.J. 1954 [1941]. *The Mind of the South*. New York: Vintage.

Castells, Manuel. 1998. *End of Millennium*. Vol. III of *The Information Age*. Malden, Mass.: Blackwell.

Castles, Stephen and Miller, Mark J. 1998 [1993]. *The Age of Migration: International Population Movements in the Modern World*. 2nd edn. Basingstoke: Macmillan.

Catterall, Bob. 2003. 'Informational Cities: Beyond Dualism and Toward Reconstruction', in Bridge and Watson 2003.

Cawthorne, Nigel. 2003. *Steel Fist: Tank Warfare 1939–45*. London: Capella.

Chaliand, Gérard. 2006 [1995]. *Les empires nomades de la Mongolie au Danube: Vᵉ siècle av. J.-C.–XVIᵉ siècle*. Paris: Perrin.

Churchill, Winston S. 1956–58. *A History of the English-speaking Peoples*, 4 vols. London: Cassell.

Clastres, Pierre. 1972. *Chronique des indiens Guayaki: ce que savent les Aché, chasseurs nomades du Paraguay*. Paris: Plon.

—— 1987. *Society Against the State: Essays in Political Anthropology* (trans. R. Hurley). New York: Zone Books.

Cocker, Mark. 1998. *Rivers of Blood, Rivers of Gold: Europe's Conflict With Tribal Peoples*. London: Cape.

Collins, Randall. 1998. *The Sociology of Philosophies: A Global Theory of Intellectual Change*. Cambridge, Mass.: Harvard University Press.

Contente Domingues, Francisco. 1998. *A Carreira da Índia* (parallel translation by P. Ingham). Lissabon: CTT Correios.

Cook, N. 2001. 'Viking genetics survey results'. http://www.bbc.co.uk/history/programmes/bloodofthevikings/genetics_results (accessed 8 July 2004).

Corbett, Julian S. 2001 [1907]. *The Seven Years War: A Study in British Combined Strategy*. London: The Folio Society.

Cox, Robert W. 1987. *Production, Power, and World Order: Social Forces in the Making of History*. New York: Columbia University Press.

—— 2002. *The Political Economy of a Plural World: Critical Reflections on Power, Morals and Civilization* (with M.G. Schechter). London: Routledge.

Curtin, Philip D. (ed.) 1971. *Imperialism: Selected Documents*. London: Macmillan.

—— 1984. *Cross-cultural trade in world history*. Cambridge: Cambridge University Press.

Cutler, A.C., Haufler, V., and Porter, T. (eds) 1999. *Private Authority and International Affairs*. Albany: State University of New York Press.

Danchev, Alex. 1999. 'Liddell Hart and the Indirect Approach'. *Journal of Military History*. 63 (2) 313–37.

Davis, Mike. 1990. *City of Quartz: Excavating the Future in Los Angeles*. London: Verso.

—— 1995. 'Los Angeles After the Storm: The Dialectic of Ordinary Disaster'. *Antipode*. 27 (3). 221–41.

—— 1999. 'Magical Urbanism: Latinos Reinvent the US Big City'. *New Left Review*. 234. 3–43.

—— 2004. 'Planet of Slums', *New Left Review* (2nd series). 26. 5–34.

Deacon, Bob. 1997. *Global Social Policy: International organizations and the future of welfare* (with Michelle Hulse and Paul Stubbs). London: Sage.

Defoe, Daniel. 1992 [1719]. *Robinson Crusoe*. London: Everyman's Library.

Deleuze, G. and Guattari, F. 1986 [1980]. *Nomadology: The War Machine* (trans. B. Massumi). New York: Semiotexte.

Delcourt, Barbara. 2006. 'International Norms in Theories of Interdependence: Towards State-less Law?' (trans. S. Rust), in Giesen and van der Pijl 2006.

Deutsch, Karl W. 1966 [1953]. *Nationalism and Social Communication: An Inquiry into the Foundations of Nationality*. 2nd edn. Cambridge, Mass.: MIT Press.

Diamond, Jared. 1998. *Guns, Germs and Steel: A Short History of Everybody For the Last 13,000 Years*. New York: Vintage.

Dickens, Peter. 1996. *Reconstructing Nature: Alienation, Emancipation and the Division of Labour*. London: Routledge.

Dijk, J.J.M. van. 1977. *Dominantiegedrag en geweld: Een multidisciplinaire visie op de veroorzaking van geweldmisdrijven.* Nijmegen: Dekker & van de Vegt.

Douglas, David C. 2002 [1969, 1976]. *The Normans* (combined edn. of *The Norman Achievement, 1050–1100* and *The Norman Fate, 1100–1154*; intro. M.T. Clanchy). London. Folio Society.

Drainville, André. 2005. 'Beyond altermondialisme: anti-capitalist dialectic of presence'. *Review of International Political Economy.* 12 (5). 884–908.

Draper, Theodore. 1997. *A Struggle for Power: The American Revolution.* London: Abacus.

Drischler, William Fr. 2006. *The Political Biography of the Young Leibniz in the Age of Secret Diplomacy.* Charleston, S.C.: BookSurge.

Duchesne, Ricardo. 2001/2. 'Between Sinocentrism and Eurocentrism: Debating André Gunder Frank's *Re-Orient: Global Economy in the Asian Age*', *Science and Society.* 64 (4). 428–463.

Duffield, Mark. 2001. *Global Governance and the New Wars: The Merging of Development and Security.* London: Zed Books.

Dumézil, Georges. 1952. *Les dieux des indo-européens.* Paris: Presses Universitaires de France.

Duncan, O.D. (ed.) 1964. *William F. Ogburn on Culture and Social Change.* Chicago: University of Chicago Press.

Eldering, Lotty. 2002. *Cultuur en opvoeding.* Rotterdam: Lemniscaat.

Elias, Norbert. 1987 [1937]. *Het civilisatieproces: Sociogenetische en psychogenetische onderzoekingen* (trans. W. Kranendonk, H. Israels, et al.). Utrecht and Antwerp: Spectrum.

Enderlin, Charles. 2006. 'Quand Israël favorisait le Hamas: Depuis trente ans, les dirigeants de l'Etat hébreu ont misé sur les islamistes pour détruire le Fatah'. *Le Monde.* 4 February. 17.

Enzensberger, Hans Magnus. 1994 [1990–93]. *Civil Wars From L.A. to Bosnia* (trans. P. Spence and M. Chalmers). New York: The New Press.

Escolar, Marcelo. 2003 [1997]. 'Exploration, Cartography, and the Modernization of State Power', in N. Brenner, B. Jessop, M. Jones, and G. MacLeod (eds). *State/Space: A Reader.* Malden, Mass.: Blackwell.

evrazia. 2006. 'The work of L.N. Gumilev as a development of the eurasist thinking'. http://www.evrazia.org/modules.php?name=News&file=article&sid=86 (accessed 22 June 2006).

Fage, J.D. 1969 [1955]. *A History of West Africa*, 4th edn. Cambridge: Cambridge University Press.

Fanon, Franz. 1968 [1961]. *The Wretched of the Earth* (preface by J.-P. Sartre, trans. C. Farrington). New York: Grove Press.

Fischer, Fritz. 1984. *Griff nach der Weltmacht: Die Kriegszielpolitik des kaiserlichen Deutschland 1914/18.* Abridged edition. Düsseldorf: Droste.

Foucart, Stéphane. 2006. 'La longue survie de l'homme de Neanderthal'. *Le Monde.* 16 September.

Frank, André Gunder. 1998. *ReOrient: Global Economy in the Asian Age.* Berkeley: University of California Press.

Freud, Sigmund. 1938 [1919]. *Totem and Taboo: Resemblances Between the Psychic Lives of Savages and Neurotics* (trans. A.A. Brill). Harmondsworth: Penguin.

—— 1967 [1939]. *Moses and Monotheism* (trans. K. Jones). New York: Vintage.

Fried, Morton H. 1967. *The Evolution of Political Society: An Essay in Political Anthropology*. New York: Random House.

Friedman, Richard E. 1997 [1987]. *Who Wrote the Bible?* 2nd edn. New York: HarperCollins.

Friman, H. Richard. 2004. 'The great escape? Globalization, immigrant entrepreneurship, and the criminal economy'. *Review of International Political Economy*. 11 (1). 98–131.

Gabriel, Christina, 2004. 'A Question of Skills: Gender, Migration Policy and the Global Political Economy', in van der Pijl, Assassi, and Wigan, 2004.

Garraty, John A. and Gay, Peter (eds). 1981 [1972]. *The Columbia History of the World*. New York: Harper & Row.

Genovese, Eugene D. 1989 [1961–65]. *The Political Economy of Slavery: Studies in the Economy and Society of the Slave South*. 2nd edn. Middletown, Conn.: Wesleyan University Press.

Gibb, H.A.R. 1962 [1933–58]. *Studies in the Civilization of Islam* (ed. S.J. Shaw and W.R. Polk). London: Routledge & Kegan Paul.

Gibbon, Edward. 1989 [1776–88]. *The History of the Decline and Fall of the Roman Empire*. 8 vols. London: Folio Society.

Giedion, Sigfried. 1987 [1948]. *Die Herrschaft der Mechanisierung: Ein Beitrag zur anonymen Geschichte* (ed. H. Ritter, postface by S. von Moos). Frankfurt: Athenäum.

Giesen, Klaus-Gerd and Pijl, Kees van der (eds). 2006. *Global Norms in the Twenty-First Century*. Newcastle: Cambridge Scholars Press.

Giles, H.A. 1915. *Confucianism and its Rivals* (Hibbert lecture, 1914). London: Williams & Norgate.

Gledhill, J. 1994. *Power and its Disguises: Anthropological Perspectives on Politics*. London: Pluto Press.

Godelier, Maurice. 1980. 'Processes of the formation, diversity and bases of the state'. *International Social Science Journal*. 32 (4). 609–24.

Gollwitzer, Heinz. 1962. *Die Gelbe Gefahr: Geschichte eines Schlagworts. Studien zum imperialistischen Denken*. Göttingen: Vandenhoeck & Ruprecht.

Gossett, Th. F. 1963. *Race: The History of an Idea in America*. Dallas: Southern Methodist University Press.

Gossweiler, Kurt. 1982. *Kapital, Reichswehr, und NSDAP, 1919–1924*. Cologne: Pahl-Rugenstein.

Gott, Richard. 2006. 'The brutal story of British empire continues to this day'. *Guardian*. 22 July. 22.

Graff, James. 2006. 'Saving Beauty'. *Time Magazine*. 15 May. 36–42.

Gramsci, Antonio. 1971. *Selections from the Prison Notebooks* (trans. and ed. Q. Hoare and G.N. Smith). New York: International Publishers (written 1929–35).

—— 1975. *Quaderni del carcere*. 4 vols (ed. V. Gerratana for the Instituto Gramsci). Turin: Einaudi (written 1929–35).

—— 1978. *Selections from Political Writings, 1921–1926* (trans. and ed. Q. Hoare). New York: International Publishers.

—— 1989 [1973]. *Letters from Prison*. 2nd edn. (trans. and ed. L. Lawner). New York: Noonday/Farrar, Strauss & Giroux.

Graz, Jean-Christophe. 2006. 'International Standardisation and Corporate Democracy', in Giesen and van der Pijl 2006.

Gumilev, L.N., 1987 [1970]. *Searches for an Imaginary Kingdom: The Legend of the Kingdom of Prester John* (trans. R.E.F. Smith). Cambridge: Cambridge University Press.

Gurney, O.R. 1952. *The Hittites*. Harmondsworth: Penguin.

Haan, Hans den. 1977. *Moedernegotie en grote vaart: Een studie over de expansie van het Hollandse handelskapitaal in he 16de en 17de eeuw*. Amsterdam: SUA.

Habermas, Jürgen. 1973. *Legitimationsprobleme im Spätkapitalismus*. Frankfurt: Suhrkamp.

Halperin, Sandra. 1997. *In the Mirror of the Third World: Capitalist Development in Modern Europe*. Ithaca, N.Y.: Cornell University Press.

Hardt, Michael, and Negri, Antonio. 2004. *Multitude: War and Democracy in the Age of Empire*. New York: Penguin.

Hattstein, M. 2000. 'Centraal-Azië: Timuriden, Shaybaniden en khan-vorstendommen. Geschiedenis', in M. Hattstein and P. Delius (eds) *Islam: Kunst en Architectuur*. (Dutch edn. trans. C. Rochow et al.). Cologne: Könemann.

Havránek, J. 1967. 'The Development of Czech Nationalism'. *Austrian History Yearbook*, iii, part 2. 223–60.

Heesterman, J.C. 1973. 'India and the Inner Conflict of Tradition'. *Daedalus*. 102 (1). 97–115.

Hegel, G.W.F. 1923 [1817]. *Encyclopädie der philosophischen Wissenschaften im Grundrisse*. 3rd edn. (ed. G. Lasson). Leipzig: Felix Meiner.

—— 1961 [1837]. *Vorlesungen über die Philosophie der Geschichte*. Stuttgart: Reclam.

Heijden, E.J.J. van der. 1958 [1933]. *Aantekeningen bij de geschiedenis van het oude vaderlandse recht*. 6th edn. (ed. B.H.D. Hermesdorf). Nijmegen: Dekker & Van de Vegt.

Herman, Zvi. 1966 [1964]. *Peoples, Seas, and Ships* (trans. L. Ortzen). London: Phoenix House.

Hobbes, Thomas. 1968 [1651]. *Leviathan* (intro. C.B. Macpherson). Harmondsworth: Penguin.

Hofstadter, Richard. 1955. *The Age of Reform: From Bryan to F.D.R.* New York: Vintage.

Houweling, H.W. and Siccama, J.G. 1993. 'The Neo-Functionalist Explanation of World Wars: A Critique and an Alternative'. *International Interactions*. 18 (4). 387–408.

Hucker, C.O. 1973. 'Political Institutions', in J.T. Meskill (ed.) *An Introduction to Chinese Civilization* (with the assistance of J.M. Gentzler). Lexington, Mass.: D.C. Heath.

Huntington, Samuel P. 1993. 'The Clash of Civilizations?'. *Foreign Affairs*. 72 (3). 22–49.

Ibn Khaldun. 1951 [1376–77]. *Ausgewählte Abschnitte aus der Muqaddima* (in German transcription, Ibn Chaldun; transl. and introd. A. Schimmel). Tübingen: J.C.B. Mohr/ Paul Siebeck.

Inayatullah, Naeem, and Blaney, David L. 2004. *International Relations and the Problem of Difference*. New York: Routledge.

Jahn, Beate. 2000. *The Cultural Construction of International Relations: The Invention of the State of Nature*. Basingstoke: Palgrave.

Jefferson, Thomas. 1969 [1803]. 'President Thomas Jefferson to Governor of the Territory of Indiana William H. Harrison, February 7, 1803', in R. Skolnik (ed.) *1803, Jefferson's Decision: The United States Purchases Louisiana*. New York: Chelsea House.

Jenkins, Dominick. 2002. *The Final Frontier: America, Science, and Terror*. London: Verso.

Johnson, Michael. 2001. *All Honourable Men: Social Origins of the War in Lebanon*. London: IB Tauris.

Jones, Stephen B. 1959. 'Boundary Concepts in the Setting of Place and Time'. *Annals of the Association of American Geographers*. 49 (3) (part 1). 241–55.

Kaldor, Mary. 1982. 'Warfare and Capitalism', in *New Left Review* (eds) *Exterminism and Cold War*. London: Verso.

Kaviraj, Sudipta. 1992. 'Marxism and the darkness of history'. *Development and Change*. 23 (3). 79–102.

Kelly, Raymond C. 2000. *Warless Societies and the Origins of War*. Ann Arbor: University of Michigan Press.

Kennedy, Paul. 1987. *The Rise and Fall of the Great Powers: Economic Change and Military Conflict from 1500 to 2000*. New York: Random House.

Khafaji, Isam al-. 2004. *Tormented Births: Passages to Modernity in Europe and the Middle East*. London: IB Tauris.

Khazanov, A. 1974 [1968]. '"Military Democracy" and the Epoch of Class Formation', in Bromley 1974b.

Klare, Michael T. 2001. *Resource Wars: The New Landscape of Global Conflict*. New York: Henry Holt Metropolitan Books.

Klein-Beekman, Chris. 1996. 'International Migration and Spatiality in the World Economy: Remapping Economic Space in an Era of Expanding Transnational Flows'. *Alternatives*. 21. 439–72.

Kloss, Heinz. 1969. *Grundfragen der Ethnopolitik im 20. Jahrhundert*. Vienna and Stuttgart: Braumüller; Bad Godesberg: VWA.

Kolko, Gabriel. 1976. *Main Currents in Modern American History*. New York: Harper & Row.

—— 1994. *Century of War: Politics, Conflicts, and Society Since 1914*. New York: The New Press.

Komroff, Manuel (ed.) 1929. *Contemporaries of Marco Polo: Consisting of the Travel Records to the Eastern Parts of the World of William of Rubruck (1253–1255); the Journey of John of Pian de Carpini (1245–1247); and the Journal of Friar Odoric (1318–1330)*. London: Jonathan Cape.

Kosta, J. 1978. *Abriss der sozialökonomischen Entwicklung der Tschechoslowakei 1945–1977*. Frankfurt: Suhrkamp.

Kühnl, Reinhard (ed.). 1980 [1975]. *Der deutsche Faschismus in Quellen und Dokumenten*. Rev. edn. Cologne: Pahl-Rugenstein.

Kuznetsov, A.M. 2006. 'The Theory of Ethnos by S.M. Shirokogorov' (ms. trans. Ekaterina Korotayeva for the author). Originally in *Ethnographicheskor Obozrenie*, 2006. 3.

Laffey, Mark, and Dean, Kathryn. 2002. 'A flexible Marxism for flexible times', in M. Rupert and H. Smith (eds) *Historical Materialism and Globalization*. London: Routledge.

Lamb, Alastair. 1968. *Asian Frontiers: Studies in a Continuing Problem*. London: Pall Mall Press.

Lasswell, Harold D. 1960 [1930]. *Psychopathology and Politics*. New York: Viking.

Lattimore, Owen. 1935. *The Mongols of Manchuria: Their Tribal Divisions, Geographical Distribution, Historical Relations with Manchus and Chinese and Present Political Problems*. London: Allen & Unwin.

—— 1951 [1940]. *Inner Asian Frontiers of China*. 2nd edn. Irvington-on-Hudson: Capitol Publishing, for the American Geographical Society.

—— 1962. *Studies in Frontier History: Collected Papers 1928–1958*. Paris: Mouton.

Lavelle, Kathryn C. 2005. 'Moving in from the periphery: Africa and the study of international political economy'. *Review of International Political Economy*. 12 (2). 364–79.

Lawrence, E.T. 1997 [1935]. *Seven Pillars of Wisdom*. London: Wordsworth Classics.

Lefebvre, Henri. 1970. *La revolution urbaine*. Paris: Gallimard.

—— 1976. *Théorie marxiste de l'Etat de Hegel à Mao*. Vol. II of *De l'Etat*. Paris: 10/18.

Lenin, Vladimir Ilitch. *Collected Works*. 39 vols. Moscow: Progress.

—— 1975. *Marxisme en staat* (Dutch translation). Amsterdam: Pegasus.

Levathes, Louise. 1994. *When China Ruled the Seas: The Treasure Fleet of the Dragon Throne, 1405–1433*. Oxford: Oxford University Press.

Lévi-Strauss, Claude. 1962. *La pensée sauvage*. Paris: Plon.

—— 1983 [1949]. 'De grondslagen van de verwantschap' (trans. from the French). *Te Elfder Ure*. 26 (3). 651–76.

—— 1987 [1953]. *Race et histoire* (ed. with a review essay by J. Pouillon). Paris: Denoël/Folio.

—— 1989 [1955]. *Tristes Tropiques* (trans. J. and D. Weightman). London: Picador.

Lewis, Bernard. 1975. *History: Remembered, Recovered, Invented*. Princeton, N.J.: Princeton University Press.

Liberman, Jean. (ed.) 2004a. *Démythifier l'universalité des valeurs américaines*. Paris: Parangon.

—— 2004b. 'Du néo-imperium de George W. Bush au passé original: un certain fil rouge', in Liberman 2004a.

Lind, Andrew W. 1969. 'Inter-Ethnic Marriage in New Guinea', monograph, *New Guinea Research Bulletin*. 31. Canberra: Australian National University.

Linklater, Andrew. 1990. *Beyond Realism and Marxism: Critical Theory and International Relations*. Basingstoke: Macmillan.

Lorenz, Konrad. 1971 [1963]. *Over agressie bij dier en mens*. Rev. edn. (trans. D. Hillenius). Amsterdam: Ploegsma.

Lubkemann, Stephen C. 2003. 'Race, Class, and Kin in the Negotiation of "Internal Strangerhood" among Portuguese Retornados, 1975–2000', in Smith 2003.

Mabey, Nick. 1999. 'Defending the Legacy of Rio: the Civil Society Campaign against the MAI', in Picciotto and Mayne 1999.

Macartney, C.A. 1969. *The Habsburg Empire 1790–1918*. London: Weidenfeld & Nicholson.

Maffesoli, Michel. 1997. *Du Nomadisme: Vagabondages initiatiques*. Paris: Librairie Générale Française/Livre de Poche.

Maiguashca, Bice. 1994. 'The transnational indigenous movement in a changing world order', in Y. Sakamoto (ed.) *Global Transformation: Challenges to the State System*. Tokyo: United Nations University Press.

Mann, Michael. 1986. *A History of Power from the Beginning to A.D. 1760*. Vol. I of *The Sources of Social Power*. Cambridge: Cambridge University Press.

Marcus, G.J. 1998 [1980]. *The Conquest of the North Atlantic*. Woodbridge: Boydell Press.

Marriott, McKim. 1955. 'Little Communities in an Indigenous Civilization', in Marriott (ed.) *Village India*. Chicago: Chicago University Press.

Marx, Karl. 1973. *Grundrisse: Introduction to the Critique of Political Economy (Rough Draft)* (introd. and trans. Martin Nicolaus). Harmondsworth: Pelican. (written 1857–58).

—— 1976. *Die ethnologischen Exzerpthefte* (ed. and introd. Lawrence Krader; trans. A. Schweikhart). Frankfurt: Suhrkamp.

—— 1983. *Geheime diplomatie in de XVIII eeuw* (trans. F. Visser). Katwijk: Servire.

Marx, Karl, and Engels, Friedrich. 1955 [1942]. *Marx en Engels over het reactionaire Pruisendom* (ed. M.B. Mitin, E.B. Kandel, and I.I. Preisz; Dutch translation). Amsterdam: Pegasus.

Masanov, Nurbulat. 2002. 'Perceptions of Ethnic and All-national Identity in Kazakhstan'. Ch. 1 of Andrei Chebotarev, Erlan Karin, Nurbulat Masanov, and Natsuko Oka. *The Nationalities Question in Post-Soviet Kazakhstan* (The Middle East Series, no. 51). Chiba, Japan: Institute of Developing Economies. http://www.ide.go.jp/English/Publish/Mes/pdf/51_cap1_pdf (accessed 23 June 2006).

Mauss, Marcel. 2002 [1950]. *The Gift: The Form and Reason of Exchange in Archaic Societies* (trans. W.D. Halls; foreword by Mary Douglas). London: Routledge.

McCarthy, Michael (ed.) 2006. 'The Day That Changed the Climate. The Stern Report: A Special Issue'. *Independent*, 31 October.

McNeill, William E. 1991 [1963]. *The Rise of the West: A History of the Human Community* (new edn. with retrospective essay). Chicago: University of Chicago Press.

Megarry, Tim. 1995. *Society in Prehistory: The Origins of Human Culture*. New York: New York University Press.

Meillassoux, Claude. 1981 [1975]. *Maidens, Meal, and Money: Capitalism and the Domestic Community* (trans. from the French). Cambridge: Cambridge University Press.

Menzies, Gavin. 2003. *1421: The Year China Discovered the World*. London: Bantam.

Merk, Jeroen. 2004. 'Regulating the Global Athletic Footwear Industry: The Collective Worker in the Product Chain', in van der Pijl, Assassi, and Wigan 2004.

—— 2007. *The Emergence of the Collective Worker in the Athletic Footwear Industry*. Ph.D. dissertation, University of Sussex.

Meskill, J.T. (ed.). 1973. *An Introduction to Chinese Civilization* (with the assistance of J.M. Gentzler). Lexington, Mass.: D.C. Heath.

MEW. Marx-Engels Werke. 35 vols. Berlin: Dietz, 1956–71. Vols. XXIII–XXV contain *Capital,* i–iii.

Migdal, Joel S. 1988. *Strong Societies and Weak States: State–Society Relations and State Capabilities in the Third World.* Princeton: Princeton University Press.

Mommsen, H. 1963. *Sozialdemokratie und die Nationalitätenfrage im habsburgischen Vielvölkerstaat,* i. Vienna: Europa Verlag.

Monbiot, George. 2003. *The Age of Consent: A Manifesto For a New World Order.* London: Flamingo.

Motley, John Lothrop. n.d. [1856]. *The rise of the Dutch Republic: A History.* 3 vols. London: George Routledge & Sons.

Müller, Claudius, and Wenzel, Jacob (eds) 2005. *Dschingis Khan und seine Erben: Das Weltreich der Mongolen.* Munich: Kunst- und Ausstellungshalle der BRD, Hirmer Verlag.

Mumford, Lewis. 1961. *The City in History: Its Origins, Its Transformations, and Its Prospects.* London: Secker & Warburg.

Naipaul, V.S. 1989. *A Turn in the South.* New York: Knopf.

Nairn, Tom. 1981. *The Break-Up of Britain: Crisis and Neo-Nationalism,* 2nd edn. London: Verso.

Nederveen Pieterse, Jan P. 1990. *Empire and Emancipation: Power and Liberation on a World Scale.* London: Pluto Press.

Neumark, S. Daniel.1964. *Foreign Trade and Economic Development in Africa.* Stanford: Food Research Institute.

Norman, E.H. 1940. *Japan's Emergence as a Modern State: Political and Economic Problems of the Meiji Period.* New York: Institute of Pacific Relations.

Oden, Michael, Wolf-Powers, Laura, and Markusen, Ann, 2003. 'Post-Cold War conversion: Gains, losses, and hidden changes in the US economy', in A. Markusen, S. DiGiovanna, and M.C. Leary (eds) *From Defense to Development? International perspectives on realizing the peace dividend.* London: Routledge.

Ogburn, W.F. 1964a [1961]. 'Race Relations and Social Change', in Duncan 1964.

—— 1964b [1950]. 'Social Evolution Reconsidered', in Duncan 1964.

Opitz, Reinhard (ed.). 1977. *Europastrategien des deutschen Kapitals 1900–1945.* Cologne: Pahl-Rugenstein.

Osiander, Andreas. 2001. 'Before sovereignty: society and politics in *ancien régime* Europe'. *Review of International Studies.* 27 (special issue). 119–45.

Ostler, Nicholas. 2006. *Empires of the Word: A Language History of the World.* London: Harper Perennial.

Ovalle-Bahamón, Ricardo E. 2003. 'The Wrinkles of Decolonization and Nationness: White Angolans as *Retornados* in Portugal', in Smith 2003.

Overbeek, Henk. 1995. 'Towards a new international migration regime: globalization, migration and the internationalization of the state', in R. Miles and D. Thränhardt (eds), *Migration and European Integration: The Dynamics of Inclusion and Exclusion.* London: Pinter; Madison: Farleigh Dickinson University Press.

Padfield, Peter. 2000. *Maritime Supremacy and the Opening of the Western Mind: Naval Campaigns that Shaped the Modern World, 1588–1782.* London: Pimlico.

Palan, Ronen. 2003. *The Offshore World: Sovereign Markets, Virtual Places, and Nomad Millionaires.* Ithaca, N.Y.: Cornell University Press.

Pallas, P.S., Johnston, Robert, and Miller, W. 1990. [1793/4, 1815 and 1803 respectively]. *Travels in 18th Century Russia: Costumes, Customs, History.* London: Studio Editions.

Pannekoek, Anton. n.d. [1938]. *Lenin als filosoof.* Amsterdam: De Vlam.

Perryman, Mark (ed.). 2001. *Hooligan Wars: Causes and Effects of Football Violence.* Edinburgh: Mainstream Publishing.

Pershits, A. 1974 [1967]. 'Early Forms of Family and Marriage in the Light of Soviet Ethnography', in Bromley 1974b.

Picciotto, Sol, and Mayne, Ruth. (eds) 1999. *Regulating International Business: Beyond Liberalization.* Basingstoke: Macmillan; New York: St. Martins (in association with Oxfam).

Pijl, Kees van der. 1984. *The Making of an Atlantic Ruling Class.* London: Verso. Also at http://www.theglobalsite.ac.uk/atlanticrulingclass/.

—— 1996. *Vordenker der Weltpolitik* (trans. W. Linsewski). Opladen: Leske+Budrich.

—— 1998. *Transnational Classes and International Relations.* London: Routledge.

—— 2004. 'Nomaden, Reiche, Staaten: Ursprünge imperialer Ideologie inner-halb der westlichen Hegemonie', in K.-G. Giesen (ed.) *Ideologien in der Weltpolitik.* Wiesbaden: Verlag für Sozialwissenschaften.

—— 2006. *Global Rivalries from the Cold War to Iraq.* London: Pluto Press; New Delhi: Sage Vistaar.

—— Assassi, Libby, and Wigan, Duncan (eds.). 2004. *Global Regulation: Managing Crises After the Imperial Turn.* Basingstoke: Palgrave Macmilllan.

Pirenne, Henri. 1937. *Mahomet et Charlemagne.* Brussels: Nouvelle Société d'Editions.

Polanyi, Karl. 1957 [1944]. *The Great Transformation: The Political and Economic Origins of Our Time.* Boston: Beacon.

Ponting, Clive. 1991. *A Green History of the World.* London: Sinclair-Stevenson.

—— 2001. *World History: A New Perspective.* London: Pimlico.

Portis, Larry. 2004. 'Les fondements culturels et structurels de l'impérialisme étatsunien', in Liberman 2004a.

Poulantzas, Nikos, 1971. *Pouvoir politique et classes sociales.* 2 vols. Paris: Maspero.

Prunier, Gérard. 2007. 'Darfour, la chronique d'un "genocide ambigu"'. *Le Monde Diplomatique* (March). 16–17.

Redmount. Carol A. 1998. 'Bitter Lives: Israel in and out of Egypt', in M. D. Coogan (ed.) *The Oxford History of the Biblical World.* Oxford: Oxford University Press.

Rey, Pierre-Philippe. 1983 [1977]. 'Klassentegenstellingen in verwantschappelijke maatschappijen' (trans. from the French). *Te Elfder Ure.* 26 (3). 578–603.

Rich, P. 1999. 'European identity and the myth of Islam: a reassessment'. *Review of International Studies.* 25 (3). 435–51.

Rischard, Jean-François. 2002. *High Noon: 20 Global Issues, 20 Years to Solve Them.* Oxford: Perseus Press.

Ritsert, Jürgen. 1973. *Probleme politisch-ökonomischer Theoriebildung.* Frankfurt: Athenäum.

Rodinson, Maxime. 1972. *Marxisme et monde musulman.* Paris: Seuil.

Rosenberg, Justin. 1994. *The Empire of Civil Society: A Critique of the Realist Theory of International Relations*. London: Verso.

Rosenstock-Huessy, Eugen. 1961 [1931]. *Die europäischen Revolutionen und der Character der Nationen*. 3rd edn. Stuttgart: Kohlhammer.

—— 1993 [1938]. *Out of Revolution· Autobiography of Western Man*. Providence, R.I.: Berg.

Rosman, Abraham, and Rubel, Paula G. 1976. 'Nomad–Sedentary Interethnic Relations in Iran and Afghanistan'. *International Journal of Middle East Studies*. 7 (4). 545–70.

Rowse, A.L. 1998 [1966]. *Bosworth Field and the Wars of the Roses*. Ware, Herts.: Wordsworth Editions.

Rufin, Jean-Christophe. 1991. *L'empire et les nouveaux barbares*. Paris: Lattès.

Rupert, Mark. 1993. 'Alienation, Capitalism, and the Inter-State System: Towards a Marxian/Gramscian Critique', in S. Gill (ed.) *Gramsci, Historical Materialism, and International Relations*. Cambridge: Cambridge University Press.

—— 2000. *Ideologies of Globalization: Contending Visions of a New World Order*. London: Routledge.

Salter, Mark B. 2004. 'And Yet It Moves: Mapping the Global Mobility Regime', in van der Pijl, Assassi, and Wigan 2004.

Samary, Cathérine. 1995. *Yugoslavia Dismembered* (trans. P. Drucker). New York: Monthly Review Press.

Schama, Simon. 1988. *The Embarrassment of Riches: An Interpretation of Dutch Culture in the Golden Age*. Berkeley: University of California Press.

—— 1990. *Citizens: A Chronicle of the French Revolution*. New York: Vintage.

Scholte, Jan Aart. 2003. *Democratizing the Global Economy: The Role of Civil Society*. Coventry: Centre for the Study of Globalisation and Regionalisation, University of Warwick.

Scott Fitzgerald, F. 1968 [1939]. *Tender is the Night: A Romance*. Harmondsworth: Penguin.

Sen, K.M. 1961. *Hinduism*. Harmondsworth: Penguin.

Seton-Watson, R.W. 1943. *A History of the Czechs and Slovaks*. London: Hutchinson.

Shaheen, S. 1956. *The Communist (Bolshevik) Theory of National Self-Determination: Its Historical Evolution up to the October Revolution*. The Hague: Van Hoeve.

Shanin, Teodor. 1986. 'Soviet Theories of Ethnicity: The Case of a Missing Term'. *New Left Review*. 158. 113–22.

Shaw, Martin. 2005. *The New Western Way of War: Risk-Transfer War and its Crisis in Iraq*. Cambridge: Polity.

Shiba, Yoxhinsobu. 1994. 'The Lower Yangtze Economy and the Trading Networks of Maritime East Asia During the Ming Dynasty: The Significance of the Transitional Age of the Sixteenth Century', in *China and the Maritime Silk Route* (*UNESCO Quangzhou International Seminar on China and the Maritime Silk Route*, vol. 2). Fujian: Fujian People's Publishing House.

Shirokogorov, S.M. 1970 [1931]. *Ethnological and Linguistical Aspects of the Ural–Altaic Hypothesis* (reprint of *Tshing Hua Journal*. 6. Beijing; transcribed as Shirokogoroff). Oosterhout: Anthropological Publications.

Shorto, Russell. 2005. *The Island at the Centre of the World: The Untold Story of Dutch Manhattan and the Founding of New York*. London: Black Swan.

Siméant, Johanna. 2005. 'What is going global? The internationalization of French NGOs "without borders"'. *Review of International Political Economy*. 12 (5). 851–83.

Slicher van Bath, B. 1980 [1960]. *De agrarische geschiedenis van West-Europa 500–1850*. Utrecht and Antwerpen: Aula.

——. 1989. *Indianen en Spanjaarden: Een ontmoeting tussen twee werelden, Latijns Amerika 1500–1800*. Amsterdam: Bert Bakker.

Smaje, Chris. 2000. *Natural Hierarchies: The Historical Sociology of Race and Caste*. Malden, Mass.: Blackwell.

Smith, Adam. 1910 [1776]. *The Wealth of Nations*. 2 vols. (introd. E.R.A. Seligman). London: Everyman's Library.

Smith, Andrea L. (ed.). 2003. *Europe's Invisible Migrants*. Amsterdam: Amsterdam University Press.

Sobel, Dava. 1998. *Longitude*. London: Fourth Estate.

Soja, Edward W. 2003. 'Putting Cities First: Remapping the Origins of Urbanism', in Bridge and Watson 2003.

Šolle, Z. 1969. 'Kontinuität und Wandel in der sozialen Entwicklung der Böhmischen Länder 1872 bis 1930', in K. Bosl (ed.) *Aktuelle Forschungsprobleme um die Erste Tschechoslowakische Republik*. Munich-Vienna: Oldenbourg.

Sorokin, Pitirim. 1985 [1957]. *Social and Cultural Dynamics: A Study of Change in Major Systems of Art, Truth, Ethics, Law, and Social Relationships* (rev. and abridged in one volume by the author, introd. M.P. Richard). New Brunswick, N.J.: Transaction Books (4 vol. edn. originally published 1937–41).

Souza, George B. 1986. *The Survival of Empire: Portuguese Trade and Society in China and the South China Sea, 1630–1754*. Cambridge: Cambridge University Press.

Spear, Percival. 1970 [1965]. *A History of India*, ii. Harmondsworth: Penguin.

Spellman, W.M. 2002. *The Global Community: Migration and the Making of the Modern World*. Stroud, Glos.: Sutton.

Spohn, W., and Bodemann, Y.M. 1989. 'Federal Republic of Germany', in T. Bottomore and R.J. Brym (eds) *The Capitalist Class: An International Study*. Hemel Hempstead: Harvester.

Stein, Aurel. 1984 [1933]. *On Ancient Central Asian Tracks: Brief Narrative of Three Expeditions in Innermost Asia and North-Western China*. Jodhpur: Scientific Publishers.

Stenton, F.M. 1966 [1927]. 'The Danes in England' in Sutherland 1966.

Stephenson, Carl. 1962 [1935]. *Mediaeval History: Europe from the Second to the Sixteenth Century*, 4th rev. edn. (ed. B. Lyon). New York: Harper & Row; Tokyo: Weatherhill.

Sterritt, Neil J., Marsden, S., Galois, R., Grant, P.R., and Overstall, R. 1998. *Tribal Boundaries in the Nass Watershed*. Vancouver: University of British Columbia Press.

Stevens, Jacob. 2006. 'Prisons of the Stateless: The Derelictions of UNHCR', *New Left Review*, (second series). 42. 53–67.

Storry, Richard. 1967 [1960]. *A History of Modern Japan*. Rev. edn. Harmondsworth: Penguin.

Strayer, J.R. 1970. *On the Mediaeval Origins of the Modern State*. Princeton: Princeton University Press.

Swaan, Abram de. 2001. *Words of the World: The Global Language System*. Cambridge: Polity.

Sutherland, Lucy S. (ed.) 1966. *Studies in History: British Academy Lectures*. London: Oxford University Press.

Tanner, Adrian. 1983. 'Algonquian Land Tenure and State Structures in the North'. *Canadian Journal of Native Studies*. 3 (2). 311–20.

Tawney, R.H. 1966 [1941]. 'Harrington's Interpretation of his Age', in Sutherland 1966.

Teschke, Benno. 2003. *The Myth of 1648: Class, Geopolitics, and the Making of Modern International Relations*. London: Verso.

Therborn, Göran. 1976. *Science, Class and Society: On the Formation of Sociology and Historical Materialism*. London: Verso.

Thompson, William R. 1988. *On Global War: Historical–Structural Approaches to World Politics*. Columbia, S.C.: University of South Carolina Press.

Tidow, S. 1999. 'Benchmarking als Leitidee: Zum Verlust des politischen in der europäischen Perspektive'. *Blätter für deutsche und internationale Politik*. 44 (3). 301–7.

Tiger, Lionel. 1970. *Men in Groups*. New York: Vintage.

Tocqueville, A. de. 1990 [1835, 1840]. *Democracy in America*. 2 vols. (Reeve/Bowen translation ed. P. Bradley, with new introduction by D.J. Boorstin). New York: Vintage.

Toynbee, A.J. 1935 [1934]. *A Study of History*. 2nd edn. 3 vols. Oxford: Oxford University Press; London: Humphrey Milford, for the Royal Institute of International Affairs.

—— 1976. *Mankind and Mother Earth: A Narrative History of the World*. Oxford: Oxford University Press.

Trotsky, Leon. 1978 [1936]. *Geschiedenis der Russische Revolutie*. 3 vols. (trans. J. Valkhoff). Amsterdam: Van Gennep.

Turner, Frederick J. 1962 [1893]. 'The Significance of the Frontier in American History', in *The Frontier in American History* (foreword by R.A. Billington). New York: Holt, Rinehart and Winston (original compilation 1920).

Velikhov, Yevgeni (ed.) 1985. *The Night After; Climatic and Biological Consequences of a Nuclear War*. Moscow: Mir Publishers.

Vieille, Paul. 1988. 'The World's Chaos and the New Paradigms of the Social Movement', in Lelio Basso Foundation (eds) *Theory and Practice of Liberation at the End of the Twentieth Century*. Brussels: Bruylant.

Vincent, Joan. 1990. *Anthropology and Politics: Visions, Traditions, and Trends*. Tucson: University of Arizona Press.

Vollmer, John E., Keal, E.J., and Nagai-Berthrong, E. 1983. *Silk Roads, China Ships*. Toronto: Royal Ontario Museum.

de Vries, Bert, and Goudsblom, Johan (eds). 2002. *Mappae Mundi: Humans and their Habitats in a Long-Term Socio-Ecological Perspective. Myths, Maps and Models*. Amsterdam: Amsterdam University Press.

Vroon, Piet. 1994 [1992]. *Wolfsklem: Over de evolutie van het menselijk gedrag*. Amsterdam: Ambo.

Wacquant, Loïc. 2002. 'From Slavery to Mass Incarceration: Rethinking the "race question" in the US'. *New Left Review* (2nd series). 13. 41–60.

Wallerstein, Immanuel. 1974. *The Modern World System: Capitalist Agriculture and the Origins of the European World Economy in the Sixteenth Century*. New York: Academic Press.

Weggel, O. 1980. '"Der Friede als revolutionäres Werk der Massen": Die Haltung der VR China zur Friedens- und Kriegsproblematik', in R. Steinweg (ed.) *Der gerechte Krieg: Christentum, Islam, Marxismus*. Frankfurt: Suhrkamp.

Werth, Alexander. 1964. *Russia at War, 1941–1945*. London: Pan.

Willems, Wim. 2003. 'No Sheltering Sky: Migrant Identities of Dutch Nationals from Indonesia', in Smith 2003.

Williams, John. 2001. 'Who You Calling a Hooligan?' in Perryman 2001.

Wittfogel, Karl A. 1977 [1957]. *Die orientalische Despotie: Eine vergleichende Untersuchung totaler Macht* (trans. F. Kool). Frankfurt: Ullstein.

Wolf, Eric R. 1997 [1982]. *Europe and the People Without History* (with a new preface). Berkeley, Calif.: University of California Press.

Wood, Frances. 1995. *Did Marco Polo go to China?* London: Secker & Warburg.

—— 2002. *The Silk Route: Two Thousand Years in the Heart of Asia*. London: Folio Society.

Wood, Michael. 2005 [1992]. *In Search of the First Civilizations*. London: BBC Books.

Wright, Robert. 2001. *Nonzero: History, Evolution, and Human Cooperation*. London: Abacus.

Zalik, Anna. 2004. 'The Peace of the Graveyard: the Voluntary Principles on Security and Human Rights in the Niger Delta', in van der Pijl, Assassi, and Wigan 2004.

Zettel, Horst. 1986. 'Deutschland und die Elbslawen im 10. Jahrhundert: Ein Beitrag zur deutschen Ostpolitik unter Heinrich I. und Otto I', in H.-J. Häßler and H. Kauffmann (eds), *Kultur gegen Krieg*. Cologne: Pahl-Rugenstein.

Zhang, Yongjin. 2001. 'System, empire and state in Chinese international relations'. *Review of International Studies*. 27 (special issue) 43–64.

Zulaika, Joseba. 1993. 'Further Encounters with the Wild Man: Of Cannibals, Dogs, and Terrorists', *Etnofoor*. 6 (2). 21–40.

Index